Capturing the News

Capturing the News

Three Decades of Reporting Crisis and Conflict

Anthony Collings

University of Missouri Press
Columbia and London

Library of Congress Cataloging-in-Publication Data

Collings, Anthony.
  Capturing the news : three decades of reporting crisis and con-
flict / by Anthony Collings.
     p. cm.
  Includes bibliographical references and index.
  ISBN 978-0-8262-1881-0 (cloth : alk. paper)
  1. Collings, Anthony. 2. Journalists—United States—Biography.
  3. Television journalists—United States—Biography. I. Title.
  PN4874.C645A3 2010
  070.92—dc22
  [B]
                        2010001404

Jacket design: Susan Ferber
Design and composition: Jennifer Cropp
Printing and binding: Thomson-Shore, Inc.
Typefaces: Minion and Myriad Pro

For Milo

Contents

Acknowledgments

I am very grateful to Professor Susan Douglas, Chair of the Department of Communication Studies at the University of Michigan, for her strong encouragement and support throughout the writing of this book. Special thanks go also to my friends Jim Barnett, Joseph Curtin, Doug Hagley, Michael Johnson, Richard Roth, Peter Stine, and Derek Vaillant, as well as to Geraldine Stewart and my sons, Andrew, Daniel, and Matthew, and my partner Alesia, for all their support. And I would like to thank the many reporters, camera operators, sound technicians, producers, and editors who helped teach me the craft of journalism and showed great dedication to the profession, including Jim Allen, Dick Blystone, Fred Coleman, Ron Dean, Mick Deane, Jane Evans, Terry Frieden, Chip Goebert, Peter Kendall, Mike Kubic, Mark Leff, Stu Loory, Doug Mason, Stan Penn, Louise Priestley, John Rafter, Rob Reynolds, Scott Schmedel, Dean Vallos, Russ Watson, and Nina Zirato.

Capturing the News

Prologue

Beirut 1981

On a clear spring morning we drove east from Beirut up into the Lebanon Mountains to a pass leading to the Bekaa Valley, and one of our few protections against danger was the word *sahafiya*. It meant "press" in Arabic. I had been told to say the magic word *sahafiya* if we got into trouble. The word was supposed to give you safe passage but it didn't always work. Other journalists had been beaten and killed here in Lebanon in the 1970s and 1980s, and I could only hope that somehow I would be spared their fate.

With me were two young men fresh from Atlanta who were my Cable News Network crew: Johnny, the camera operator, and his sidekick, the sound technician, each in white T-shirt and blue jeans. I wore a brand-new television correspondent's outfit, a safari suit, having joined CNN from *Newsweek* the month before and being a novice on the television side of the news business. With us also was our driver, Abed, a short, cheerful, chubby, smiling Lebanese Muslim, balding and paunchy in his dark-blue sports shirt worn outside his slacks, a cherubic middle-aged man who always had a friendly nod and wave. Abed would begin each day by carefully canvassing members of his family and other people he knew to gain vital information about what had happened during the previous night's fighting among rival armed gangs in West Beirut. Each morning there were new turfs established, and that meant a new alignment of streets that were safe or unsafe. Abed did an excellent job of gathering this information and letting me know where we could go and where we could not go, as I told him about stories we wanted to cover. I trusted him to get us safely there and back in his Mercedes taxi.

I enjoyed Abed's whimsical sense of humor and his ability to set people at ease despite the pressure-cooker environment of guns and rivalries. When we would take trips south of Beirut and we were stopped at UN checkpoints, Abed would wave to the tall Fijian soldiers wearing the pale blue helmets of UN

1

peacekeepers and he would smile and call out: *"Boola boola!"* In the Fijian language it meant "Hello!"

Now, in May 1981, as we drove east through the mountain pass on the road from Beirut to Damascus, I saw a place by the side of the road with a panoramic view of the Bekaa Valley and asked Abed to park there. I wanted to get an "establishing shot," a wide-angle view of the valley that we might be able to use as the opening scene for our CNN news report about a missile crisis. And, should we be unsuccessful in finding the Syrian missiles that were the cause of the current showdown with Israel, at least we would have pictures of the general location of the missile crisis. One way or another, it should be useful.

Spread out below us in the morning spring sun were hillside apple orchards and, beyond them, green fields of plants including hashish. On the far side of the valley to the east lay the Anti-Lebanon Mountains, which formed the border with Syria, and beyond that lay Damascus. Somewhere down here in the valley just below us were the missiles that were dominating the news and threatening an outbreak of war.

We stepped out of Abed's Mercedes and set up the tripod near the edge of the flat area by the side of the road, just above the slope that led down to the orchards and fields. Before Johnny could place his television camera on the tripod, two dusty Mercedes sedans pulled up beside us. I felt uneasy but hoped they were just curiosity seekers, intrigued by the tripod.

Six men in civilian clothes stepped out. Five wore jeans and short-sleeved shirts. To my alarm I saw that they carried AK's, the Kalashnikov AK-47 assault rifles seen all over the Middle East, the semi-automatics with the distinctive curved banana clip for ammunition. The sixth man, a handsome man of about forty with long dark hair, wore a three-piece pinstriped dark-blue suit with bell-bottom trousers. The length of his hair and the flare of his bellbottoms had once been fashionable, although that day had come and gone. I didn't know if the men were Palestinian or Syrian or Lebanese. Without identifying themselves, they demanded to know who we were and what we were doing. I said, *"Sahafiya."* Abed smiled and told them in Arabic that we were American television journalists doing a story about the Bekaa Valley. He did not mention the missiles.

One of the gunmen screamed something at Abed and struck him in the face with his fist. It was all happening so fast that I did not know what to do other than to repeat the word *sahafiya*. They didn't seem impressed by the word.

"Get in the car," the dapper man with the long hair told us, in English.

I got into his car and sat in the passenger seat in front, my crew in the back seat, and he drove. A gunman got into Abed's car and he followed behind us. The rest of the men got into the third car to follow Abed. We drove down the winding mountain road that descended to the town of Shtaura. We parked outside a yellow stucco building that was four stories tall. My heart was beating hard, and I could not think straight. Part of me was annoyed that we had been interrupted in our reporting. Part of me was worried for our safety.

The dusty yellow building was being used as a headquarters for Syrian troops who occupied part of the Bekaa Valley. Although in theory Lebanon was an independent state, in practice it was carved up into chunks of territory ruled by whoever had enough guns, and this part of Lebanon was ruled by Syria. The Syrians recently had added Soviet-made surface-to-air missiles to their armaments in the valley and had rejected Israeli demands to remove them.

The crew and I were taken to a room upstairs. The dapper man demanded we give him our American passports, which we did. Abed was taken to another room for interrogation. We were prisoners, and I realized that we had to be very careful what we did and said, so that we did not make things even worse. I told the crew to say nothing about missiles but keep repeating that we were journalists doing our job reporting the facts.

Being held in a room in one of the most dangerous parts of the world was a far cry from what I had known. At the age of forty-two I had been hired away from *Newsweek* by Cable News Network during its first year, as part of an effort to improve CNN's news coverage. Whatever experience I may have had covering Russian and European politics and economics had not prepared me for news coverage in Beirut. I was accustomed to the safe and secure environment of the *Newsweek* bureau on Upper Brook Street in London, near the American Embassy and the Marble Arch corner of Hyde Park. The office building was a narrow, delicate, pleasant structure with a tiny, phone-booth-sized elevator and a bay window on the second floor out of which I could catch a glimpse of Hyde Park when I glanced up from my typewriter.

My days consisted of typing up four-thousand-word "files" for *Newsweek* writers to use as raw material for the finished prose that they churned out each week in New York. I made phone calls to sources, and took pleasant London taxi rides to interviews, to gather information for files on the latest up or down trend of the dollar against European currencies, or some scientific breakthrough such as the Louise Brown test tube baby, the foibles of the royal family, or the emergence of Margaret Thatcher as she prepared to sweep to power in elections. It was all comfortable and secure, and Londoners were polite and considerate. Not that the job was cushy. There was the usual stress of deadline pressure and competition with *Time* for exclusive tidbits of information and dealing with sometimes testy editors in New York. But by and large it was an environment that was stable and safe.

In addition, I had my family: my wife, Geraldine, and my three young sons, Andy, Danny, and Mattie. We lived in a four-floor townhouse with a beautiful back yard on a street called The Vale in the fashionable Chelsea district southwest of the Houses of Parliament and a short walk from the Thames. Half a block away were the lively boutiques and pubs of the Kings Road. There were the pleasures of watching quality programming on the BBC and the other television network, ITV, and reading intelligent, thoughtful commentary on world events in such newspapers as the London *Sunday Times* and listening to jazz and classical music in our attractive living room with French doors that opened out to a charming little garden that was sunny when the clouds parted, which did not happen often but was enjoyable when it did.

Everything safe and stable and secure and comfortable was now far behind me.

The man who spoke English entered the room where we were held in Shtaura. He identified himself as an agent of Syrian intelligence, although I could not tell if that meant he was Syrian or Lebanese.

"Who are you?" he asked.

"American journalists," I said. "CNN."

"Who are you really?" the man asked.

"We are American journalists." I showed him my CNN identity card but, of course, back in May 1981 CNN was still in its first year and meant nothing to most people.

He looked at it with suspicion and I worried that he saw us as possible Israeli spies.

I knew that meant we could be imprisoned and even executed.

The dapper, long-haired translator left the room and then came back with a Syrian soldier carrying a rifle.

"Come," he said.

He led us, followed by the soldier, down the stairs to the office of a Syrian officer whose rank I could not identify. I assumed he was a senior officer, at least a major or colonel, possibly a general, because of his age, probably late fifties, with a bald head and a spreading paunch that strained at his khaki blouse, and because of the size of his office, with a big desk and a conference table that adjoined it and formed a T. Whoever he was, this senior Syrian officer had our lives in his hands.

He gestured for us to sit around the conference table, with the English-speaking man across from me on the left; Abed, his pudgy face bruised, sitting across from me on the right; the sound man at the far end of the table on my right; Johnny the cameraman next to me on my immediate right; and the Syrian officer on my left seated at his desk.

He spoke in Arabic, and the dapper man translated into English.

"You were caught taking photographs without permission," he said. "We know very well who you are and what you were doing."

The words were chilling. We were in more trouble than I had thought.

"We are American journalists," I insisted.

But the Syrian officer seemed unmoved.

He beckoned to the soldier who was standing off to one side and said something to him. The soldier left the room.

My feeling of dread deepened now. In a moment of panic, I wondered if the officer had ordered the soldier to go outside and prepare a firing squad. We sat in silence.

At last the soldier came back into the room. Instead of escorting us outside to face execution, he carried a large round brass tray. On it were red, white, and black packs of Marlboros and small glasses of tea.

He went around the room, placing in front of each person one pack of Marlboros and one glass of tea.

At first I felt relief. Perhaps we had been spared. But then another thought occurred: was this a last meal? In films and cartoons, didn't they offer a condemned man a last meal and a cigarette just before blindfolding him, tying him to a post, and shooting him?

The Syrian officer lifted his glass.

I turned to the crew and said, "Do whatever he does."

We lifted our glasses.

He sipped at his tea.

We sipped at our tea.

He opened his pack of Marlboros.

We opened our packs of Marlboros.

He lit a cigarette.

We went around the room, lighting our cigarettes: the translator, Abed, the sound man, and me.

But Johnny, the cameraman on my right, did not light his cigarette.

"What's the matter?" I asked.

"I don't smoke," he said.

I thought to myself: *Today you smoke.*

"Just light it and hold it."

He shrugged and lit the cigarette and held it in his fingers.

And then the atmosphere changed. The Syrian officer puffed on his cigarette and took more sips of tea. For the first time, he smiled. He told us that we were guests in this part of the country, and he wanted to welcome us.

I was dumbfounded. Why all this display of hospitality? Was this some trick? I didn't know what to think, but slowly I began to hope that we would get out of this unharmed.

The Syrian said he would release us, and that he wanted us to see some of the nearby sites. Confused, relieved, unsure what was happening, we were asked to enter the dapper man's Mercedes. He drove us from Shtaura along a road that led southward through fields and orchards. Eerily, he began singing "Raindrops Keep Fallin' On My Head," the theme song from *Butch Cassidy and the Sundance Kid*. Even more eerily, as we drove along I noticed that farm workers in the orchards and fields bowed as we drove past. Was he a feudal lord?

He took us to his villa and showed us around inside. He fed us lunch and chatted easily. He said we were free to go back to Beirut. He even said we could come back here any time and take any pictures we wanted to. Then he insisted on personally driving us all the way back to the Commodore Hotel in West Beirut, the hotel used by journalists. Abed followed us in his taxi.

Later, over badly needed cognacs in the hotel bar, Johnny asked me if we should accept the invitation to go back. I said we should not. The mood had changed quickly today, and it could change quickly in another direction tomorrow.

Today, more than twenty-eight years later, as a lecturer in communication studies at the University of Michigan, I think back over my lifetime as a journalist and I keep returning to that incident in the Bekaa Valley. I replay in my memory the image of the gunmen getting out of their Mercedes sedans, their AK-47s, the beating of Abed, the locked room in Shtaura. I wonder why I was willing to take such a risk for a story. It must be the simple fact that, for a journalist, the story is everything.

So many other things in your life just get pushed to the side in your pursuit of what you see as the one great tale that will amaze and enlighten the world. In a sense, you are a seeker of truth. You are an adventurer who overcomes the obstacles to truth and brings it back as a trophy. To this holy grail of the great story you subordinate family and friends, the comforts of home, the trappings of normality, membership in society. In their place you plunge yourself into the unusual and new. As a journalist you often have that feeling of strangeness, occasionally asking yourself: *What am I doing here?* When you're with the people you cover, you're an outsider, a nonparticipant, disengaged. Often you don't speak their language. You haven't shared their experiences. You're only with these people for a short time. You're the stranger at the door.

The incident in the Bekaa Valley was typical of many experiences I had in thirty-four years as a journalist, first for the *Wall Street Journal* in New York, then for the AP in Russia and Western Europe, then for *Newsweek* in Europe and the Middle East, and finally for CNN in Europe, the Middle East, and Washington. There was the feeling of strangeness, voyaging into the unknown, encountering surprise, enjoying humor ("I don't smoke," Johnny had said), sometimes fearing danger, and always facing obstacles to the truth. The obstacles could be external, as in the case of the gunmen in the Bekaa Valley, or internal, involving my own subjectivity. I would encounter many obstacles to the truth in my life as a journalist and, as I tried to overcome them, there would be many surprises along the way. The first surprise came in Russia . . .

Part I

Overseas

Chapter One

No Building Collapsed

Peaceful empty white snowfields shone brilliant and beautiful in the morning sun, seen from the train speeding toward Moscow from Brest, yet superimposed on the quiet empty fields were the explosions of tank fire and the shouts of Red Army soldiers fighting Nazi German invaders. There were no tanks on the snowfields spread out before us. There were no Red Army soldiers, no German invaders. And this was 1967, not 1941. The sounds of tanks and soldiers came from loudspeakers built into the ceiling of our Soviet railroad car, loudspeakers blaring a Soviet radio program reliving the battles of what had been known here as the Great Patriotic War, World War II on the Russian front, and we heard the sounds of war as we gazed out at the fields of peace blurring past us.

This was the scene as my wife, Geraldine, and I and our one-year-old baby, Andy, arrived in Russia by train from London in January of 1967 to begin my first foreign posting, a three-year tour in the Moscow bureau of the Associated Press, the American news agency. I was twenty-eight years old and thrilled to be a full-fledged foreign correspondent, a position I had dreamed about while a high school sophomore at the International School in Geneva and later at Beverly Hills High School. I had imagined myself being sent to exotic places to cover the great events of history. As a teenager growing up in Southern California, and as a college student spending hours writing for the *Daily Princetonian,* I had admired such journalists as James Reston of the *New York Times* and Edward R. Murrow of CBS News. As a cub reporter at the *Wall Street Journal* in New York, before going into the army for two years, I had learned some of the skills of the trade but always I had dreamed of writing under foreign datelines. Now here I was at last, a real live foreign correspondent, traveling with my family on a train to Moscow.

The train trip from London took two days, and it was worth it. We could have flown, of course, but we would not have gained such a great sense of the distance of Moscow from the capitals of the West. It took one full day just to get to Warsaw, Poland, and then another full day to reach Moscow. Russia extended across the map in such a massive expanse of land that the only way to appreciate it fully was by surface travel.

Moscow was a great distance away from London not only geographically but also culturally and economically, and the voyage by rail exemplified that cultural and economic divide. When we began our voyage in London our British Rail car was new, clean, modern, fairly quiet, and pleasant. We traveled to Harwich, where we took a ferry across the North Sea to Hook of Holland, in the Netherlands, and boarded a Dutch railroad car that was fairly new, clean, modern, quiet, and pleasant. We dined in a comfortable dining car, ordering from a full menu printed on glossy paper. We traveled eastward across Holland, West Germany, and East Germany to the border with Poland, where our Dutch railroad car was replaced by a Polish one. This Polish railroad car was old, shabby, dirty, and noisy, with the heating system not working well, and we forced ourselves to eat unpleasant food in a cheaply made dining car from a limited menu printed on cheap paper that felt like thin cardboard.

When we arrived at Brest, on the Soviet border, in the middle of the night, we had to transfer to another train with the broader-gauge wheels of the Russian railroad system. Our car on the Russian train was older and shabbier than the Polish car, smelled bad, and offered little to eat other than bread and sausages, and basically *chai* (tea) to drink, dispensed from a *samovar* tea-maker built into one corner of the corridor. So, as we moved from left to right across the great map of Europe, from west to east, our standard of living gradually declined, giving us a sense of the relatively poorer conditions you encountered the farther east you traveled.

Not only a great distance and cultural and economic divide separated Russia from the world we knew, but also an obsession with secrecy, one of my first encounters with obstacles to truth during my voyage of discovery. We were plunged into a largely closed society, so unlike the American openness we were accustomed to. As foreigners, we were forced to live in Soviet government housing, in a high-rise beige prefab apartment building surrounded by a fence and manned by a gray-coated policeman in a guard box at the gate, to keep Russians away and to keep them uninformed about the truth of the outside world. Secrecy at all costs. There were odd clicks on our phone that suggested tapping. (We knew that the phones of foreigners were tapped because one time a dissident intellectual phoned the AP office and announced the time and place of a protest demonstration, and within minutes a Soviet official called us to warn us not to go to the demo. The only way the official could have known was by someone listening in to our calls.) That was another way to keep Russians from contacting us and to keep them in the dark.

Russians were forbidden to have any personal contact with foreigners unless they had been given specific permission from the government or the Communist Party, so the only local people we met legally were our translators (provided to the AP by the government agency UPDK), our driver, other AP staff, a Russian language teacher who came to our apartment, and Soviet officials, usually from the Press Department of the Ministry of Foreign Affairs, where "spokesmen" usually refused all comment on all subjects, in keeping with the official policy of secrecy above and beyond all reason. The few times they did offer any kind of comment, sometimes they were wrong.

One absurd example came during a Soviet space shot. TASS, the Soviet "news" agency controlled by the government, our main source of breaking news announcements, reported that a Soviet unmanned probe had been launched. Its destination was not revealed, but at Jodrell Bank radio telescope in England a British scientist said it was on a trajectory toward the moon and appeared to be intended to go into orbit around the moon. When I saw the AP report from Jodrell Bank, I called up a man named Simonov at the Press Department of the Soviet Foreign Ministry and asked if he could comment on the British report that the Soviet space shot was heading for lunar orbit.

Simonov replied, *"Eta utka."* Translation: "That is a canard." (*Utka,* pronounced "OOT-kuh," means either "duck" or "canard" in the sense of hoax.)

I dutifully updated our Moscow-dateline story including the official denial that the Soviet space shot was headed moonward, and of course within a few hours came a TASS report that it had gone into orbit around the moon. Simonov obviously was uninformed, and presumably said *"utka"* as a knee-jerk reaction to any report from the West no matter how accurate.

Denying what was obviously true was part of the way of life in the Soviet world. One evening I was working at the AP office on Ulitsa Narodnaya, a quiet street on the eastern side of Moscow, rewriting TASS reports, when I heard a loud explosion from a district to the south, on the other side of the Moscow River. I jumped into my car and headed in the direction of the explosion. There was a stream of ambulances and police cars and Soviet army trucks heading in the same direction, and I followed them. At last, ahead of me at the end of the street, I could see arc lights of rescue workers and cranes and smoke rising into the evening sky. A Soviet Army private manned a roadblock and did not permit me to enter the area, so I parked nearby and walked back to the roadblock. The soldier was standing facing me, with his back to what was obviously a collapsed apartment building a few blocks behind him, the scene of frenetic activity by rescue workers brilliantly illuminated by emergency arc lights.

"Can I get through?" I asked in Russian.

"Nyet."

I showed him my *udostoverenye,* my accreditation from the Soviet government as an American journalist authorized to report from Moscow.

"*Nyet,*" he replied to my repeated request to get past him to the scene.

"I need to get through," I said.

"There is nothing to see," he said.

"I want to see the building that collapsed."

He looked at me and said, flatly: "No building collapsed. Go home."

This instinctive Russian response to deny what was obviously true in hopes that nothing negative would be reported was a product of the kind of secrecy I had never experienced and could not even imagine existed on such a scale. With all this secrecy we lived in relative isolation, at our foreigners-only compound on the drab, wide boulevard called Kutuzovsky Prospekt (named after General Kutuzov, who had commanded Russian troops against Napoleon's invading army outside Moscow), on the western side of the capital. In the center of the map of Moscow, like a bull's-eye, was the Kremlin, and on the eastern side of Moscow was the AP office on Ulitsa Narodnaya (People's Street), in another foreigners-only building with a policeman outside to keep Russians away, except for government-approved translators and staff, and to monitor our comings and goings.

All this effort to isolate us from Russians was frustrating for me, especially since I spoke the language. My father, Leon, was Russian. He had been raised in the southern city of Maikop, near the border with Soviet Georgia, and had fled during the civil war after the Bolshevik Revolution and made his way to Paris, where he was working as a journalist for Russian-language publications when he met my mother, Martha, an American writer. They married in France and moved to Los Angeles, where I was born in 1938. I remember as a child hearing him curse in Russian during traffic jams on Hollywood Boulevard. Later, his letters to me would end with the words *krepko obnimayu i tseluyu tebya* ("I give you a big hug and kiss"). Fascinated by the Russian language, I studied it in school and took a Berlitz language course while working at the AP in New York, and then studied Russian more intensively once we were living in Moscow. But, sadly, speaking the language was not enough to overcome the other barriers.

The few times ordinary Russians dared say anything to us (sometimes after consuming inhibition-easing vodkas at their tables next to ours at restaurants), they were friendly and exchanged phone numbers but never called us later, presumably realizing when sober that this was too dangerous. They could be fired, deported from the relatively better living conditions of Moscow to someplace undesirable, or even arrested and imprisoned.

The one time a Russian couple did befriend us was because my American brother-in-law knew them. They had met at a scientific conference and had stayed in touch. The couple, the Lubovskys, were friendly when I first called them up. We met at a restaurant and immediately hit it off, a Russian couple eager to learn about the West, and an American couple eager to learn about the East. I felt sure that we would be able to develop our friendship and that it would not cause political problems for them because they had already been allowed to attend scientific conferences abroad, which meant that they were considered loyal and not likely to defect.

The Lubovskys invited us over to their small apartment for dinner, in a cheap prefab building like ours. I remember that as we entered the living room the television was on, and the Soviet announcer of a "news" program was denouncing "American imperialist aggressors in Vietnam." Being Americans at a time of such escalated anti-American rhetoric, my wife and I felt uncomfortable at the dinner table that evening, and it was a reminder that politics would trump normal human relations in this paranoid, Big Brother police state. We made small talk, insisted that they visit us next time, and left.

Later we invited them to our place for dinner, and they did accept the invitation. They drove past the policeman at the gate to our compound, where their arrival, I'm sure, was duly noted in their files, and probably they were questioned later at their scientific institutes as to why they associated with suspected agents of imperialist aggressors. The dinner that evening at our apartment was strained, and we assumed that microphones picked up our conversation, but we tried to make the best of it.

At the end of the evening, we said we would meet again but we never did. Both couples wanted to meet again, but the Lubovskys dared not. The entire three years we were in Moscow, we never heard from them again—with one exception. On New Year's Eve, when he must have felt that the police state had relaxed slightly for the celebration, Vladimir got up the nerve to call me at home and say, "*S Novim Godom*" ("Happy New Year"). I could hear in his voice the isolation and frustration of a good man beaten down by the system yet adamant that he be allowed at least some freedom.

The system's paranoia and secrecy took other odd forms.

One evening as I worked at the AP office on Ulitsa Narodnaya I heard an explosion, very close to the building. I soon found out that the VW Beetle of the AP bureau chief, parked downstairs in our parking lot, had been damaged by a small blast, but it was unclear whether it was by an explosive device or some other cause. The bureau chief, Henry Bradsher, lived across the hall from the AP office, but had been away at the time, using another car. I made some phone calls to the American Embassy and to some journalists.

Then our phone rang.

It was Viktor Louis, a mysterious Russian who spoke good English and had a number of jobs including work as correspondent for a London evening paper, and who was reputed to be unusually well informed about the inner workings of the KGB, the Soviet counterpart to the CIA. Before I could say anything I heard his voice telling me: "It was the heater." Then he hung up.

A later investigation determined that a faulty heater in the Beetle had caused the explosion. But how did Viktor Louis know about the incident, and how did he know it was the heater? And more important, why did he call the AP to pass on this information? Was the KGB sending a message: *It wasn't us?* One can only speculate, but the incident was chilling.

Even more chilling was my detention by the KGB.

This was in May 1969. Like several other Westerners in Moscow, I and my wife had befriended a young dissident intellectual Russian named Andrei Amalrik, a historian, and his lovely wife, Gyuzel, a painter. Andrei was a small, wiry, boyish man with angular features, a wide jaw, brown hair in a brush cut, and glasses. He had an ironic smile as he defied the Soviet rules forbidding unauthorized contacts with foreigners. As an author of *samizdat* (self-published) works that circulated secretly among dissidents, he had been in trouble with the authorities a number of times. Instead of being cowed by the repression, he laughed at it. One of his books was entitled *An Involuntary Journey to Siberia* and was about being sent to Siberia for "parasitism" (lacking a steady job). A 1969 book, quite prescient, was entitled *Will the Soviet Union Survive Until 1984?* Actually the Communist state lasted a bit longer, until 1991, but Andrei was absolutely right that it could not survive, and he correctly predicted the breakup along ethnic lines. For writing that book he was later sentenced to three years' hard labor in Siberia.

His wife, Gyuzel, was a Tatar beauty with high cheekbones, eyes set wide apart, and a lovely figure. She could have been a film star or a model living in luxury in the West, but instead lived in modest conditions in Moscow in one room of a communal apartment with other families, all of them sharing the bathroom and kitchen. At the end of a long, narrow hallway Andrei and Gyuzel had a separate room to themselves that was bedroom and living room, and on its walls were her paintings. There was always the smell of cabbage in the air when I visited. The apartment was in a drab, dark gray building on the west side of Moscow, near the Soviet Foreign Ministry, on the other side of the river from our own apartment.

In May 1969 Andrei called me one day to say that he and Gyuzel were about to go on a vacation and he wanted to see me that day before they left. I rang the doorbell of the communal apartment. Usually Andrei would open the door and take me down the internal hall past the communal kitchen to his room, but this time a stranger, a middle-aged man with suit and tie, short red hair, and a managerial air, opened the door.

"What do you want?" he asked in Russian.

"I'm visiting my friends. They invited me."

"Who are you?"

"Tony Collings. I'm an American correspondent."

"Let me see your accreditation," he demanded.

I showed him my *udostoverenye,* mounted in a small blue-vinyl folder that fit into the palm of my hand. Then I asked him for his own identification. He reached into a suit pocket and pulled out a palm-sized red-vinyl folder and opened it to reveal a card that had his name under the Russian words *Komitet Gosudarstvennoy Byezopastnosti*—KGB.

He ordered me to come into the communal apartment, and I realized with dismay that I was now in their control and that there was no way of predicting what they would do with me. I was not under arrest but I was being detained by them, and if things went badly enough it could lead to actual arrest and either imprisonment or expulsion from the Soviet Union. Whatever it was, it was not good.

The KGB man escorted me down the internal hallway to Andrei's room, where a younger KGB man in a dark suit was seated in one chair facing four other seated persons: Andrei, Gyuzel, the *New York Times* correspondent Henry Kamm, and the wife of the *Washington Post* correspondent. Henry was demanding that he be allowed to contact the American Embassy. The young KGB agent ignored him and shifted his attention to me as I took a seat.

"How long have you known the Amalriks?" he asked, in fairly good English.

"I don't remember," I said, figuring the less I said the better.

"For a 'journalist' you don't seem to have a very good memory," he said, his tone of voice putting quotation marks around the word "journalist" as if that was merely what I was *claiming* to be whereas in fact I was something sinister, such as a spy. He was clearly using an interrogation technique intended to intimidate me and panic me into talking. Unsure what to do, I kept to my insistence that I could not remember how long I had known Andrei and Gyuzel or other details of our relationship.

Henry also refused to provide information and kept insisting that the American Embassy be notified that Americans were being detained against their will for no good reason. While in general we Americans were obviously at risk of being arrested at any time in a police state like this, one thing that protected us was reciprocity. Over time, the United States and the Soviet Union had developed a pattern of tit-for-tat behavior, so that if a journalist from one country would be detained, a journalist from the other country would also be detained in retaliation, and that meant that if we three Americans were going to be held in Moscow, the United States Government might do the same thing in Washington to three Soviet "journalists." (I put quotation marks around this word because a number of them really were spies, unlike us.) Perhaps the implied threat of reciprocity worked, but in any case we were let go after a few hours.

A few days later I was summoned to the Soviet Foreign Ministry, where Mr. Simonov, from the Press Department, chastised me for having gone to the apartment of "a certain Amalrik, who has a dark past." By chastising me and accusing me of not being an objective journalist, Simonov was implying a warning that if I continued in this way I could be expelled. Later I told Andrei about the stilted, bureaucratic language that Simonov had used, and I repeated his words: "a certain Amalrik, who has a dark past." "But," Andrei quipped, "a bright future." That was a joke about Communist propaganda, which always promised the people a bright future but never delivered on it.

Andrei and Gyuzel eventually were forced to emigrate and lived in the West for a while. In 1980 I was shocked to read the news of his death in Spain in a car accident. He had been on his way to protest Soviet refusal to discuss human rights at an international conference. Although Andrei had been regarded with suspicion by the KGB, there was no evidence that it was anything other than an accident.

During my three years in Moscow I continued to meet with dissidents and to write stories about their protests against Soviet censorship and against the harassment and imprisonment of fellow writers, scientists, and other intellectuals. Some of the stories told of hunger strikes by prisoners to protest human rights violations. Others told about protest statements circulated underground or even the staging of a rare unauthorized demonstration. While I tried to be objective and detached, I could not help feeling sympathy for their cause. After all, the Soviet government was brutal in its violations of human rights, and I admired the courage of these few dissidents who stood up to the regime.

The Kremlin was not pleased by my many stories about the dissident intellectuals. After I and an Italian correspondent named Ennio Caretto wrote about protesters who chained themselves to a railing at a department store, Ennio was expelled by the Soviet government and a January 1970 *Pravda* article denouncing him (under the headline, "Provocation") also mentioned me as being "very similar" to Ennio—implying I could be expelled, too. *Pravda* said Collings "also breathes fire and sulphur in regard to the U.S.S.R., a man who is very far from being interested in a serious study of this country." Despite being compared to a fire-breathing dragon, I ignored the implied threat of expulsion and continued covering the dissident movement. (I never was expelled, but five years later, when I was an AP correspondent in Bonn and *Newsweek* hired me to go back to Moscow as their correspondent, the Soviets refused to give me a visa, without explanation—apparently as punishment for all those stories about the protesters.)

The stories that I and other Western correspondents in Moscow wrote about the dissident movement reached a wide audience not only outside the Soviet Union but also inside, despite government censorship. Typically, a dissident would contact me and give me a bit of news. I would write a story and send it by Telex from Moscow to London. (Telex was a system of typewriting machines connected by wires to transmit texts from one country to another, similar to telegraphs. This was before the Internet, of course.) From London it would go to New York, and then to all AP subscribers around the world, including radio stations. Then a Western shortwave radio service in the Russian language, such as the Voice of America, the BBC World Service, or Deutsche Welle of West Germany, would translate my AP story into Russian and broadcast it that evening back into Russia, and people in Russia who had shortwave radios powerful enough and with enough different wavebands to evade the jamming would hear the news that the dissident had wanted the public to hear.

Sometimes the dissidents assumed, incorrectly, that Western journalists were part of their movement. In fact, although my heart went out to them and I wrote many stories that benefited their cause, as a journalist I had a duty to be as objective as possible (meaning I had to stick to the facts and not let my emotions get in the way). I had a duty to report their statements only if they were newsworthy and if they provided useful information about conditions in the Soviet Union, rather than letting myself become a propagandist for the dissident movement. This made for agonizing decisions.

One day I received a phone call from Viktor Krasin, a wiry economist and very tough character. He asked to meet me. We had an agreed-upon location for meetings, near a subway station on the western side of Moscow, and he always surveyed the area ahead of time to make sure there were no KGB. At this meeting, he told me that an obscure dissident was on hunger strike at a prison. I had done many stories such as this in the past, and there didn't seem to be anything particularly noteworthy about this hunger strike. The prisoner was a minor figure, unknown in the outside world, not even well known inside Russia, and the reason for his protest was unclear. I thanked Viktor and went to the AP office, where, after some soul-searching, I decided not to do the story.

The next time I saw Viktor he was angry.

"I didn't hear any story on the radio about the hunger strike," he said.

"I didn't do it."

"Why not?"

"It just wasn't big enough for a news story."

"Tony," he said, barely able to control his rage, "whose side are you on?"

That indicated the deep divide between journalists and sources, especially here in Russia in the 1960s, a country without a free press, a country where frustrated dissident intellectuals like Viktor depended on Western reporters to get their messages to the Russian public through the roundabout route of outgoing wire service stories and incoming shortwave broadcasts. It made no sense to Viktor that I as a human being could sympathize with the cause of democracy and freedom of expression, and could admire the courage of the dissidents, yet I as a journalist would not always do his bidding. He didn't grasp the concept of independent journalism.

Of course, even in the United States, with probably the freest press in the world, there were editors who expected me to take sides in controversies instead of keeping to the ideals of impartiality and independence. Before going to Moscow I had edited foreign stories that came into the Cables Desk at AP headquarters in Rockefeller Center, Manhattan, and I was under AP orders to make sure our Vietnam War stories included certain wording. For example, whenever we quoted the Vietnam News Agency, the propaganda unit of the North Vietnamese government, as reporting a Communist victory in a battle, we were required to add the sentence: "There was no independent confirmation of the claim." I told one of the older editors that I thought we should insert the same sentence after any U.S. government claim of an American victory. The editor gave me a look as if to ask me the same question that Viktor Krasin was to ask later: "Whose side are you on?"

I also complained about propagandistic clichés in U.S. news stories about the war, such as the phrase "Communist-infested." A war dispatch would refer to "the Communist-infested Mekong Delta." I told my AP colleagues that that didn't sound objective, and facetiously proposed that, if we were going to continue to do this, for balance we should also say "American-infested Da Nang."

One of the biggest news events while I was in Moscow was the defection to the West by Stalin's daughter, Svetlana Alliluyeva, while on a visit to India in 1967. In the supercharged atmosphere of the Cold War, this was a major propaganda setback to the Communists, coming as it did on the eve of the fiftieth anniversary of the Bolshevik Revolution. It dominated the news for days, leading the radio and television news reports, garnering banner headlines in newspapers and magazines around the world—everywhere except in the Soviet sphere of influence. There, official news media were silent.

Totally silent.

Not one word about Stalin's daughter defecting.

In Moscow, the translators and I scoured every publication, no matter how obscure, in a fruitless effort to find even the slightest or most indirect mention of this world event. I went to the apartment of Svetlana's brother, near the Kremlin, in an unsuccessful effort to speak to him and get a reaction. I wrote AP stories saying the Soviet government and Soviet Communist Party remained silent.

One day Boris, one of our translators, a short, wide-faced man with a sardonic grin, said from his desk facing mine: "Tony, look at *Pravda*. Page five."

At first I couldn't find the item. Then I found it, so small, at the bottom of the page, that it was almost not there. The headline was guaranteed not to attract attention, a headline in almost comically stark contrast to the screaming sensational headlines of mass-circulation newspapers in the West.

The tiny headline said: "S. Alliluyeva."

And the news item itself, a product of days of cogitation by the propaganda department of the Central Committee of the Soviet Communist Party, and obviously approved at the highest level, was stunningly lacking in detail. In its entirety, all it said was:

"*Soviet citizen S. Alliluyeva is living abroad. How long she remains there is a personal matter.*"

That's it.

Nothing more.

If you were an average Soviet citizen you would have no idea what this item referred to, since almost no one knew that Alliluyeva was her married name. (Russians knew that her first name was Svetlana. There was even a perfume named after her. But the *Pravda* item gave only the initial "S.")

If you were a better-educated Soviet citizen with a bit of savvy, you would know several things: It must refer to someone very important, and whatever that person had done must be very embarrassing to the party.

And if you were a better-educated Soviet citizen with a bit of savvy who also had access to an unjammed Western shortwave radio broadcast, you would have known about Stalin's daughter's defection to the West while in India and her denunciations of the Soviet system, and then if you happened to come across this microscopic item buried at the bottom of page five of *Pravda* you would know that the party leadership was furious at what it obviously saw as a betrayal. But you would also note that there was no attack on her as a traitor, and you would say to yourself that the current Soviet leaders were products of Stalin's purges, were Stalin's men, and could not bring themselves to attack anyone in Stalin's family.

For me, as an American journalist in Moscow, it was amazing to see how difficult it was for the Soviet leaders to say anything other than those few bitterly chosen words, and, of course, by saying so little it revealed how much of a blow it had been that even Stalin's daughter preferred life in the West.

As journalists we occasionally got the briefest of glimpses of members of the Soviet elite, usually at carefully structured events. In Moscow in 1967 there was a city council "election" (in which the Communist candidates were the only candidates). I went to a polling station to observe the ritual voting by dignitaries including Stalin's foreign minister Vyacheslav Molotov (a man best known for giving his name to an improvised bomb called the Molotov cocktail) and his wife, Polina, bundled up in fur-trimmed winter coats. While taking photos of other voters I accidentally backed into someone and heard a woman cry out in pain, and when I turned around I realized that I had just trod on Mrs.

Molotov's feet. I know that journalists are supposed to step on a few toes, figuratively, but this was going too far.

Another year former Soviet leader Nikita Khrushchev voted in an election, and we Western journalists went to another polling station so that we could see how he looked, since he had not been seen in public for years. We lined up along the pale green wall of a hallway leading into the schoolroom where he would vote. A black Chaika limousine pulled up outside, and men in black coats and grim faces stepped out. One of the men shoved me against the wall as if I were a sack of flour. My colleagues got the same treatment from the other men. The security detail having immobilized the press corps, the short figures of Khrushchev and his wife made their way down the hall and into the voting room. I had planned to shout out a question, but it all happened so fast that I never got a chance.

As an AP reporter I had one brief moment to interview Leonid Brezhnev, although it hardly provided any great insights into Kremlin thinking. It happened in 1973, three years after I had left Moscow, when Brezhnev made the first visit of a Soviet leader to Bonn. Brezhnev was on a charm offensive, apparently in hopes of increasing trade deals. On a pleasant spring morning in May I stood with a small group of reporters at the side of a winding road that led to the Petersberg Hotel, atop a hill across the Rhine River from Bonn. Brezhnev and his entourage got out of their limousines and began walking along the road. Remembering a few words of Russian from my days in Moscow, I shouted: "Mr. Brezhnev, what are your first impressions of West Germany?" He turned and walked over to me and said he was very favorably impressed. Then he smiled, squeezed my arm, and left. The other reporters asked me to translate from the Russian, and dutifully wrote down his words. It is a measure of the secrecy of the Kremlin in those days that I never could have asked even such an innocuous question of him when I was in Moscow.

The drabness of life in Russia was relieved somewhat by opportunities to interview visiting film stars. Claudia Cardinale was in Moscow to film *The Red Tent* and I was so taken by her beauty that my throat was dry and the questions came out as croaks. I fared even worse when I interviewed Sophia Loren in her trailer on the set of *Sunflower*. My glasses steamed up, and all I could see of her was a pile of hair and two black blobs of mascara for eyes. (Her press agent, by the way, was one of the funniest and wisest people I ever met. Over coffee in the restaurant of the Rossiya Hotel, on Red Square, a brand-new white marble structure that was already shabby and in disrepair, he said to me, in words that mocked the Cold War mentality of the West: "If the Red Army is run as badly as this hotel, what are we so worried about?")

Gloria Swanson came to Moscow for a semi-private showing of the film *Sunset Boulevard*. I interviewed her at the Metropole Hotel, across from the Bolshoi Theater. She impressed me with her dignity and charm, and her alert mind at the age of seventy, and my AP profile of her was played across the back page of the *International Herald Tribune*. I say that her film had a "semi-private" screening because it was shown to a carefully selected audience of producers, directors, writers, cultural bureaucrats, and other Soviet film figures at the Dom Kino (House of Cinema) and was not open to the general Russian public. This restrictive approach was typical of the Soviet politicization of culture, playing up movies made in the Communist world and playing down movies made in the West. Very few American films were ever shown in Moscow and usually they were movies that took critical looks at life in the United States. (I was so starved for American culture that I actually wept when I saw *Up the Down Staircase* at a Moscow film festival.)

At the Dom Kino showing of *Sunset Boulevard*, the Soviets used a very crude method of translating from English into Russian. Instead of dubbing the film or using subtitles, they had a translator stand at the back of the theater with a copy of the script and a microphone in her hand. She did a running ad lib translation, often out of sync with what was happening on the screen. And the way she translated the dialogue left much to be desired. For example, when William Holden, playing the role of a film writer staying at the home of Gloria Swanson, tells of his secret affair with a young female script writer at Paramount Studios, he says, in English: "I was playing hookey every evening." The Soviet translator at the back of the theater said, in Russian: "Every evening I played hockey."

But seeing a few film stars provided only a brief respite from the dreariness and oppression of Moscow. More often than not we were reminded that this was not an open society.

In the atmosphere of fear caused by the police state, the Russian translators in our AP office dared not speak their minds, for fear of being overheard by the inevitable microphones. But in subtle ways they sometimes made their views known.

In the late summer and fall of 1968, Volodya, one of our translators, a kindly, chubby young man who favored beige turtleneck sweaters, helped me translate government-controlled newspaper articles about the Soviet-led Warsaw Pact invasion and occupation of Czechoslovakia, actions taken by Moscow to strangle the reform movement there, known as the Prague Spring, a reform movement that later came back in the form of the Velvet Revolution of 1989 which finally succeeded. But in 1968 it was suppressed by force. I was curious to know how a Russian like Volodya felt about seeing his country's leaders ordering the imprisonment of Czech leaders such as Alexander Dubcek, who had tried to permit more freedom.

Volodya, sitting across from me in the AP office, would read aloud from articles, translating into English from editorials in *Pravda*, which were filled with lies, as usual, about the "fraternal assistance" rendered to the Czechoslovak people to free them from the "counterrevolutionaries." Because Volodya saw the stories we wrote in English, he knew the truth but could never talk about it. I would ask Volodya what *Pravda* was saying, and he would say, "You see, Tony, *Pravda* is saying that we have provided fraternal Socialist assistance at the invitation of our Czech comrades to help them overcome the counterrevolutionaries," and he would say this with a straight face while I smiled with disbelief. The closest Volodya would come to revealing how he truly felt would be in an exchange such as this:

"But, Volodya," I would ask, "how do you as a Russian feel about this?"

"You see, Tony, the situation is very complex."

Those were code words. It was as close as Volodya could come to saying that he was against what the Soviet government was doing. I would have to read it in his eyes, and between the lines, which was the way people conveyed their feelings in those days without risking arrest. It was wording that dated back to censorship in World War II, when official Soviet military communiqués omitted mention of any battlefield losses against the Germans but hinted at problems by saying that "the situation is complex."

Sixteen years after Volodya's coded conversation with me, there was still a Soviet government in Moscow but it was losing its grip, and on a return visit I was amazed how freely people now expressed themselves.

In the winter of 1984 I returned as a CNN correspondent from Rome, for a brief two-week spell to fill in for the vacationing Moscow bureau chief of CNN, Stu Loory. While I was there, mostly doing feature stories about a Soviet actress or a heated outdoor swimming pool near the Kremlin (I did a "standup" on-camera report while swimming in it in the winter), one morning I was awakened by a phone call from CNN headquarters.

Someone on the foreign desk in Atlanta said the wires were reporting that official Soviet radio stations had replaced normal broadcasting with nonstop classical music, usually a sign that someone in the Politburo had died.

I turned on the radio. It was playing Mendelssohn. Kremlinologists had long tried, without much success, to figure out, in such situations, whether you could tell which Politburo figure had died by which classical composer's music was played on Soviet radio. If it was Beethoven, was that the foreign minister? If it was Schubert, was that the head of the Komsomol, the party's youth wing? Who knew? It was all so mysterious. All I knew is that today it was Mendelssohn.

I went to the CNN office, across the courtyard from the apartment building where I was staying, on Kutuzovsky Prospekt. The TASS machine had stopped producing any reports of any kind. It was motionless and silent, a roll of blank paper in its rollers. The leadership was waiting to break the news and probably there was a power struggle going on behind the scenes. Usually when the death of one of the ruling Politburo members was announced there was also a line in the TASS announcement about who was heading up the funeral committee, and that person probably would be the new leader. They didn't want to say who headed up the funeral committee yet because they didn't know who the new leader was, so they said nothing.

CNN had me keep an open phone line to Atlanta (we didn't have live television feeds in those days) so I could get the news out fast whenever the announcement was made. Finally, at 1 p.m. that day, the TASS machine's motor hummed and its light came on. I told CNN to stand by to put me live on the air. The TASS machine began printing out a story: Soviet leader Yuri Andropov had died. I ripped the printout from the machine, ran to the phone, and reported the news, giving CNN the edge on our competition as we reported it first. What happened next in the CNN office in Moscow amazed me.

The translator and the driver began speculating, openly and without fear of the microphones, as to who the new leader might be, whether it would be Gorbachev or his rival Chernenko. Not only that, but the translator, Andrei, actually said: "I hope it's Gorbachev."

I was stunned.

Back in the 1960s when I was first in Moscow, he could have been arrested for saying that. In those days no one dared express any opinion about politics other than the officially approved party line. But now here was Andrei openly siding with one of the competing politicians, and not afraid to say it. Things had changed. As it turned out, Gorbachev did not get it this time, but a year later Chernenko, the new leader, died, and finally Gorbachev did become party leader and brought about the reforms of *glasnost,* which relaxed censorship, and *perestroika,* which permitted a more market-based economy, and then he finally presided over the collapse of the entire Soviet empire.

Hearing Andrei talk about politics in 1984 in the open way that we took for granted in the West made me realize that fundamental changes were under way in Russia. Although many problems remained, some of the secrecy and paranoia of the past seemed to be gone, and with them the obstacles to truth that had frustrated me in the 1960s in Moscow.

Chapter Two

Christmas Presents

Our flight from Rome was the last plane to arrive in the snow-covered Polish capital of Warsaw that cold and dark Saturday evening. In fact, although we didn't know it at the time, our flight was the last regularly scheduled flight allowed into the country for weeks. Purely by chance, we would soon be cut off from the outside world and plunged into the middle of a world event.

It was December 12, 1981. There were three of us from CNN: me, in my first year at CNN after leaving *Newsweek;* our camera operator Jim Allen, a wiry, chain-smoking, no-nonsense Texan with years of experience; and Ron Dean, our sound technician, a style-conscious, fun-loving younger man from Atlanta. We thought we would be doing feature stories about the Christmas season in Poland. The country was in the news because of Soviet pressures to crack down on the pro-democracy movement. Perhaps we could produce some profiles of people as they reacted to the tension.

We were greeted at the airport by Ela Volkmer, a slim, bespectacled Warsaw University student who worked as a translator for Interpress, the government agency that dealt with foreign journalists. Ela was bright, savvy, and courageous. Even though she was an employee of the Communist-run government, she, like many Poles, sympathized with the anti-Communists of the pro-democracy movement known as *Solidarność* or Solidarity. On the taxi drive to the modernistic Victoria Hotel, Ela told us that Solidarity leaders including Lech Walesa would be meeting soon in Gdansk, to the north. We made tentative plans to go there the next day.

As we arrived at the hotel, we did not know it but preparations were under way to shut down airports across the country. Borders were being closed. Communications with the outside world were being cut off. In fact, when I got to my hotel room, I picked up the phone to call Atlanta, as usual, to let the foreign desk know that we had arrived, but I was unable to get through. I assumed that there was some technical problem and went to bed.

Next morning the phone was still dead. I turned on my shortwave radio to get the news, the usual way to begin the day. I heard static on most shortwave bands. I wondered if there might be some hotel equipment in use causing interference. I kept trying to tune in different stations until at last I got a strong signal that turned out to be a shortwave broadcast of Polish state radio in English beamed to the outside world. The announcer was in the middle of an item, something about a "state of war," and at first I could not figure out which country he was talking about. Some country in Africa? Slowly it dawned on me that he was talking about Poland. We were in the middle of a "state of war," whatever that meant. Had the Russians invaded?

I went downstairs to the lobby and found Ela, looking tense. She said that shortly after midnight the Polish government had proclaimed martial law (badly translated from the Polish language as "state of war" on the state radio). The army had rounded up the leaders of the pro-democracy movement and cut off all communication with the outside world. There were tanks in the streets. There was a curfew. Jim and Ron and I huddled with Ela. We really had almost no idea what to do. Would it be safe to travel around the city? Were our competitors already on the air with their reports, beating us badly? Being unable to contact Atlanta or anyplace else outside this country, we were in near-total ignorance.

We hired a taxi outside the hotel entrance and I asked Ela to tell the driver to take us around the city center, to see what we could see. It was a bright, sunny Sunday morning, cold and crisp. Jim slumped down in the back seat, cradling his television camera in his lap as low as possible so as not to attract attention, and occasionally raised it and aimed it through the window. At first the streets seemed normal. Pedestrians were bundled up in overcoats and fur hats, trudging down the streets, going to church or wherever. Taxis and buses and trucks were moving along. Then I saw an olive-drab tank with a long gun looming over the cars and buses and trucks. Jim saw it, too. Ela said it was a Polish tank, not a Soviet one. Although Ela had made some wisecracks about the government, I did not know her well enough yet to trust her completely, so to be on the safe side I communicated with Jim in brief, obscure phrases, indicating things to include in our story without tipping off what might be a government agent paid to keep an eye on us and steer us away from sensitive news. I did not want Ela to stop us from our work. (As it turned out, she never would have done that. She was supportive, and even joined us in our many ploys to outwit the censors. And I do not want to imply that she said or did anything at first to make me suspicious. It was just my unfamiliarity with her in the beginning, and my perhaps excessive caution.)

We drove around some more, and Jim snuck shots of more tanks, and of martial-law proclamations that had been plastered to buildings. There was even one proclamation stuck onto the door of a Catholic church, which was ironic, since the church supported Solidarity. The whole time we were in the taxi I was worrying if we were pushing our luck, if we were staying out too long, if we were greatly increasing our chances of being arrested and imprisoned.

A police car stopped us.

Jim slid the camera to the floor. I prayed they had not seen him sneaking shots. The driver of the police car rolled down his window and spoke to Ela. He asked who we were and she told him.

"What are you doing?" he said, according to her translation for us.

"We're showing life in the streets," I said, and she translated.

Then the policeman said something in Polish.

I asked Ela what he had said.

"He said, 'Stop fooling around and go back to the hotel,'" she said.

I was relieved that we had not been arrested, but also I was frustrated. We were interrupted and would have to stop our coverage. What else was going on that we hadn't seen yet? We had no way of knowing, and now we wouldn't be able to find out. I had a sinking feeling that we were going to get very badly beaten by our competitors, who had permanent bureaus in Warsaw and had had weeks to get ready.

But I should have been thankful that the policeman sent us back to the hotel, because it was there that we got one of the best shots of all.

We arrived at the Victoria Hotel just before noon that day, Sunday, December 13. The snow was bright white in the powerful sunlight of Victory Square, right in front of the hotel. As we got out, a small unit of Polish soldiers armed with rifles and bayonets goose-stepped past us as they marched slowly across the square toward the tomb of the unknown soldier on our left. It was the changing-of-the-guard ceremony, something that took place every day and was usually perfectly normal. But today it took on a special meaning. It was a reminder that the military had seized power from the civilian government. We decided to get a shot of it, and thank God we did. While the martial-law restrictions might forbid our getting shots of military activities in the streets, there was nothing to stop us from shooting a perfectly routine, standard ceremony, the daily changing of the guard.

Jim framed the shot several ways. One was a wide shot, showing all of the soldiers as they goose-stepped. Another even more important shot zoomed in to a close-up (a "tight shot," in television terms) of just their black boots tromping on the white snow. I could imagine that shot in a finished, edited television news report—if only we could transmit it to Atlanta. But Ela had said all travel and communications were shut off. How could we get our tape out?

In one of the hotel rooms we did a "rough cut," prepared a tape that contained the best pictures, not yet in final edited form but arranged in the right order so that a CNN editor somewhere—Atlanta? London?—could shorten each shot and drop it into a finished news package. We had the tank, the martial-law proclamation, and the changing of the guard, as well as street scenes. Next we did a "stand-up"—my on-camera closing commentary. We shot it in the hotel room because we did not want to go outside again and risk arrest. I don't remember what I said on camera, but probably it was something about the uncertain future of Poland now that martial law had been proclaimed in an effort to stamp out the pro-democracy movement.

The final element was a "track": an audio recording of my voice reading the story I had written, to provide context for the pictures and sound, sort of a glorified caption. We didn't have a recording studio setup, with proper sound-absorbing wall paneling to avoid echoes, so we used the field-expedient method of those days, which was for me to pull my blazer over my head and use this mini-tent as a recording booth. The track was recorded onto the rough-cut tape as one of the elements now available for some editor somewhere in the world. Now we had to try to get the tape to that editor, without any means of communicating with CNN.

While we had been putting together the rough cut, Ela had been making inquiries. She discovered that, although airports were shut, roads were closed, and borders were nominally sealed, there was one train still leaving the country. It was going from Warsaw to East Berlin. And it was leaving this evening—soon.

She and I jumped into a taxi and raced to the Wschodni Station. I had the tape in a manila envelope, and I hoped it did not look suspicious. Martial-law authorities had forbidden any communications with the outside world, to prevent the pro-democracy activists from trying to make political statements and stir public opinion abroad, and anyone trying to smuggle a videotape out of the country would be suspected of law violation. The penalties could be serious.

In the dim, cramped waiting room of the train station I saw men in heavy winter coats and fur hats sitting and reading, waiting to board the train to Berlin. I needed a "pigeon"—a passenger who would agree to carry our tape with him. It had to be someone I could trust, but I didn't know any of these people. Any one of them could have been a government agent, or at the very least an individual who might feel it his duty to turn me in as a suspected spy or saboteur. I tried to find someone who might be Western, and about the only way I had of telling was their clothes. Most of the men wore the cheap, shabby clothing available in Eastern Europe. But one man was better dressed, wearing a dark-blue overcoat. He seemed better fed, also, with a healthy, ruddy color in his boyish face. He seemed to be in his mid-thirties. I went up to him.

I introduced myself and found out that he was British, a computer software salesman on his way home from a business trip to Krakow. He planned to go to East Berlin and then cross over into West Berlin. I told him I wanted to ask a favor.

"I have a videotape for American television reporting the news of the martial-law proclamation. Would you be willing to take it with you?"

"Sure," he said, in a cheerful voice.

"I have to warn you it could be dangerous. You could be searched at the border, by Polish customs and the East Germans. If they found it you could be arrested and put in prison."

"No problem."

I studied his face. He seemed to realize what I had been warning him, so I felt reassured that I had not misled him. He seemed almost to enjoy the sport of it.

But could I trust him? He was a total stranger. I had no idea if he were telling the truth about being a software salesman. There was paranoia in the air, and I didn't know whom I could trust other than Jim and Ron—and, increasingly with time, Ela.

He opened his duffle bag. Inside were computer disks and tapes, all jumbled together. This was perfect. One more tape wouldn't attract notice, even if a videotape cassette were a different format from the other tapes. I had to hope that the border guards wouldn't be that sophisticated to know the difference. I gave him the envelope with the tape and he put it in the duffle bag and zipped it shut.

I handed him a slip of paper with a telephone number on it.

"When you get to West Berlin, call this number in London, collect. Ask for Françoise. She'll tell you what to do."

Françoise Husson was the London bureau chief of CNN. A Frenchwoman who spoke in accented English, she was shrewd, tough, and hard working. She had helped create the foreign newsgathering operation of CNN. If anyone could complete the safe delivery of this precious package, she could. But so many things could go wrong. The pigeon could be arrested at the border. The tape could be confiscated. I might have written down the wrong phone number. The more I thought about it, in the taxi back to the hotel, the more I realized our chances of success were slim.

We had made a backup copy of the rough-cut tape, and I tried to find another pigeon somewhere, for insurance, but without luck. All I could think was that the established networks with their huge news operations—CBS, NBC, ABC—were beating us badly and CNN had nothing to show for its presence in Warsaw. We were miserable failures, and Chicken Noodle News, as they called us, was once again the laughingstock of the news trade.

Each day we went out in a taxi and got whatever shots we could, put together a rough cut in the hotel room, and tried different techniques that I knew were hopeless for smuggling the tape out. Several times we used passengers at the same train station. One of them demanded money. One time I gave the tape to a French airline pilot who managed to get permission to fly to Paris, as martial law eased a bit. One time the Norwegian ambassador agreed to put the tape in the diplomatic pouch; I included a note for anyone in Oslo to call Françoise, but this seemed like a long shot.

There was a food shortage, and for some odd reason the only meat available in the hotel restaurant was buffalo, so we had buffalo burgers and buffalo steak until we couldn't face the idea of yet another buffalo meal. I don't know if the food shortage was related to martial law, but it seemed that way. In any case, it added to the eeriness of our situation. After a week of tension and uncertainty, the martial-law authorities relaxed their grip slightly. We were allowed to send one message to the outside world, but could not receive any message back from the outside. And, of course, we knew that any message we sent would have to be carefully worded so as not to reveal what we had been doing and land us in jail or risk expulsion.

The means of transmission for the message was Telex. The Telex transmission office for journalists was located across Victory Square from our hotel, in the headquarters of Interpress, the agency where Ela worked as a translator. On the day that we were told we could send brief outgoing Telex messages, I went over to the Interpress office and gave the Telex operator this message to send to Françoise in London:

WE ARE FINE. HOPE THE CHRISTMAS PRESENTS ARRIVED.

To my amazement, after the Polish operator transmitted the message, Françoise found some way to keep the line open and sent a reply, even though two-way communication was forbidden.

I'll never forget the words she sent us:

CHRISTMAS PRESENTS ARRIVED.

CHILDREN HAVE BEEN PLAYING WITH THEM FROM MORNING TILL NIGHT.

I knew that Françoise, a single woman, affectionately referred to the Sony videotape machines in the London office as her "children." When I told Jim and Ron, and Ela, they were overjoyed at this great good news. Somehow or other, our smuggled tapes had made it to the outside world, and were being played over and over again on CNN. We later found out that the AP took a photo of a television screen showing one frame from our first tape when it was broadcast by CNN, a frame showing the Polish troops with bayonets tromping in the snow, the honor guard we had videotaped that first Sunday of martial law, and this photo was widely used by newspapers around the world.

Reassured that our packages were making it to the outside, we continued to go out into the streets each day to cover developments. One day we shot footage at a Mass at a Warsaw church attended by Solidarity supporters. One day we went to a cemetery for the funeral of a Solidarity figure. Events such as these—a Mass, a funeral—were borderline illegal protest demonstrations but were tolerated by the martial-law authorities (and their Soviet sponsors) because the authorities had no choice. The country was overwhelmingly Catholic and the church was anti-Communist. At the funeral I was impressed that a news photographer had a small black camera tucked just inside his jacket, with a piece of black adhesive tape over the white letters of the word OLYMPUS so that his camera would not attract attention, and he would quickly lower the zipper of his jacket and sneak a picture while, at the back of the crowd standing at the cemetery plot, plainclothesmen watched. There was constant danger for journalists.

Day after day we would cover the story, prepare rough cuts, and smuggle the tapes out, ending the day with the inevitable dinner of buffalo at the Victoria Hotel restaurant. As Christmas approached, I told Jim and Ron and Ela that we could get some good footage of Poles praying on Christmas Day, and I was thinking how this coverage would help us do a good job as journalists when to my surprise Jim said we would not do that. We quarreled. Jim said he and Ron and Ela were entitled to have Christmas as a day off. I had been so wrapped up in the daily story that I had failed to realize something: there was more to life than covering a news story. There was such a thing as having a day off and resting, especially on Christmas. But I was slow to realize that. Our argument spilled over into my hotel room, where Jim found me in my bathroom and would not let me out, held me there as a captive audience while he lectured me on my uncaring ways, his voice raised nearly to a shout. We were all exhausted and the tension was getting to us. I agreed we should take the day off.

At around this time John Cochran, then the correspondent of NBC News, did something I will never forget. Although CNN and NBC competed intensely and each of us tried to beat the other to a story, he put that rivalry aside for one day and invited me and the crew to share a Christmas dinner in his hotel suite at the Victoria. (Ela dined with her family.) At the time, NBC and the other big networks continued to disparage and disrespect poor little Chicken Noodle News and to deprive us of certain privileges such as the occasional pooling of resources, but John put all that aside and welcomed us. He is an intelligent, thoughtful person who seems incapable of an unkind word, a warm and caring man, and his kindness came at the moment when we needed it. It was an evening that is tucked away in my memory as one to keep for as long as I can remember. And, for once, I think we had turkey or goose and not buffalo meat. John later went on to ABC as a White House correspondent. He continued to do a fine job being a vigorous competitor yet still dignified and humane despite the vulgar circus of our business.

We had entered Poland on two-week visas, and now they were running out. The government refused our requests to renew them. It was time to leave. We decided to depart in stages, one each day, with Jim going last, so that we could keep getting pictures for as long as possible. I went first (a reminder that, although the correspondent gets the credit for the story, in some ways he or she is the least important member of the team in television, where the picture is everything or nearly everything). In my suitcase was yet another rough-cut tape, and when my train arrived at the border with East Germany, Polish border guards came down the corridor and one of them came into my compartment. He was young and seemed to be fresh off a farm. He asked for my passport and examined it, then pointed to my suitcase. *Uh-oh,* I thought. In Polish he demanded I open it. I stalled for time by pretending I did not understand and asked a fellow passenger in the compartment for a translation. Anything to delay things and perhaps kill enough time so that the young border guard might lose interest and move on. But he seemed determined. Martial law was still in effect. The crackdown was continuing and authorities were on guard against anyone trying to pass secret messages to the outside world from the Solidarity forces. If he found that tape, I could end up in prison instead of back home with my family.

I opened my suitcase. He pointed to the gray Sony box containing the videocassette tape. He said something in Polish.

I turned slowly to the other passenger and took my time asking, "What did he say?"

"He said, 'open it.'"

I feigned horror and pointed to the overhead light in the compartment.

"Oh, no. I can't do that," I said. "The film will be ruined if it's exposed to the light."

The passenger gave me a look but dutifully translated this bogus argument. I held my breath. Anyone who knew anything about videotapes would see through this ploy, but I was counting on this guard being unaware of what was then a relatively new technology.

The guard looked at the box and glanced up at the light, then back to me.

He shrugged and handed the box to me and left the compartment. I slumped back against my seat.

From Berlin I flew to Rome, my home base for CNN. The bureau fed the tape on that afternoon's satellite transmission to Atlanta. I was very glad to see my family, and they were relieved to finally know for sure that I was all right. We had a belated Christmas celebration at our three-story apartment in the northern suburb of La Giustiniana, a wonderful place with a tile roof and wrought-iron balcony railings and a view eastward of a small valley with Italian houses and small farms and cypresses and pines, bright and colorful in the sun, far away from drab, gray, cold Poland.

While in Rome I did the first live shot of my life. I had been with CNN since April, and this was now the end of December, and I was finally doing what most other television correspondents did all the time, appear live on camera without the safety net of tape and the possibility of doing it over. Our live shot from Rome was done in a studio of RAI, the Italian state radio and television company, and, like many beginners at this trade, I was overprepared. I wrote too long a script, had too many notes spread out on the desk in front of me, didn't make use of videotaped pictures, and tried to memorize too much instead of doing what I later found out works better: keep it short and simple, do it off the top of your head, look into the camera lens, and connect with your audience. To make it worse, there was no TelePrompTer so I kept looking down at my notes instead of up into the lens.

It was a disaster, in my opinion, but no one at CNN said anything one way or the other. They were just glad to have someone fresh from Poland able to appear on their air, and I'm sure the producers in Atlanta were too busy with the next story to conduct any postmortems.

The president of CNN, an assertive, eccentric character named Reese Schonfeld who loved the news business, had hired me in the spring. Now, at the end of December, Reese called me in Rome and asked for me and my family to come to Atlanta, as soon as possible, at CNN's expense, because he wanted me to do more live shots in Atlanta and to prepare a one-hour special on Poland. We packed our warm clothes and headed to cold, snow-blown Atlanta, where we stayed in a motel. For several days I shut myself in an edit bay and logged tapes and wrote a script and then worked with a tape editor to put together this enormous project, knowing it would have to be done quickly if it were to have any timeliness. "Quick and dirty" was one of our informal mottoes at CNN, and that described this product. We made use of what we had. I discovered that Atlanta had almost every tape we had smuggled out, and we were able to use almost every shot on those tapes, as well as other tapes obtained from other sources such as the video news agency Visnews in London. I had not been able to do a special standup in Warsaw for this project, since I had not known about it until I got out, so we did the standups in the studio in the former Jewish country club on Techwood Drive in Atlanta that was the first CNN headquarters.

Probably the kindest thing you could say about our one-hour special report is that it was earnest and well intentioned, but in truth it was crude and amateurish, quickly slapped together, and without slick production values. I blame myself, not the fine CNN video editors and producers who worked long hours to put the special together. I should have written a better script, and I should have gathered better visual elements to tell the story. And I should have done a better job getting my facts right. I realized how many gaps in my knowledge there were, including no clear idea exactly how many Solidarity people had been rounded up and put in internment centers. The government underestimated the number, while priests I interviewed, who were eager to make the pro-Communist government look bad, overstated the number. Later Western news reports put the total at about ten thousand rounded up during the crackdown.

We lacked many elements for a complete report. But one thing we did have was some excellent footage to capture the mood of martial law, including those shots of the Polish honor guard at the changing-of-the-guard ceremony. We began the one-hour program with a shot of Lech Walesa speaking at a podium and then gradually superimposed the sound of marching boots and Jim's tight shot of those black boots against the white snow until Walesa's voice and image disappeared and the boots remained. It was a simplified view of what had happened, the military trying to silence Solidarity, perhaps oversimplified, but it worked visually and helped tell the story. I thought again about the policeman who had stopped us and said, "Stop fooling around and go back to your hotel," and how grateful I was that he had done that and made it possible for us to get this shot.

Almost a year later, in November 1982, I was back in Poland. This time Ron Dean had been promoted from sound technician to camera operator, and the new sound technician was Mick Deane, a tall, blond, cheery Englishman who previously had been a roustabout for the Goodyear blimp station outside Rome. I liked working with both of them, because they cared about covering the news well and were good companions on the road. We were in Poland for the expected release of Lech Walesa from eleven months of internment near the Soviet border, and what turned out to be a bigger story than we had anticipated.

We did not know exactly when Walesea would be released, but we knew where to be: at the entrance to his ordinary-looking, working-class apartment building in the Baltic shipyard city of Gdansk. When we arrived in early evening and parked in the lot in front of the building, there were several other camera crews already there. We set up our tripod in a good position, with the building entrance behind us and the driveway in front of us, a position where Ron should be able to shoot a car arriving, Walesa stepping out and being greeted, and Walesa walking through the entrance into his building. ABC's tripod was next to ours. I could see that ABC also had a second camera position at a window on the floor above us, with what looked like a good high-angle view of the scene below.

Then we waited.

And waited.

And waited.

It was midnight, and still no Walesa. It was bitter cold, one of the coldest November nights in recent memory, the chill worsened by a wet Baltic wind. We stayed inside our car for warmth but kept our eyes focused on the likely approach route, so that we could spring out and run to the tripod as soon as we knew that he was arriving.

We waited.

It was two in the morning, three, four. Still nothing. We catnapped, in turns, so that at least one of us would be awake when the moment arrived. Then it was dawn, and eight o'clock, and still nothing. Local residents who were glad to have us on hand gave us gifts of apples and candy, and one man let me borrow his razor and a bowl of hot water, and I shaved outside the car, using the rearview mirror to see. It went on, hour after hour, waiting, waiting. We sent someone out to get takeaway food. A growing weariness crept over us, but we dared not let down our guard. We had to be alert enough for the money shot, Walesa freed and welcomed home.

It grew dark on that second day, and still we waited, and still nothing. The hours went by. Nine o'clock. Ten. Midnight. One in the morning. A crowd gathered, based on a rumor that that was it, but nothing happened. We noticed that among the crowd were men who were clearly plainclothes police, and they were watching us, ready to arrest us and confiscate our tape if this turned into any kind of illegal political demonstration. Martial law was still in force, although it was being relaxed enough to permit the release of Walesa and other leaders of Solidarity.

Three in the morning. Four. We catnapped. More apples from well-wishers. Dawn. Again I shaved outside the car. The daylight hours passed. At last it was late in the afternoon, nearly forty-eight hours since we had first arrived, and a motorcade loomed. This was really it. We and the other journalists from around the world raced to the entrance of the building. I could hear the ABC camera operator complaining about something, but I did not pay much attention. I was focused on witnessing the scene as a car door opened and the short, beefy Walesa with his walrus mustache stepped out holding a bouquet and waving to his friends and neighbors in the crowd. The symbolism was powerful. Martial law, under Soviet pressure, had failed to break Solidarity's grip, and in fact had made its leaders martyrs and all the more popular for their defiance. In its way, this moment in November 1982 was one of the steps that led to the collapse of the Soviet empire by the end of that decade, and with it the removal of the Berlin Wall and the eventual death of the Soviet Union and its totalitarian system. It could not have been more historic.

I looked at Ron. He was squinting into the viewfinder and panning left as Walesa walked into the building. Afterward Ron said he thought he got the shot, and we were OK. But the ABC camera operator was dejected. At the crucial moment of the money shot, his camera had malfunctioned. He didn't get the shot. And then his producer made an odd request. He asked me for a copy of our tape, declaring what he called a "technical pool." This was a term that meant one camera would be used for all the networks, if there were a technical problem preventing all of them from competing with one another. But usually such pool arrangements were made in advance, not after the fact, and in this case he was asking for it to apply only to the benefit of ABC and not the others. At first I considered refusing, thinking to myself: *Why should we help our competitor? We have a great shot and they don't.* But then I thought of something.

"I'll make a deal with you," I said, and pointed to the other ABC camera overhead in the second-floor window. "You make a copy of that tape for us, and we'll make a copy of our tape for you."

"Done."

And that is what happened. By the time all of the networks fed their stories from the satellite ground station in Gdansk that night, anyone closely watching the transmissions would have noticed that ABC and CNN had suspiciously identical shots of Walesa at ground level and at second-floor-window level, but the two stories were different enough in their order of shots and the voice narration of the correspondents that no one complained.

Walesa, the rumpled shipyard electrician and union leader, had become a symbol of populist resistance to the government, and he was dominating the news around the world. (Later he became president of Poland.) We journalists attended an informal, impromptu press conference that he held in the small, low-ceilinged living room of his apartment, sitting on his couch with cameras and reporters huddled around him. But Ela, translating from Polish, could hardly hear what he was saying, because an American television reporter from a local Chicago station was doing a "stand-up" (his on-camera commentary, to establish a "presence" at the scene of the story) in front of Walesa as Walesa sat addressing us from his couch. The world news figure Walesa was saying something about continuing to resist oppression, and the local Chicago reporter was shouting into a microphone: "And so Lech Walesa continues his fight. . . ." The scene was chaotic.

When we got back to Warsaw, the story had shifted to antigovernment street protests that were continuing day after day. We covered demonstrations by university students, and one evening we got pictures through one of our hotel room windows of candles and flowers arranged in the snow in the form of a huge cross in the middle of Victory Square. While Ron was shooting the protest display, there was a knock on our door. I opened it to find two plainclothes police officers who spoke English. I spoke in a loud voice to warn Ron what was happening. While I stalled for time asking the police what they wanted, Ron ejected the videotape from his camera and put a blank one into the camera in its place and then went into the bathroom and hid the tape in the ceiling. The police demanded that I let them in the room. Reluctantly, once I had seen that Ron was done, I opened the door wider and let them in. They went over to the camera and saw that it was pointed toward the cross of flowers and candles. They demanded that Ron give him the tape from the camera. He feigned indignation and adamantly refused, saying it was impossible to give them the tape. They insisted, and with a great display of disgust he ejected the blank tape and gave it to them. We were counting on their not being able to find out that there was nothing on the tape they had confiscated.

The police ordered us to come with them, and I worried that we would be arrested, but as it turned out they were friendly and all they did was march us across the square to the Interpress office, where an official spent an hour lecturing to us that we were forbidden to take such provocative pictures and that we should be more objective in our reporting. I told him we were very sorry and it would not happen again. That was a lie, of course, but at that point I would have said anything to avoid our being arrested and being unable to keep reporting. The police marched us back across the square to the hotel, where Ron retrieved the tape he had hidden in the ceiling and resumed shooting the cross of flowers and candles.

The fact that the police had been friendly, and had merely slapped us on the wrist, made me think that perhaps martial law would be eased even more. It was clear that the Polish government could not count on the loyalty of its regular police force, since many of their members were friends with people in Solidarity and some police were Solidarity supporters themselves. The government could not expect regular police to crack down very hard on the pro-democracy demonstrators. That was when it brought in the Zomo.

The Zomo were special police assault troops who came from the provinces, presumably not infected with the pro-democracy feelings of city dwellers. There were rumors that the Zomos were hopped up on drugs and were told they could beat anyone on sight with impunity. We soon saw evidence that these were no ordinary police.

University students were marching, chanting, and holding antigovernment signs at a major intersection of a wide boulevard and a cross street in downtown Warsaw. Ron and Mick and I parked our car nearby, and we walked quickly to the site of the demonstration. Ron and Mick were shooting videotape of the nighttime scene when suddenly we heard the loud sound of engines and saw a line of armored personnel carriers pull up. There was the popping sound of teargas canisters being propelled in our direction. The night air fogged with teargas. The hatches of the armored cars opened and out climbed Zomos wearing gas masks and wielding truncheons, looking like nothing less than Martians in a low-budget sci-fi film. But this was no film, and the reality of it became clear when the Zomos began beating everyone in sight, from students to journalists. The crowd dispersed and people ran in all directions. Cut off from Ron and Mick, I ran back to the car and crouched down inside. Fortunately for me, this street remained dark and deserted, while in the distance I could hear shouts from the clashes on other streets. Later when it was safe I went back but could find no sign of Ron and Mick or anyone else. Eventually they rejoined me back at the hotel, and I saw that they both had been beaten. The blood on Ron's face, and welts on Mick's back, bore evidence of their treatment at the hands of the Zomo. The two had been thrown into the back of a truck with students, had been repeatedly beaten, and had been held for hours at a police station. Their equipment was confiscated. They got the camera back but not the BVU, the separate unit used in those days for audio recording (now the two units are combined into one camcorder). We went to the American Embassy, which lodged a formal protest at the brutal treatment of journalists. We told CNN in Atlanta that we needed someone to bring in another BVU to replace the one stolen by police, and were told by someone in the CNN hierarchy that first we needed to file an insurance claim so that CNN could get enough money to buy another BVU. The claim form they faxed to us required that local police confirm our statement that the equipment was stolen and that they had been unable to retrieve it. I laughed. It was the police who had stolen it in the first place.

All in all, those first two years at CNN, 1981 and 1982, were tumultuous for me, from the perils of Beirut to the tension of covering Poland and the other stories in Europe and the Middle East. Many years later, in the mid-1990s, I received a telephone call at my office in the CNN bureau in Washington, D.C., where I was now covering political developments in a much calmer atmosphere. It was Ela. She was now a student at the University of Pennsylvania Law School, and was coming to DC to visit two friends. The four of us had a wonderful dinner at the America Restaurant in Union Station, near Capitol Hill, and Ela and I laughed as we recalled the smuggled tapes. Later I learned that she had landed a good job at a pharmaceutical company in New Jersey. I was happy for her. She is a fine, brave woman who had risked her safety to help Chicken Noodle News cover a world event. She deserved a happy ending.

Chapter Three

The Pope Has VD

The phone rang in our Rome bureau. I recognized the musical voice of a producer in Atlanta. This producer was famous for odd story assignments, so I braced for this one.

"Is that Tony?"

Here it comes, I thought.

"Yes. Hi. How are you?"

"There's a story we want you to work on."

Uh-oh.

"OK," I said, a feeling of dread beginning to grow.

"We understand from our sources that the Pope has VD. We want you to check it out and do a story." (VD, or venereal disease, is what people in those days called sexually transmitted disease.)

"What?!"

Of all the conversations I had with the producer, this one was by far the most bizarre. I should have pretended that there was interference on the transatlantic phone line. I should have pretended I couldn't hear. I should have hung up and run like hell. But instead I continued this conversation.

"Is this an April Fool's joke?" I asked, although it was not April. It was June 1981, my third month at CNN.

"Our sources are strong on this one. We're going to do it."

"There's no way this could be true," I said in desperation.

"We feel good about our sources."

"In Atlanta? The Pope is *here.*"

"You heard me."

The lilt was gone from the voice, and now there was a tough edge. The producer was determined to get the story. Normally this would be an admirable quality in an executive of a news organization. It helps provide the momentum to make sure all obstacles are overcome so that the news is covered and your organization beats the competition. But the obstacles to this particular story seemed to me at this moment to be overwhelming, starting with the fact that it couldn't possibly be true. If you wrote the most fanciful novel and included such a notion, no publisher would publish it. An even greater obstacle was that if CNN did run such a preposterous, blasphemous, and indecent story, the Vatican would never again provide us access to St. Peter's or return our phone calls or have any dealings with us of any kind whatsoever. It was only two months since the Pope had been wounded by a gunshot from a would-be assassin. Waves of sympathy had been pouring in as he lay recuperating in Gemelli Hospital in Rome. At a time like this, if we ran a story claiming that the Holy Father had a sexually transmitted disease, hundreds of millions of Catholics around the world would be outraged, and many probably would boycott CNN and its advertisers. You couldn't possibly achieve any greater disaster.

"OK," I said. "Let me see if there's anything to it."

I hung up.

Unbelievable, I thought. *This can't be happening.*

I racked my brains trying to think of a way out of this nightmarish assignment. The fact that I was in such a predicament made me wonder if I had made the right career move, joining this network. I had thought that two of my previous employers, the AP and *Newsweek,* were sensationalistic at times, but they paled in comparison with CNN. There was the time Jim Miklaszewski in the CNN Dallas bureau had illustrated a heat-wave story by doing a standup in which he fell backward into a tub of chopped ice. There was the time CNN owner Ted Turner did an on-air editorial in which he claimed that the people who should be put on trial for the 1981 attempted assassination of President Reagan were not John Hinckley, the man charged with the shooting, but the producers of the film *Taxi Driver* because Hinckley had said he did it to impress Jodie Foster, one of the stars of that movie. (Ted himself, our founding father, came to Rome on a visit that first year, accompanied by a young woman who was not his wife. She later was given her own show on our network. Over dinner with her and me and my wife at a restaurant, Ted read aloud clippings from *Fortune* and other magazines about the one subject apparently dearest to his heart—himself. I was amazed at his cheerful egotism.)

Even I became caught up in the silliness of CNN. One time the crew and I went on location to the Italian health spa of Saturnia where we showed people taking mud baths, and for my standup I began with my back to the camera while I said, "No one knows if this health cure works, . . ." and then I turned and faced the camera, revealing mud all over my face, and added, ". . . but some people will try anything. Anthony Collings, CNN, Saturnia, Italy." Actually, that standup never got used. It was too silly even for CNN. But it shows you what the circus atmosphere was like in those days.

To be sure, most of our stories were legitimate news items—disasters, economic policy, summits, terrorism. But there were enough oddball reports to make me wonder if CNN would ever be taken seriously. There was something distinctly nutty about this little network, and I should have known it from the way I was hired.

My friend Dick Blystone, from the AP London bureau, had joined CNN when it began in June 1980 and said I should follow suit. By March 1981 he had me convinced. There was an opening in Rome as bureau chief, and I applied for the job. Soon I found myself in the Atlanta office of Reese Schonfeld, the CNN president and cofounder of the network, a grinning New Yorker known for his uninhibited behavior. (I was told by one producer that Schonfeld had shouted an obscenity at errant producers as he ran across the set behind two anchors during a live broadcast, his on-screen appearance startling viewers and anchors alike.) As he talked to me from behind his desk, I could see behind him television sets tuned in to the major networks as well as CNN itself. On the CNN screen was a woman standing in front of a courthouse somewhere in California, doing a live shot. I could hear her talking about a trial taking place concerning the teaching of evolution in school. She seemed to be talking a lot, and her live shot seemed to be endless. I realized that Reese was not totally focused on my conversational skills when I saw him pick up a phone from his desk and, keeping his eyes on me, say something into it, apparently an order to get her off the air. Within a few seconds the reporter disappeared from the screen.

If Reese was tall, flamboyant, and animated, his vice president Burt Reinhardt was short, glum, and poker faced. Burt reminded me of a wooden Indian. He was renowned for his ability to pinch pennies, a quality much in demand at a network with meager resources as it tried to compete with the big boys. Those who knew him advised me to prepare for some hard bargaining over salary. I decided to ask for as much money as I could, and be prepared to be haggled down to a much lower amount. Burt took me to dinner at an Atlanta restaurant and asked me how much money I wanted to be paid. I gave him a high figure and said it was based on the fact that in those days CNN had no fringe benefits of any kind: no health insurance, no travel allowance, no cost of living adjustment for the higher housing costs abroad, no foreign exchange rate fluctuation adjustment, no schooling allowance. I had calculated how much it would cost me to create all these benefits myself, and added this to a base salary comparable to what I was making as *Newsweek* bureau chief in London, and told Burt.

"We don't have that kind of money," he said bluntly.

"Well, then I guess we don't have a deal," I said.

"I guess not."

I told Burt that in that case I would return to London. He said to wait a day. Next day we met again and he offered me a salary that was five thousand dollars *more* than I had asked for. This made no sense. I had been fully prepared to accept much less than that. Was this some trick? Had Burt forgotten how much I had asked for? Had he lost his vaunted negotiating skills? Whatever the reason, I accepted immediately before he had time to change his mind. Soon I was studying a contract that was placed before me. The idea of having a contract was novel for me. At my previous journalistic jobs, at the *Wall Street Journal,* AP, and *Newsweek,* there had been a handshake and a letter, but now in the television business there was a contract. Parts of it were strange, such as the clause that said I could not change my facial appearance (for example, growing a beard) without network approval, or the clause that said Turner Communications had worldwide rights to the use of my voice and image. (In later years, as Ted Turner's empire expanded, the wording in my contracts was changed to say that they had those rights throughout the Earth "and the cosmos." Were they expecting cable operators on Mars?)

Soon after being hired I was back in Atlanta for two weeks' training. One day I was sitting in an edit bay beside a video editor, a teenager who was selecting shots from various tapes and electronically pasting them in sequence into an edited taped news report. On a monitor overhead I could see the anchor at his set next to us, and I could hear his voice. It suddenly dawned on me that the anchor was introducing the very news report that the video editor with me was still working on, but the report wasn't ready yet. The anchor was "stretching," stalling for time by ad-libbing extended commentary. A frantic producer came to the doorway of our edit room and asked for the tape. "I've got a few more shots to lay in," the editor said casually. With time running out, he found the shots, laid them in, ejected the tape, and handed it to the producer, who ran off. Within a few seconds the story appeared on air.

I got the impression that this sort of frantic, last-minute behavior was commonplace at CNN. There didn't seem to be a huge amount of planning going on. One night just before midnight I was in the newsroom when a young woman ran up to me and asked: "Can you anchor?" I was brand new and had never done live television other than brief guest shots as a *Newsweek* or AP reporter appearing on British, German, and Hungarian television. She said the anchor had failed to show up that evening and they were on the air in a few minutes and were desperate. Bewildered but not wanting to let the team down, I agreed to try it. Someone started dabbing makeup on me, but fortunately the regular anchor showed up at the very last minute and went on the air. I didn't have to humiliate myself. Still, the fact that whoever just happened to be in the newsroom might end up anchoring a news hour told me a lot about how this network operated. It was so slapdash, but there was something about it I liked.

In contrast to the self-important *Newsweek* editors, these kids were eager and dedicated. There was an energy and excitement that had been missing from the established news organizations I knew.

The makeshift approach to news carried over to my first CNN story. I was assigned to cover two unrelated events: a memorial for Martin Luther King, Jr., and a continuing Atlanta police investigation into the mysterious deaths of young black boys. Neither event was big enough for a story itself, but the thought was that these two half-big events combined might amount to enough for an edited package. In any case, they were the only newsworthy things that were happening in Atlanta that day, and the Atlanta bureau, like all CNN bureaus, was expected to produce one package every day.

With me was a local camera operator named Lenny, who was short and squat and built like a fireplug. Lenny taught me a lot about television news, the main lesson being that the story doesn't have to make much sense as long as you have good pictures. First we went to the MLK memorial where a ceremony marked the thirteenth anniversary of his shooting death in Memphis. Then Lenny told me to do a "standup bridge"—a brief statement to camera that would be inserted into the middle of the edited package.

"What do I say?" I asked him as he extended the legs of his tripod and placed the camera on top of it.

"Say 'While the King memorial service was taking place, the investigation continued into the missing and murdered children in Atlanta.'"

"But the two have nothing to do with each other."

"Just say it."

This was what we at *Newsweek* had called a neck-snapping transition, a sentence that tried to link two unrelated thoughts. Just about the only thing the two events had in common was that they were both taking place in Atlanta that day. I suppose there was also the slight connection that both events were of concern to African Americans. But as a reporter my gut told me that this linkage made no sense. Still, the show had to go on, we had an appointment for an interview with police across town, time was running out, and I couldn't think of anything better to say. I did the standup bridge using Lenny's wording, and that was my first story for Chicken Noodle News.

Once I began working in the Rome bureau, I realized that you could do stories about almost anything as long as you had good pictures. Story ideas would come from scouring the local newspapers including *La Repubblica* and seeing what was on RAI, Italian television. Louise Priestley, our bureau manager/producer, a voluble, vivacious woman whose emotional outbursts contrasted with my shy demeanor, would clip something out of the paper, make a few phone calls in her fluent Italian, charm some official in her flirtatious manner, set up a shoot for us, and off we would go, out into the streets to get our story. Louise, along with Mark

Leff, an NBC correspondent, had helped create the Rome bureau, and they had pulled off a miracle in fighting both Italian red tape and Burt Reinhardt's miserly budget allocations to create this tiny CNN office, which was hardly much more than a glorified closet in an RAI building on Via dei Robilant in north Rome off the little square called Piazzale di Ponte Milvio.

We did stories on almost anything. One day it was an Italian heat wave. One day it was topless beaches. One day it was how Italians make pasta (including a shot of our neighbor's dog, Beggy, eating a bowl of *pasta per cani*—pasta for dogs). One day it was how the Vatican wants priests to dress better. One day it was how terrible the traffic is. For that story we wanted to get a shot of one of the busiest intersections, where traffic from Via del Corso, Rome's main downtown street, pours into the huge square known as Piazza Venezia. There in the middle of it was a photogenic Rome policeman in a white pith helmet and white gloves with gauntlets who stood on a platform and directed traffic like an orchestra conductor with elaborate, ornate gestures. We had to have that shot. It would be perfect for this story. So we parked our car to one side and carried the tripod and camera and BVU audio recorder to a good vantage point and began to set up. We were interrupted by a policewoman who demanded to see written permission for us to shoot this scene. Of course, we had none. We begged her to let us get the shot. She emphatically shook her head. Not possible. *Niente da fare*—nothing could be done about it. We slumped in dejection. Then we noticed something. The officer who had been directing traffic finished his shift and left, and the policewoman replaced him atop the conductor's stand and began directing traffic herself. She turned and looked at us and smiled and nodded and beckoned to us, and I finally realized what was going on. She didn't want us photographing *him;* she wanted us to photograph *her.* And so we got the shot.

We were constantly dashing off to cover stories in Rome, usually running late and slapping things together at the last minute. One time we dashed out of the Via dei Robilant office and into our car and raced off to cover some event. Chip, the camera operator that time, was sitting in the back seat chatting with me and the sound operator about the story and about upcoming assignments and other matters when suddenly he asked: "Where's the camera?"

Each of us said he thought the other had loaded the camera into the car. All the other equipment—the tripod, the batteries, the cables, the reflector, the tapes—all of it was in the car, but not the camera.

Our sixty-thousand-dollar Sony broadcast videocamera.

If we had left it out somewhere, it would certainly be gone by now, given the widespread extent of theft in Rome. CNN would dock Chip's pay, taking out a certain amount each month until the replacement cost had been covered. It was a disaster. Hoping against hope, we raced back through Rome traffic to the building on Via dei Robilant. We looked out the window—and saw the camera where we had left it, right on the sidewalk. I figured that a would-be thief must have said to himself: *No, it can't be. It's too good to be true. Got to be a trick of some kind.*

Then there was the story of Valentino and the french fries. The world-famous Italian fashion designer Valentino Garavani had his atelier on the top floor of a building in the Centro Storico, the historic old center of Rome next to the foot of the Spanish Steps. He had worked there happily for years until McDonald's opened its first Italian restaurant on the ground floor of his building. Now he was suing McDonald's for damages. Apparently, according to the maestro, the smell of french fries was so powerful that it penetrated several stories up into his workplace and made it impossible for him to create his great fashion designs. We covered the farcical trial in a courtroom where everyone, including the judge, smoked cigarettes during the hearing. Lawyers for the two sides delivered melodramatic perorations, complete with sweeping gestures of their berobed arms, as if this were one of the great legal issues of our time. At last the judge said he would appoint an expert with a keen nose to go to the atelier of the fashion genius and smell for himself whether the odor was so disturbing as to thwart the progress of Italian fashion. (I don't know what the expert later reported, as I was gone by then. But we did cover the amazing opening of the trial.)

Silly stories from Rome provided comic relief from the deadly wars and violence that we covered so often in the Middle East, and that mix of the serious and the trivial was all part of being a foreign correspondent. I enjoyed some of the more trivial stories partly because they came closer to showing Americans what ordinary life was like for people in other countries. We journalists needed to do more of that. We needed to show everyday life, how people work and relax in other countries, so that Americans could get away from demonizing or idolizing foreigners and not think about them only in such clichés as the eccentric English or the ooh la la French, and to get away from only showing the exceptional and the unusual—earthquakes, mudslides, revolutions—and only profiling officials. We needed to cover non-news: everyday lives of ordinary people. In fact, to CNN's credit, the network did use some of our feature stories about daily life abroad.

We did a series about Palestinians, their values, culture, music, history. We focused on one family living in Nabatiya, southern Lebanon, near the Israeli border. We included such details as the key from their former home in what is now Israel, hanging inside the house by the front door of their current home in southern Lebanon, a visual reminder that despite the fact that Arabs had lost the 1948 war with Israel, and that Palestinians had fled the area, there were many Palestinians who refused to give up on the unlikely idea that someday they would move back into their old homes. This was a story that I thought might upset some Americans because it did not portray all Palestinians as bad and all Israelis as good, and it tried to explain why Palestinians felt the way they did without taking sides ourselves. My feeling was that sometimes a journalist had to upset or at least challenge his viewers, to stretch their minds and force them to go beyond narrow stereotypical views of the world.

We also did a story in Moscow about a Russian family although this family was not typical: the daughter was Yevgeniya Simonova, a famous Soviet actress, and the father was a scientist and they had some privileges including travel abroad and a shorter wait to buy a car. One reason I chose this family was that they were allowed to meet with foreigners, so there would be less danger of their being in trouble for talking to us. Another reason, I have to admit, is that she was beautiful, and having her in the story increased the chances that CNN would use it. (She was so beautiful, in fact, that, before we left the office to go interview her, our translator Andrei fussed over his appearance and brushed his teeth.)

We should have done more stories like that about humanity rather than politics, disasters, and oddities. Too often we provided what Atlanta wanted: novelties, good pictures for their own sake, video versions of AP stories, and exclusive bits of information that were not really important but helped CNN promote itself. Too often we did these journalistic bread-and-butter stories and did not serve the greater cause of Truth. But to his credit Ted Turner wanted feature stories from all over the world, partly due to his exchange agreements with other countries, swapping free CNN satellite dishes and free CNN service for free television news reports produced by foreign networks, but also partly due to idealism. He thought in global terms. In fact, he forbade us from ever using the word "foreign" (we had to pay a one-hundred-dollar fine each time we slipped and used it) because he felt that we were all part of one big world, and that non-American CNN subscribers should not be considered alien, and that CNN should provide more than just the American version of the day's events. To avoid being fined, we had to make do without such phrases as "foreign relations," "foreign affairs," or "foreign policy," all of which is not easy for a foreign correspondent. We had to substitute "world," "international," "abroad," "overseas," or "non-American" for the forbidden f-word.

We were a little network with big ambitions, but our desire to be taken seriously was constantly undercut by our own nuttiness. So it was in this context that I faced my predicament after the producer in Atlanta informed me that their sources had told them that His Holiness the Pope had contracted a sexually transmitted disease. I agonized over what to do. At last I telephoned Gemelli Hospital and spoke to a doctor who was serving as press spokesperson for the duration of the Pope's recovery from his gunshot wounds and abdominal surgery.

"This is Tony Collings from CNN," I said.

"Yes?"

"I have a question."

"Yes?"

I took a deep breath.

"After his surgery, the Pope has had blood transfusions, right?"

"That's correct."

"And obviously the hospital makes sure that the blood is not contaminated by anything, right?"

"Anything such as what?" the doctor asked.

"Oh, I don't know . . . Anything." I couldn't bring myself to say it.

"There is no problem with the blood supply," he said.

"So the Pope has not contracted any diseases?"

"No."

"Thank you, doctor."

I called the producer and said that I had received an official denial. Strictly speaking, this was not exactly true, but I had gone as far as I could. Luckily, the producer had lost interest in the story by this time and had gone on to something else. We had dodged a bullet.

Chapter Four

Line of Death

They called it the Line of Death.

It was an imaginary line drawn on the map by Colonel Muammar el-Qaddafi, the Libyan leader. The line went across the mouth of the 150,000-square-mile Gulf of Sidra, a huge indentation in the coastline of Libya. Although the area south of the line was clearly in international air and sea space, Qaddafi claimed it as Libyan. He said that any plane or ship that crossed that line would be attacked. Calling his bluff, the United States sent an armada including three aircraft carriers into that portion of the western Mediterranean and made it clear that it intended to enforce its right to enter international waters and airspace. Newspaper commentators envisioned U.S. and Libyan warplanes in deadly dogfights, and there were fears of a wider war.

So when I was told that CNN and three other networks—CBS, NBC, and Independent News Network—had decided to jointly charter a plane and fly to the area near the Line of Death, I thought that was a good idea. I had no idea how dangerous it was. I should have, but I didn't. Perhaps I was too focused on how we would do the story, what elements we would shoot, how we would get the footage to Atlanta. It seemed like a great story.

On Tuesday morning, March 25, 1986, the Cessna Citation charter plane was waiting for us at Ciampino, one of Rome's airports. Mark Phillips, a fine correspondent for CBS, a man with a mustache and a wry sense of humor (he once did a standup in front of an aquarium full of sharks for a story about lawyers), accompanied me and our camera crew aboard the small twin-engine jet. We took off and headed south high above the Mediterranean. After flying for a while we saw, far below us like a toy boat in a bathtub, the USS *America*. Our camera operator got shots of the aircraft carrier. There were other American warships nearby.

Suddenly a jet fighter plane appeared off our right side. We could see that it was a U.S. Navy interceptor, from the carrier, with air-to-air missiles mounted under its wings. The plane was very close. Its wingtip appeared to be almost touching the tip of ours. Mark and I, peering through our window, could see the American pilot in his helmet. He was speaking and making hand signals. "He's giving us his radio frequency," our pilot said. Our pilot tuned in and put the sound on a loudspeaker so we could hear.

"Who are you?" the Navy pilot asked.

"Charter from Rome. American television," our pilot said.

To which the Navy pilot replied, in chilling words: "I suggest you stay well away."

He was making it clear that he had orders to keep all non-Navy planes away from the carrier, and would use force if he had to. Then he soared up and away in a hard right banking turn.

We didn't need any more convincing. We decided to heed his advice and stay well away. Three U.S. Navy jets escorted us back toward Italy.

When we returned to Ciampino with our aerial footage of the American aircraft carrier and the Navy jet that had flown so close to us, I used the airport pay phone to call Atlanta. A CNN producer immediately put me on the air, and I gave a quick report on the U.S. Navy's presence near the Line of Death. Then I went to the CNN bureau on Via dei Robilant and worked with our video editor to put together a complete package that we fed by satellite to Atlanta.

Our adventure became a news item itself. The *Washington Post* headlined: "The Networks' Libyan Fly-By; Plane Escorted From Combat Zone." The story referred to our flight as "a bit of daring that made even some war correspondents shudder with concern." It added: "Network and government sources said that besides the worry that U.S. forces might mistake a small plane for a new form of Libyan kamikaze, there was also considerable concern that Libyan planes and missiles could find the slower twin-engine plane a more attractive target than the American military jets." When I read this, I realized that I had had no real idea how dangerous our flight was.

Dangerous, yes. But was it worth it? I think so. We obtained aerial views of part of the huge American armada in the western Mediterranean, as well as shots of the fighter jet that came so close to our civilian plane. We gave viewers at least some idea of what was going on in the confrontation between U.S. and Libyan forces. The alternative would be to rely solely on the Pentagon for access to the scene, and that, of course, would mean giving the Pentagon total control over what journalists could see.

As it turned out, the American presence and some skirmishes including the U.S. bombing of a Libyan patrol boat and radar facility were enough to make Qaddafi back down, and there was no major armed conflict. Eventually the crisis went away.

But there was always another crisis somewhere in the Middle East in those years, and I covered some of them, first as a *Newsweek* correspondent and later as a CNN reporter. Probably the most dangerous story to cover was the Israeli bombing of Beirut.

The year was 1982. The PLO—the Palestine Liberation Organization, led by Yasser Arafat—had found a new headquarters in West Beirut, and its office was near Arab University. It was the main leadership group for the Palestinian diaspora. Many Palestinians had wandered from one country to another. First they fled to Jordan from what was once the British mandate of Palestine after the creation of Israel. Then, in September 1970 (Black September, the Palestinians call it), King Hussein of Jordan had his army destroy the bases in Jordan of Palestinian guerrillas who were taking over parts of his country. Then Hussein ordered the Palestinians to leave his country and many went to Lebanon. Their arrival in this multiethnic country created a new situation. Critics said the Palestinians upset the delicate balance of Lebanese Maronite Christians and Lebanese Muslims and other ethnicities. No one knew the exact numbers of each ethnic group; the subject was so sensitive that the country had stopped conducting a census. In any case, after the Palestinians arrived, with many living in filthy refugee camps around Beirut and in southern Lebanon, tensions rose, and in 1975 a terrible civil war destroyed what peace and harmony had existed and left parts of Beirut in ruins. A number of Lebanese believed the Palestinian presence created problems. Another opponent of a continued Palestinian presence in Lebanon was the Israeli government of Prime Minister Menachem Begin. It saw the Palestinians as a security threat, and pointed to the Katyusha rocket attacks from Palestinian positions in southern Lebanon on Israeli towns near the border. Begin wanted the PLO out of Lebanon. Arafat refused. To force him to comply, the Israelis began bombing PLO positions in West Beirut.

I was sent to West Beirut to relieve CNN correspondent Peter Arnett, who had been there for several weeks and done an outstanding job and now was taking a breather. Peter was a hero of mine. Seventeen years earlier I had been a rewrite editor at the AP in New York, working on the Cables Desk from midnight to 7 a.m., and part of my job was to read the incoming stories from our Saigon bureau and do any rewriting necessary. Whenever the story was from Peter Arnett, it needed no rewriting. It was beautifully reported and beautifully written. I admired his courage in covering combat, and his attempt to be as objective as possible, reporting only what he saw with his own eyes and not assuming that official U.S. statements bore any relationship to reality (many of them were lies, as we now know). He broke the story of American looting during the incursion into Cambodia, a story that was so sensitive that at first the AP spiked it, with the lame excuses that such looting was normal and not news, and that negative news about our fighting troops would hurt the war effort. I was outraged that the AP would refuse to run this story, and relieved when the AP finally did release it. It was an example of honest, important reporting by a Pulitzer Prize–winning correspondent. Arnett saw war for what it was: not a fun adventure, not a glorious campaign for a noble cause, but an ugly form of organized human activity in which each side tried to kill as many soldiers as possible on the other side and in the process caused unspeakable suffering.

Many years later, Peter made some bad decisions and hurt his reputation as an honorable journalist. He agreed to put his name on a disastrous CNN story, written by others, called "Valley of Death." It claimed that during a commando raid called Operation Tailwind, U.S. troops used nerve gas in Laos and were sent to kill American defectors, and he narrated the story and helped promote it. Soon it turned out that the main source for the wild allegations was an eccentric veteran who had written an entire book about the incident and never once mentioned nerve gas or defectors. He claimed to have "repressed memory" problems. There were many other problems with sources and lack of clear evidence. Two producers were fired by CNN. Peter was lucky to get off with a reprimand that time, but his luck ran out during the 2003 U.S. invasion of Iraq. While working for NBC, Peter made the disastrous decision to give an interview to state-controlled Iraqi television and to let them use his opinion that the Americans were getting bogged down. NBC fired him, and he admitted he had made a misjudgment. Arnett was wrong to let himself be used by the propaganda arm of a country deemed the enemy by the U.S. government. I can't excuse his behavior in Tailwind and in the Iraq war of 2003, and I'm saddened to see his demise, but I still remember all the great stories he did covering other wars.

So when I arrived in West Beirut in August 1982 I was there to relieve the short, tough man with a New Zealand accent and an easy laugh who was one of my heroes in journalism at that time. Peter briefed me on the situation, telling me who our tape couriers were, where our cameras could go to get views of the bombing (the best location was the rooftop of our hotel, the Commodore), and the names and phone numbers of key contacts including the PLO spokesperson and Lebanese government officials and U.S. Embassy officials. The bombing was taking place in the context of complex negotiations. Because at that time Israel did not recognize Arafat as a legitimate leader, its government refused direct negotiations with him. Instead, Israel negotiated with a special U.S. envoy named Philip Habib. Israel would tell him its position. Then Habib would go to Beirut and meet with Lebanese Muslim politicians who supported Arafat and relay Israel's position to them (since the United States also did not recognize Arafat as leader) and the Lebanese politicians would then tell Arafat. Habib would shuttle back and forth between Beirut and Jerusalem, conducting these proxy negotiations.

I discovered that there was a pattern that linked the negotiations with the bombing. Habib would meet with Begin in Jerusalem, then fly to Damascus (the Beirut airport was closed), drive to Baabda, the district of Beirut where the American ambassador's heavily fortified residence was located, meet with

Lebanese politicians to give Arafat the latest Israeli negotiating position, listen to the Lebanese politicians give Arafat's reply, then drive to Damascus and fly to Jerusalem and meet with Begin to give him Arafat's position. Then we would brace for another round of Israeli bombing, which seemed to be Israel's way of replying to an unacceptable Palestinian demand. In fact, as we journalists waited on the rooftop of the Commodore Hotel late in the afternoon, one journalist said, "I wonder what the Israeli response will be to Arafat's position," and I nodded toward the eastern Mediterranean and said, "I think we're about to find out." Israeli bombers were approaching out of the setting sun.

I'll never forget the sound of those Israeli planes, sent to Beirut by the government of Menachem Begin. It was an odd rumbling sound, like a giant marble rolling on a sheet of zinc, slow and menacing. On that rooftop, television cameras from CNN, ABC, NBC, CBS, and British, French, German, Japanese, and many other news organizations pointed toward the approaching planes. Their microphones picked up the rumbling thunder of the engines and the explosions of PLO antiaircraft fire, the explosions growing more numerous and more intense as the bombers flew closer and closer, coming in out of the sun to make it hard for Palestinian air defense to see them. There would be the whoosh and flash of Soviet-made surface-to-air missiles fired by the Palestinians in hopes of hitting the planes. There would be the bright pinpoints of light darting out from the planes and slowly falling as the Israeli pilots expelled heat balloons to deflect the heat-seeking missiles, and there would be the curves of the missiles' trajectories away from the plane. And then the planes would make their sharp dives and bombing runs and climb sharply just as the bombs exploded near the PLO headquarters south of our hotel. Sometimes the bombs landed so near us that our building shook. After the bombs exploded you could see tall columns of black smoke that rose from the targeted buildings and lingered over West Beirut.

The bombing happened almost every day during the most intensive weeks. Some wag among the journalists created T-shirts that said APPEARING NIGHTLY: BEGIN AND THE JETS. Gallows humor helped us get through the tension.

Being on the Commodore rooftop usually was relatively safe, as the planes did not target buildings on our street, although it was close enough that we could feel the impact. Some camera operators took the risk of getting closer to the target area near PLO headquarters, but I felt this was far too dangerous. Some days the Israelis shifted their targets closer to our hotel, and then it was dangerous to be in a part of Beirut that earlier we had thought was relatively safe. Palestinians speculated that the Israelis were trying to kill Arafat, who slept in a different building during the daytime each day and moved around at night, and that the Israelis were bombing certain buildings near us in West

Beirut based on tips from informants as to where Arafat was staying. The bombs were a special type that caused buildings to implode, to fall inward, apparently to maximize the possibility of killing everyone inside, or at least that was what some Palestinians and Muslim Lebanese believed. One day one of the bombs hit a building on Cleopatra Street, which was only a few blocks from our hotel, and the blast rattled our windows and shook our building so hard and the thunderous explosion was so loud that it felt as if the bomb had exploded right next door. I was terrified. Still shaking, I joined our camera crew and we went to the building on Cleopatra Street and got pictures and sound of the rescue operations by Lebanese emergency workers and the Red Crescent Society, the Palestinian version of the Red Cross. The whole time that we video-taped dead bodies and the wounded, covered in blood, being pulled from rubble, I worried that the Israeli planes would come back for another bombing run and that we would be in the center of the target. The minute the camera operator said he had enough footage, we left as fast as possible.

Under my short-sleeved shirt I wore a bulletproof vest made of Kevlar, reinforced by a small steel plate that slid into a pocket over my heart. If a bomb had gone off nearby, the vest probably would have protected my heart from shrapnel but would not have protected my head, arms, legs, or other parts of my body, so wearing a vest was more psychological than anything else. I talked myself into believing I was doing everything I could to be as safe as possible, but that was not true. The safest thing would have been to not be there at all.

In addition to the bombing, the Israelis besieged West Beirut, intermittently cutting off electricity and water, from their positions in East Beirut where Maronite Christian armies welcomed the invading Israeli army as an ally against the Palestinians. The siege was designed to pressure the PLO into leaving. The Commodore Hotel and those other people in West Beirut who could afford it had diesel-powered generators and arrangements with private suppliers of water. But the less fortunate had to live without modern appliances and water for hours at a time. We did stories about life in the siege. In one of them, I did a standup next to an outdoor water tap. I lifted the lever that opened the faucet. No water came out. I let the lever fall back with a loud clink, a bit of audio designed to be available to the video editor as "natural sound" to provide emphasis and a presence, one of the ways a television news report brings the viewer into the scene.

One of the most sought-after stories was any comment by PLO leader Yasser Arafat as to whether he would give in to Israeli pressure or continue to resist. Communications with the PLO were haphazard, and it was dangerous to go to their office because it was in the bull's-eye of Israeli bombing, so I worried that we didn't always know what Arafat was doing. He might be off somewhere talking to journalists and we would miss the story. One day that did happen. I got an urgent Telex message from CNN in Atlanta that CBS had broadcast an exclusive interview with Arafat saying he would not compromise. A message like that from your home office is known in the trade as a "rocket," meaning a projectile that travels up a certain part of your anatomy. A rocket is what you don't want to get if you want to be successful and have a good reputation for competing with the other news organizations. When I read the Telex my stomach churned. We were badly beaten on an important story. What could we do to recoup?

I tried reaching the PLO but could not get through to anyone to request our own interview with Arafat. I asked Abed, our driver and fixer, if he had any ideas. Abed noted that one of the key interlocutors in these proxy negotiations was Saeb Salam, a former Lebanese prime minister.

"Let's go to his house and maybe you can interview him," Abed said.

"Good idea."

What did we have to lose? Interviewing Saeb Salam would be better than nothing, I thought, as the camera crew and I got into Abed's car and drove to an upscale residential neighborhood of West Beirut and the mansion of Saeb Salam. It had a wrought-iron fence and a garden in front, where water sprinklers were working (no sign of siege here), and the building had sweeping Moorish arches with ornate inlaid marble decorations. It was a different world from the dusty poverty of the Palestinian refugee camps. Abed told a servant that we were from American television and that we would like a brief interview with Saeb Salam, the former prime minister.

We were ushered into a library on the right side of the entrance hall. We waited a long time. Nothing happened. Then we heard the sound of vehicles approaching on the street, and people getting out of the vehicles and entering the building. We looked and saw a group of men in fatigues in the entrance hall, and in the middle of them was Yasser Arafat in his familiar khaki uniform and *keffiyeh,* a checkered headdress. By pure chance, we had arrived here just before him. The camera crew began filming, and I knew instantly that at the very least we had fresh pictures of the Palestinian leader, and clear evidence that he had survived the latest bombing. We got a brief interview with him, on camera, in the entrance hall, an interview in which he said he was fine and denounced the bombing and demanded that the Israelis withdraw. No outward sign of change in his negotiating position, to be sure, so it was not that exciting a story, but still it was news: Arafat was alive and well and was showing no signs of giving in to Israeli demands. We found another driver to take the tape to "Dixie," the journalists' code word for Israel to the south of us (we didn't want suspicious Palestinians hearing us talk about Israel and mistakenly thinking we were spies), and in place of the earlier rocket from Atlanta this time we got congratulations.

One of the challenges in covering Arafat was to avoid being exploited by him. He was a survivor, a shrewd politician, a master of propaganda, and he knew how to manipulate the press. One time we interviewed him in the middle of the night. Plans for the interview kept changing, apparently for security reasons. We were told by his press officer at 9 p.m. to wait in the Commodore Hotel. Finally the press officer came to get us at 2 a.m. We were driven around West Beirut, taken from one building to another, until finally we were told to set up our camera gear in the basement of a building. We waited for another hour, and at last Arafat entered the basement. During the interview, in his heavily accented English, he ducked one question after another, despite my efforts to get him to address the burning questions of the day. When I asked, "Will you recognize Israel?" he answered with a question: "Should I?" I got very little out of him, but he got a lot out of us: publicity. At the end, the cameraman handed a still camera to one of Arafat's aides and asked him to take a souvenir picture of the crew with Arafat. I was about to join the group posing for the picture when I noticed Arafat putting his arm around the cameraman's waist, as if they were great friends. My journalistic instinct told me to keep my distance. I didn't want critics of the news media waving this photo around as alleged proof of pro-Palestinian bias by CNN.

(A few years later a similar issue came up when we were in Tunisia and wanted to interview Arafat or any other PLO official on his reaction to an Israeli bombing raid on their temporary headquarters in Tunis. The PLO press officer insisted that I make a formal request, in writing, for the interview. I had no CNN letterhead stationery with me, so I had to use his office's stationery, but it had the official slogan of the Palestine Liberation Organization on it. After I wrote the letter I was embarrassed to see my signature on a document headed *Revolution Until Victory*. So much for journalistic detachment.)

Back in August 1982 in West Beirut my crew and I covered the Israeli bombing for a month, then rotated out of West Beirut and another CNN team came in. We relocated to the Alexandre Hotel in East Beirut and continued to cover the story from this new vantage point, getting footage from the hotel rooftop as Israeli artillery batteries positioned in the hills of East Beirut behind us fired shells and rockets at targets in West Beirut.

One day, after intensive shelling, Lebanese sources said that three hundred civilians had been killed. This type of casualty claim was almost impossible to verify independently, and all that the journalists could do was make sure to attribute the claim to as specific a source as possible (the PLO or Lebanese Muslim political parties that supported the PLO or sometimes a hospital or police office) and see if an Israeli army press officer hanging out at the Alexandre Hotel would have any reaction. At night we could see the tracer fire from

Israeli heavy machine guns arcing like sparks as the bullets headed for targets in West Beirut. The rooftop vantage point became a gathering place for journalists from around the world. John Chancellor, the anchor of NBC, was there, and so was Peter Jennings, the anchor of ABC. We journalists assumed that the armies of the Israelis and their Lebanese Christian supporters and the armies of the PLO and their Lebanese Muslim supporters knew that the Alexandre was the journalists' hotel. We assumed that neither side would target us. Being there in East Beirut seemed safer than being in West Beirut—until the morning of Thursday, August 5, 1982.

I was resting on my bed in my room in the Alexandre Hotel in East Beirut that morning, hot and uncomfortable in my bulletproof vest and safari suit, when what sounded like a clap of thunder exploded and the panes of glass in my window shattered and shards of glass flew across the room. I got under the bed in case this was the start of a barrage, in case for some reason one of the armies had decided to target our hotel for shelling, but nothing more happened. It was quiet. Finally I got up and went downstairs and saw that a bomb placed in a container in the parking lot in front of the hotel had exploded, wounding several journalists and badly damaging thirty-five cars. Our driver had a bloody bandage on his head, and said he had just left the pharmacy next to the hotel when the bomb went off and that if he had been a few minutes later he would have been dead.

A bunch of us milled about in the parking lot, and our camera crews got footage of the burned-out remains of the cars and the blown-out windows of our hotel. I remember seeing the familiar face of Peter Jennings, and discovered that he was as friendly and nice in person as he appeared to be on-screen. He even was kind enough to tell me that he liked the CNN story that Peter Arnett and his crew had done about a Palestinian mental hospital that had been hit by Israeli shelling.

Most journalists are highly competitive, and if they compliment a rival network it is sometimes done grudgingly or sarcastically, but Peter Jennings's compliment seemed genuine. Jennings had spent more time as a foreign correspondent than his counterparts, the anchors Tom Brokaw at NBC and Dan Rather at CBS, and ABC's news programs seemed to devote more time to foreign news than the other over-the-air commercial networks, and that one meeting I had with Jennings gave me the feeling that he cared about foreign news and wanted to see as much of it on air as possible. In later years I noticed how much more foreign news (some of it picked up from the BBC) was broadcast by ABC than the others. It's still inadequate, of course, but a two-minute package from Beirut is better than no minutes at all.

That bomb in the parking lot of the hotel in East Beirut was typical of the dangers for reporters in Lebanon. It was all part of a strange way of life for

Western correspondents. Much of the time we lived in West Beirut at the Commodore Hotel, in the Hamra district near the U.S. Embassy and the American University of Beirut. Earlier, Western journalists had lived in more luxurious hotels along the Mediterranean but after the civil war in the 1970s they had relocated farther inland to the Commodore. Some of the exotic characters frequenting the Commodore seemed to have stepped off the screen from Rick's Café Américain in the film *Casablanca.* The lobby was sometimes filled with intriguing politicians such as Walid Jumblatt, leader of the Druze Muslims, Lebanese mountain villagers known as fierce warriors. Mysterious people were rumored to be spies. One old man I saw sitting on a sofa in the lobby was rumored to have assassinated King Abdullah of Jordan in 1951.

Despite the intrigue and danger, we felt relatively safe, partly because Fuad, the Palestinian Christian manager of the hotel, paid bribes to local Muslim militias to stay away from our neighborhood. He didn't want them launching mortar attacks from our street, which would have invited return fire from Maronite Christian militias on the other side of town in East Beirut. Correspondents checking into the hotel preferred rooms on a middle level—not so low as to be hit by shrapnel from car bombs, not so high as to be hit by shells that exploded on the roof. Coco, the African gray parrot in the pool garden in the back, terrified newly arrived reporters like me with his imitation of an incoming shell, a descending whistle that caused some guests to scramble for shelter.

Whoever had trained Coco to imitate mortar shells may have seen life here as grimly humorous, but at times there was little to laugh about. Akram, a Lebanese audio technician I hired on the spot one day in the lobby, told me he had been kidnapped and beaten by Syrian troops. Although still a young man, his hair was now white. Sean Toolan, a forty-three-year-old Irish freelance reporter who reported for ABC and the London *Observer,* had laughed and told stories in the bar of the Commodore Hotel the first time I visited West Beirut. On my second visit a month later when I asked about his absence I was told that Sean had been murdered on a street near the hotel. He had been beaten, stabbed with an ice pick, and shot three times by unknown assailants.

They called it Dodge City, because Beirut was wide open in those days in the early 1980s. There was no functioning government, no single authority. No one was in charge of this sprawling city that extended eastward from the edge of the Mediterranean to the hills of Baabda, with Mount Lebanon in the distance, this once-beautiful, once-thriving city that some had called the Paris of the Orient and now was partly in ruins, the banks closed, tourists scared off, guns sold openly on the street, the airport largely abandoned and cratered by shells, the metropolis Balkanized into nasty, well-armed feudal fiefdoms. There was a bewildering array of competing militias, some of them little more than street gangs of shabby, dirty kids riding around in pickups and toting AK's. Their militias had names such as the Phalange or the Mourabitouns (the wisecracking press called them the Looney Toons), and they were interconnected with Lebanese ethnic/religious clans such as the Druze, the Maronites, the Shiite Muslims, the rival Sunni Muslims, and outsiders such as the Palestinians. Beirut's main square, the Place des Martyrs, had been battered into ruins by the shelling of the midseventies civil war.

There were reminders everywhere of that civil war. When I first entered the Commodore Hotel in 1981, it was filled with journalists who had covered the previous conflict. Someone had put a cynical sign in the lobby that said WELCOME BACK CLASS OF 1975. At the National Museum was the Green Line, the city's no-man's-land between Muslim west and Christian east, a dividing line that had resulted from the civil war, a gauntlet you raced down at your peril, flooring your accelerator, knowing you might be in a sniper's sights.

There were hints of a hedonistic, affluent past. One day, exploring back rooms of the dilapidated Commodore Hotel, I came across a vast empty chamber. In the darkened room I could make out a stage and maroon and gold curtains and a dance floor. I imagined this night club in its heyday, and with it Beirut in its heyday, a place where strictly religious Gulf sheikhs escaped to play, to sin a bit, to mix with exotic cultures. Now it was abandoned, and abandoned with it was much of the old Beirut, taken over by kids with guns and by the vengeful older men who ruled them.

When I first arrived in Beirut in April 1981 I was surprised how tough and unfeeling and even selfish the American and other foreign journalists seemed to be toward one another, in contrast to the kindness and generosity shown by my colleagues in cities in Europe. It took me a while to realize that this hard shell was a defense, a protection against the tension. I can remember how that tension affected me from time to time. One afternoon I lay on my bed at the Commodore Hotel and hallucinated that the ceiling was about to collapse, that it would crush me, and that I would lie there slowly dying, my body pinned down, rescuers unable to reach me. It was a waking nightmare.

One day our driver Abed, the crew, and I drove to a building in West Beirut being used as a clinic by the Lebanese leftist Sunni Muslim militia known as the Mourabitouns. We wanted to do a story about how this militia provided medical services to people in the district it controlled. This was during a resurgence of artillery exchanges between Maronite Christian militias in East Beirut and Muslim militias such as the Mourabitouns in West Beirut.

I had obtained permission from a Mourabitoun press contact for us to get "b-roll" (noninterview video shots) of activities at the clinic. I wasn't quite sure how it would add up to a story, but I soon found out the answer. While I was inside on the second floor with the crew, the building came under mortar fire.

Someone shouted for me to get away from the windows and to seek protection on the stairway in the center of the building. I huddled on the stairway with other people and could see the entryway on the ground floor at the bottom of the stairs. Shells exploded close to the entrance. Glass from the front doors exploded. Shards rattled on the entryway floor. The mortar rounds were coming in from somewhere in East Beirut, and we could hear the answering mortar fire from the Mourabitoun position right outside our building. That meant our building was in the center of the attack, the prime target. Suddenly I saw a man running into the entryway below us, blood soaking his trousers. More wounded people took the risk of running into the building. They came here despite the risk because it was a clinic. They needed urgent care.

The mortars crashed on all sides around us and the sound was like cracks of thunder, over and over again, relentless, brutal. Carefully we made our way up the stairs and the cameraman pointed his camera into a room at the clinic to show patients being treated. A woman sitting in a chair did something I will never forget.

She opened her mouth wide and her body shook, in the manner of a person laughing.

I could not believe my eyes.

Why would anyone be laughing at such a time? Could she be enjoying this? Yet that is what I saw: a woman laughing with delight. Her mouth was wide open in a sign of pleasure. Her body rocked back and forth and shook with merriment. Or so it seemed. I looked more closely and saw fear and disbelief in her eyes. I began to realize that it was not pleasure but terror that she was experiencing. She was hysterical.

The tension affected other people, too. Sam was an American journalist for the Associated Press. One day he and I and other journalists were riding in someone's car, driving up the hill to Baabda past pine trees and palms to attend a press briefing at the American ambassador's residence near the Lebanese president's palace. As we drove along, hearing the distant sounds of shelling exchanged by the ragtag militias of east and west, Sam told me that earlier that day there had been a car bomb explosion near Hamra, the main street, and he had interviewed a woman who had been an eyewitness. Sam told me that after his interview with her, which took place alongside some other cars parked on the same street, he began walking away and he heard an explosion, and when he turned around he saw that another car bomb had gone off. The explosion had cut the woman in half. "If I had stayed with her a few minutes longer . . ." he said, and shook his head in disbelief that he could have come so close to being killed himself.

Sam stared ahead, clearly shaken, and even as he told this story we felt the tremendous blast of an explosion behind us as an artillery shell detonated on the road. Then another shell exploded just in front of our car. Our driver swerved and drove off the road into some bushes. We were in the middle of a barrage of shelling. Perhaps our car was the target. We were stuck, trapped, unable to move. Sam was shaking more now. I couldn't blame him. I was shaking myself. I've heard military experts say that despite all the changes in warfare it is artillery shelling that remains the strongest force for undermining an enemy army's morale. There is the thunder of it, seemingly unending, seemingly everywhere, closer and closer, making it impossible to think, impossible to feel safe and sheltered.

Another time I and our crew were in a white car that was heading along the coastal road in southern Lebanon, moving away from an area near the Israeli border and heading toward Beirut to the north. Suddenly I heard an explosion behind us. I looked around to see what had happened, and off to my left, in the Mediterranean, I saw an Israeli gunboat fire another shell, and this time it landed in front of us. I realized what was happening. When I had been in the army, in the early 1960s, at artillery school at Fort Sill, Oklahoma, we had learned about something called bracketing. You fired one round behind a target, and one round in front of it, and then you split the difference and your next round would be right on the target. So that meant that the Israeli forward observer for the gunboat was probably telling the crew on the ship to split the difference between the settings of their firings for the shell that landed behind us and the shell that landed in front of us. The next shell should land right on us. And there was no way for me to signal to the Israelis that we were press. There were no press markings on the car. As far as the Israelis were concerned, this was a white car speeding northward through a part of Lebanon populated by Palestinians hostile to Israel and those inside the car might well be members of groups that Israel considered to be terrorists. The only thing I had going for me was that we were driving fast and the forward observer probably did not always have a clear view of us as we passed behind buildings and hills.

As it turned out the next round landed off the road, way off target, and there was no round after that. For whatever reason, we were off the hook. Perhaps because I was in a car and moving fast I did not feel as vulnerable as I had in the Mourabitoun clinic. It was only afterward when I thought about it that a deeper fear set in.

Then, in 1983, came the Marine barracks bombing, and I saw what the tension can do even to hardened combat veterans.

In October of that year there were U.S. Marines deployed in Lebanon by the Reagan administration in the mistaken belief that they could impose American will and bring about peace and order to Lebanon, after the Israelis withdrew. Young Marines were dug in on a flat coastal plain near Beirut International

Airport, south of the capital. In the hills above them, to the east, were hostile armed groups—Amal, Druze, Syrians—and the American soldiers were sitting ducks for mortars fired from the high ground. That made daily life treacherous. They took casualties. But worse was to come.

At 6:20 a.m. on Sunday, October 23, a suicide driver sped his yellow Mercedes-Benz delivery truck through the gate of the Marine barracks compound near the airport. The bomb he exploded killed 241 Marines and other service members, many of them in their late teens or early twenties, as they slept in their barracks building. The United States later said it was the largest non-nuclear explosion since World War II. We flew from Rome to Beirut the next day and joined another CNN crew covering the aftermath. At the airport we saw coffins. What I will never forget is how the bombing affected a tough old Marine major who escorted us as we shot footage of rescue workers trying to see if there were any more survivors pinned down in the wreckage. There were no more survivors, only bodies to be pulled from the collapsed building and put in bags and taken away. The major was describing the rescue and cleanup operation when suddenly he stopped speaking. I saw tears in his eyes. He tried to speak but his voice broke.

Later he took us to a tent in a makeshift new compound. There were rows of telephones on tables. Young Marines, many of them hardly more than boys, were seated and holding the telephones and talking. These were the survivors. Each was allowed a free call home. The Pentagon wanted us to show the positive side, that these Marines were well, and the military hope was that visually this would say that the United States was undaunted. But even as we videotaped the scene there were plans in Washington to evacuate the Marines to a ship offshore, claiming at first it was only temporary, but ultimately it became permanent and the United States was forced to give up its attempt to impose its will on a country still in civil war. I thought how unsuccessful we Americans were, so many times, in trying to impose our values on other countries, and I thought of the sadness we inflicted on others, and the sadness that others inflicted on us, and the suffering felt by so many on all sides.

Now, in the aftermath of the barracks bombing, here was one of the stories, and there was something deeply troubling and touching about the scene in this tent, all the voices and twangs and southern accents and midwestern accents and the other regional cadences in the voices of these boys.

Our camera zoomed in on one as he ended his phone call: "Good-bye, Mom. I love you."

Chapter Five

Welcome to Tripoli

The plane descended to a desolate runway at Tripoli International Airport in Libya on a dark evening, the view out the airplane window bleak, mostly flat land, and here and there a dim light. It was 1985, a dangerous year, a time of wave after wave of terrorist attacks, with Americans abroad increasingly concerned for their safety, and here we were arriving in the capital of the Great Socialist People's Libyan Arab Jamahiriya (state of the masses), the North African country the United States had identified as the instigator and hiding place of terrorists bent on killing Americans, a country so dangerous that we had been discouraged by the State Department from making this trip. In our passports was the notation that we would not be protected if we traveled to certain countries. One of them was Libya.

The Alitalia plane, on a flight from Rome, was largely empty. Who in their right mind would want to fly to Tripoli, Libya?

As the plane touched down and raced along the runway in the darkness, I heard a voice next to me. It was my wisecracking producer, Richard Roth. In his best imitation of an Ian Fleming villain, complete with low voice and menacing foreign accent, Richard leaned closer and said: *"Welcome to Tripoli, Mr. Bond."*

His dark joke helped ease the tension. It captured the moment perfectly and raised the legitimate question: What were we doing here? The Libyan leader Muammar el-Qaddafi, an eccentric figure branded by the U.S. government as a sponsor of terrorist crimes, had agreed to a CNN interview in his capital, and we assumed that no harm would come to us while we were in his country to record his views and broadcast them to the world. But there was no question that we were the enemy, not least because our country supported Israel. Qaddafi was militantly opposed to the Jewish state. In fact, when I had gone to the villa in Rome that was the Libyan embassy to get a visa stamped in my American passport, I noticed on the embassy grounds a large billboard. On it was painted a green map of the Middle East, green being the color of Islam. The countries of the region were clearly identified, their state borders drawn, and the names of the countries written in Arabic and Latin lettering: Libya, Sudan, Egypt, Lebanon, Syria, Jordan, Saudi Arabia. But there was something wrong with the map. I looked closer.

No Israel.

As far as the map—and its Libyan creator—were concerned, there was no such country. This was his distorted view of reality, and now we were about to step into his world and depend on him for our safety. Richard was right: there was a kind of James Bondian mood to our arrival, and in fact deep inside me was a fantasy of living the life of 007, an absurd and juvenile fantasy. I'm not really the type. "Dashing" would not be the right word to describe me. I'm shy and quiet. I like to curl up with a good book or a crossword puzzle. Loud noises scare me, which is a real handicap if you cover wars and other violence. I loved my family and enjoyed the peaceful quiet of our home. But at the same time I did have pretensions of living the adventurous life. I was conflicted. Like many other expatriates, part of me wanted to get away from the repressive conformity of American life, yet part of me also wanted to be a member of American society. Part of me identified with foreigners, felt more comfortable with them than with fellow Americans, and yet at the same time I did not really fit in abroad. In some ways I was like the protagonist of the film *Lawrence of Arabia*, the oddball Englishman who didn't fit in at home and didn't really fit in abroad. Not that I was Collings of Arabia, but I had some of the same conflicted feelings. In my own country I felt uncomfortable at parties where provincial people spoke of dull things in a smug, satisfied, consumerist way. In foreign countries, I either didn't speak the language well or didn't speak it at all. I hadn't grown up there. I didn't get the jokes. Like a lot of foreigners, I smiled to show I was friendly since I couldn't express it well in words, but I didn't really belong there. I didn't belong anywhere. Or so I felt at times.

Among the few other passengers on our Alitalia flight was a middle-aged American named Skender Brame and his wife, Carol, and their young son. Richard, our producer, befriended them during the flight and learned that they were living in Libya despite the government's hostility toward Americans. Skender was recreation director at a school for the children of foreign oil industry workers and his wife was a school administrator. Richard persuaded them to let us do a story about their life in Libya, which turned out to be a good idea as we found out that we had a lot of time on our hands and needed things to do.

In Tripoli, the Libyan capital, we waited day after day at the Al-Kabir Hotel for our interview with Qaddafi (known as The Leader), but day after day we were told by an official of the government's information ministry that we must wait and that we would be told when the time came. The official was our "minder," someone who would keep an eye on us, preventing us from seeing whatever the government did not want us to see and discouraging Libyans from saying anything to us that sounded critical of The Leader.

Every day our minder would meet us in the lobby of our hotel and tell us that he had no information on our interview with The Leader. We would ask him for permission to shoot street scenes, and usually he would say no. In effect we were stuck in our hotel, with little to do. Being a strictly Islamic country, Libya did not permit alcoholic beverages to be consumed, so we were limited to the one type of drink that was served at the hotel: juniper berry juice. On the walls of the hotel, as on the walls of many other buildings, were quotations from The Leader. For example: *"NATIONS WHOSE NATIONALISM IS DESTROYED ARE SUBJECT TO RUIN."* There wasn't much to do other than drink juniper berry juice and read quotations from The Leader, and we soon grew bored.

While waiting for our interview with Qaddafi, Richard followed up on his contact with the Brames, the American family he had met on the plane, and got their permission for us to visit their home and profile them. I admired Richard for doing this. While I had been thinking more in terms of stories about geopolitics, terrorism, oil prices, and Qaddafi's impact on American foreign policy, Richard was thinking in terms of real people and how they live their lives, and he was right. It made a good story.

We shot footage of the Brames's stucco house with its small garden behind a wall, and we shot footage of the Oil Companies School, the international school for the children of foreigners who worked for petroleum companies, where Skender taught gym and Carol worked in the administration office. (As a sign of the tense times they lived in, the name of their school was later changed to the College of U.S. Aggression Martyrs, after the April 1986 U.S. bombing of Tripoli and Benghazi.) We showed Skender coaching a soccer team, out on their field. We showed Carol and their son at home. We included a shot of Carol listening to uncensored news from the BBC on their shortwave radio in their kitchen. We showed Skender and his son playing catch on the front lawn, and I interviewed the three of them sitting on their front step. They seemed a very typical American family (at least, in the popular image of typical), well fed, good humored, optimistic, and outgoing, with the only untypical thing being that they were living in the capital of a country run by a dictator deemed by the State Department as a financial backer of terrorists bent on killing Americans.

Our talented producer Richard Roth was the right person for finding human-interest stories such as this one. He is an interesting human himself. Tall and lanky, with glasses and curly gray hair and an occasional disregard for sartorial elegance, Richard is a kind-hearted, jokey New Yorker who is crazy about sports and movies, talks a blue streak, has a machine-gun-rapid comic patter punctuated by bursts of laughter and abrupt silences, and enjoys events such as his annual marble-rolling contest in the New York bureau of CNN (the marbles roll down an inclined board with holes in it, and wagering is permitted). People take to him right away, as I did, and they often agree to his requests for interviews simply because his friendliness and openness helps them overcome their nervousness about being on-camera.

An actor later played the part of Richard Roth in the HBO fictional film, *Live from Baghdad*, about CNN's coverage of the 1991 Gulf War. In one scene, the actor conveyed Richard's love of sports, as he talks baseball with a nervous American who is, in effect, a hostage because he cannot leave Iraq. The "Richard" in the film is so unthreatening and comically obsessed with sports that the American agrees to chat with him on camera—and "Richard" gets an exclusive interview. That was the way Richard was in real life.

I remember him visiting me and my wife and three sons at our apartment north of Rome as one of our guests at a Sunday afternoon party, and, while the rest of the guests sat in the living room chatting, Richard sat in the dining room, headphones clamped to his ears, listening to an Italian soccer game that he had bet on. (He took part in the national craze of Totocalcio, the small bets that Italians made on the outcomes of Sunday soccer matches.) I remember Richard entering the CNN office with his scruffy Dalmatian, Souness, named after a Scottish soccer star. We would feed Souness bits of our breakfast rolls as we read the morning papers.

Anyway, people took to our Richard Roth as soon as they met him. The Brames took to him right away, too, and in Tripoli we were granted access to their unusual world. I put together a feature story showing the field where the children of the Americans and Europeans living in Tripoli played soccer under Skender's supervision. We showed the Brames cooking in their kitchen, watching videotapes of American TV shows, and sitting on their front stoop talking about hamburgers and school and life in Libya. Again, we were trying to get beyond politics and show ordinary life.

But we were here to do a highly political story, and finally the word came that we would get our interview with Qaddafi. We gathered up our gear and drove with our minder to the Azziziya military compound in Tripoli. We were thoroughly searched, and our equipment was inspected carefully, before we were allowed to proceed further to an isolated building where we were told our interview would take place. There was a well-furnished office with high ceilings and tall windows. It looked like a living room. We set up our tripod and lights and other gear, checked all our settings, arranged two chairs facing each other (for what is called a knee-to-knee interview), and waited . . . and waited.

An hour went by. At last we heard a motorcade arrive. A door to the outside opened, and the familiar face and figure of Qaddafi appeared in the doorway, wearing a gray military tunic. He seemed smaller and quieter than I had expected. During the interview, which was conducted in Arabic and translated into English, he had the odd habit of lolling his head on his shoulders and rolling his eyes, almost as if he were on some drugs. I asked him every tough and topical question I could think of, especially on his alleged support of terrorism and his refusal to recognize Israel, and he deflected all of them with nonanswers. I tried to ask tough follow-up questions, but the time required for the translation of each question and answer broke up the momentum and gave him plenty of opportunity to fudge his answers and spout meaningless generalities. In other words, he didn't really say much at all. But still it was interesting to hear his defense of his militantly anti-Israeli position and to see that there was no hint of any readiness at compromise or accommodation.

Qaddafi in his gray military tunic didn't seem as evil as the Reagan administration had portrayed him, although he was eccentric, his speech rambling, head lolling, eyes focused somewhere beyond me. And while the Reagan administration may have demonized him for its own political purposes, Libya in the 1980s was indeed involved in support of violent groups. Qaddafi had supported the IRA guerrillas in Northern Ireland. And we found out later his role in the PanAm 103 bombing. After years of denying involvement, in 2003 Libya agreed to pay $2.7 billion to families of victims in a statement that accepted responsibility for the actions of its officials, in effect accepting responsibility for the 1988 airplane bombing over Lockerbie, Scotland, that killed 270 people. So the Qaddafi I was interviewing was not above dabbling in terror, and his unpredictability made me uneasy. And I remembered that the American government had made it clear that should anything happen to us in Libya we were on our own—we were not protected.

However, I assumed that Qaddafi saw it in his interest to make use of CNN and to get his messages out to the world through our network and that therefore he would not let us be harmed. And Qaddafi used CNN a great deal to get his messages out. In fact, later, during the 1991 Gulf War, when CNN became a household name around the world, one day Qaddafi personally called the CNN foreign desk in Atlanta and asked to be interviewed by phone, live on the air, which CNN did, after first verifying that this was not a hoax. So because Qaddafi saw it in his interest to use us, I didn't feel too insecure in his country, but at the same time I did not feel totally safe. There was an element of danger. In fact, the Azziziya compound in Tripoli where we interviewed Qaddafi in 1985 was later bombed by U.S. planes in April 1986.

I interviewed Qaddafi twice. That first time was with Richard Roth as producer. The second time, a year later, it was just me and a crew, and without Richard it was a lot more difficult—especially when it came time to leave.

Once again we stayed at the Al-Kabir Hotel, and waited and waited for the interview. This time our minder was a man of about thirty who always had bits of spittle on his lips, causing Doug, our sound technician, to nickname him the Spitter. One day the Spitter told us that there would be a meeting that afternoon of a district People's Assembly in one part of Tripoli, and we could videotape it. I wondered whether this would be worth covering, since people's assemblies were useless rubber-stamp legislatures that were intended to create the impression of a town-hall-type democracy. I asked if The Leader would be there, and our minder said yes, he would. That sounded interesting, and I figured that at the very least we could get some "b-roll" (video shots to supplement interview footage) that could be edited into our final story somehow. (The term "b-roll" comes from the early days of television news when everything was on film. Crews usually shot two rolls of film, from which editors selected shots and put them into a news package. The a-roll was for interviews and the correspondent's standup, and the b-roll was for all other pictures.) In addition to b-roll, perhaps while we were there we could buttonhole The Leader for a quick informal quote to supplement whatever formal quotes we would obtain later whenever he finally sat down for our interview.

Encouraged by this prospect, we packed up our tripod, our lights, our batteries, our cables, our reflectors, and other gear and loaded them into a car along with our camera. Accompanied by the Spitter, we drove through the streets of Tripoli, past the palm trees and the many pictures of The Leader and the quotes from him displayed on billboards. At last we arrived at a run-down local government building and were ushered into an auditorium. It was filled with men, many of them late middle-aged or elderly. Some of them wore shabby clothes and seemed in need of medical attention, such as one man who seemed to have an eye infection. We set up our gear. The Spitter translated the speeches for me. The members of this pseudo-grassroots assembly, carefully controlled and scripted by the government, were discussing the powers of the United Nations, for some odd reason. We shot close-ups of speakers, wide shots of the audience, and close-up details of the room, including placards with quotations from The Leader. We had everything except the one thing we wanted most.

I turned to our minder.

"When do you think The Leader will be arriving?"

"He is here," the minder said.

"Oh. Great." I looked around the auditorium. No sign of Qaddafi or his entourage. "I don't see him. Could you point him out? Where is he standing?"

The minder replied calmly: "He is everywhere."

He is everywhere. I stared at our minder. Had something got lost in translation? Were people in this country living in a dream world? Or did words have different meanings in this culture? I began to realize that perhaps, for some people in this part of the world, what they said was not expected to be taken literally but was true only in a figurative or poetical sense. "The Leader will be there" was not intended to mean that Qaddafi would actually show up in person but rather that his ideas would be felt by everyone in the room—a nice thought, perhaps, but useless to an American television news crew trying to base its coverage plans on Western versions of reality.

There were other instances of this different approach to "truth" in the Middle East. One time in Beirut we were told by the press spokesman of the Palestine Liberation Organization—the PLO—that the next day we would be taken to a guerrilla outpost in Nabatiya near the southern Lebanese border with Israel. But when we showed up the next morning for the trip, he said he knew nothing about it and acted as if no such trip had ever been planned.

So in Libya the expression "he is everywhere" was part of that same mentality, perhaps. I've often wondered whether this might be part of the Middle East problem, that the way language is used does not lend itself to cautious, careful, tentative, precise statements as to what is reality, and instead the culture encourages people to make wild, sweeping statements with no empirical basis whatsoever (all Jews are bad, all Arabs are good), statements that are not subject to independent verification, a condition ideal for breeding intolerance, absolutism, and violence. Another television producer, puzzling over Middle Eastern irrationality, once wisecracked, "These people have different chemicals in their brains," but I think a more useful way of looking at it is to study the culture and history of the region, including the beautiful poetic wording of the Koran, to try to understand how that influences language and communication, and then to see how statements that mean one thing to one person mean something totally different to another.

After days of waiting we finally did get our second interview with Qaddafi. Once again he spouted generalities denouncing Israel and the Reagan administration and denying involvement in terrorism. I was disappointed that he didn't have anything new to say. But I was even more upset when something happened as we were trying to leave Tripoli and go home to Rome.

At the chaotic, crowded airport, late in the afternoon, we had to submit case after case of equipment to Libyan customs inspections, which took more than an hour. I was worried we might miss our flight, the only flight to Rome that day. Then we had to go through Libyan immigration, which took another hour. Our American passports were stamped with Libyan stamps stating that we had left the territory of the Great Socialist People's Libyan Arab Jamahiriya, and we passed through a door into a kind of no-man's-land at the airport, where technically we were neither in Libya nor out of Libya. If we missed our flight, we would not be permitted back into the country and we would have no place to stay, so the need to get on that one and only flight to Rome was uppermost in my mind.

We went through more security and at last came to the gate for our flight. A Libyan official at the gate said that we could not proceed further. He gave no reason and refused to say what the problem was. We showed him our Alitalia tickets and our passports and our customs declarations, all in order, all properly stamped. He said no, we could not proceed further. We demanded to know why not, and he refused to answer the question. I wondered: was Qaddafi angry about our interview? Were we going to be taken into custody? The gate closed and the flight to Rome took off without us.

"What are we going to do?" the cameraman asked.

I looked to the left. There was another gate for some other flight going somewhere. No one seemed to be in charge at that gate.

I pointed to the other gate. "We're getting on that plane."

"Where's it going?"

"Who cares? It's leaving Libya, isn't it?"

At that point, all I wanted to do was leave this country and as soon as possible.

Amazingly, no one checked our tickets. We boarded the plane easily. There seemed to be extremes here at the airport: extreme control at one gate, and no control at the other.

As we waited to take off, an Alitalia stewardess came down the aisle. I raised my hand to get her attention.

"Excuse me."

"Yes, sir?"

"Could I ask a question?"

"Certainly."

"Where is this plane going?"

"Milan."

That was fine. At least it was in the same country as our intended destination. We would be able to make an easy connection to Rome, and our checked luggage on the other flight would get to us within a few days. When the plane took off, we had our first beers in a week (no more juniper berry juice) and gratefully headed for home.

Chapter Six

Call the Palace

We were stuck in the middle of the desert, on the border between Jordan and Iraq, unable to move forward and unable to move back. We sat on a bench in a remote, forlorn building, looking at the fly specks on the dusty windows, and the one person who could get us out of there was asleep on a cot in his office. Israel had bombed a nuclear reactor in Baghdad the day before. It was the top story in the world, but we couldn't get to Baghdad to cover the aftermath because we couldn't get out of a bureaucratic nightmare.

It all began on Monday, June 8, 1981. I was with a crew in Beirut when Israel announced that Israeli F-15 bombers and F-16 fighters had destroyed the French-built Osirak reactor twelve miles south of Baghdad the day before in the world's first air strike against a nuclear plant. Israel said the Iraqis had planned to make nuclear weapons to destroy Israel. No one knew how Iraq or the rest of the Middle East would react, and war jitters filled the air. The CNN foreign editor told me that I and my crew should cover any reaction in Baghdad. There was only one problem: the airport in Baghdad was closed because of the crisis.

We decided that we would try to drive in. My crew and I flew from Beirut to Amman, Jordan, arriving at Amman airport in the early evening that Monday. We got all our boxes of television gear from baggage, put them on carts, and went out to the taxi rank in front of the airport on a steamy evening. I found a driver, a Jordanian man in his thirties who spoke German but not English. Since I did not speak Arabic other than a few basic words, but I did speak German, this would have to do. I explained to him in German that we were American television and we wanted to cross the desert to Baghdad, a trip of 535 miles, and we wanted to do it at night. He had an air-conditioned Mercedes station wagon, but if we drove across the desert in the daytime then whenever we had to get out of the car for rest stops or other reasons we would suffer in summer heat of over a hundred degrees. Driving at night would make it more bearable. We haggled over the price, and at last a deal was struck. He and the crew and

I loaded the gear into his Mercedes, bought bottles of water, and we headed northeast. It was about 10 p.m. by the time we set off. We drove for some five hours until we arrived at the border at three in the morning.

And that is when the trouble began.

At the border of the Hashemite Kingdom of Jordan, there was a lonely shack of a building housing the Jordanian customs and immigration office for that crossing point. It was not crowded at that hour, and I assumed that the formalities would be routine and we would be on our way in an hour or so. One formality we had to go through was getting our carnet stamped. The carnet is a kind of passport for television equipment. It is a thick sheaf of papers testifying to the origin and place of purchase of each of our many items of gear, from the TDK camera and the BVU recorder to the tripod, lights, microphones, batteries, cables, tapes, edit gear, and other items. Sometimes, even though the carnet format has been worked out by international agreement, a country's customs officer will try to charge duty on a piece of equipment because the officer does not understand that anything on the carnet may be brought in for work purposes and no duty is charged.

At the Jordanian border I braced for possible trouble over the carnet, but to my relief there was none. The only official at the border outport was a paunchy unshaven man in khaki uniform who sat behind a desk. With a bored expression on his face, he routinely stamped our carnet, then examined our passports and returned them to us without even looking up. I relaxed. This was going to be easy. But then the official began asking our driver questions. Our driver showed him a document. Soon both men were raising their voices. The slovenly officer said, *"La,"* which I knew meant "No" in Arabic. I asked our driver, in German, what was the problem.

"My taxi driver's license," he said.

"What about it?"

"He says it's expired."

"So do you have to pay a fine or something?"

"No. He says I can't drive the taxi."

"That's ridiculous. Tell him we have to get to Baghdad. There's a press conference this afternoon at the Foreign Ministry."

The two men argued some more in Arabic, voices raised even further, the slovenly customs and immigration officer apparently saying something insulting and then waving his hand dismissively and turning his back and walking out of the room. To my amazement, I saw him lie down on a cot in the next room and fall asleep.

I began to feel like a character in an existentialist play: in the middle of the desert, on our way to achieve a goal, we couldn't go forward, we couldn't go back, and the only person who could make a decision about our fate didn't speak English, didn't care about us, and had just gone to sleep on a cot. The fly specks on the windows loomed larger. Time slipped by. We sat on a hard bench and debated our fate. Could we go back to Amman and find another taxi and driver? No, because the officer had said that this driver could not drive his taxi one direction or the other. He was grounded. And there was no other taxi here, and no other means of transportation. Could we call a taxi from here? No, because the officer had said we could not use his phone.

Outside the sky was beginning to lighten.

We sat there and went over every possibility we could think of. If we had been in Lebanon we might have been able to slip a hundred-dollar bill into each of our passports and hand them to the border official and we would get through, but this was not Lebanon. There had to be a solution to this dilemma, but what was it?

I turned to Dean Vallos, our cameraman, a strapping man with long dark hair. He had been to Jordan before. I asked Dean if he knew anybody who could help us. He said he knew the chief press officer for King Hussein.

"There's only one thing to do," I said. "We've got to call the palace. That's the only thing that will move this guy." I looked through the doorway to the paunchy man snoring on the cot.

"But he said we can't drive anywhere," Dean said. "How are we going to get to a phone?"

"We'll find a way."

After another hour or so the creature on the cot began stirring. Slowly, he sat up, rubbed his eyes, stood, went into a bathroom, relieved himself, then shaved.

Time passed slowly.

At last he tucked his shirt in and tightened his belt buckle and came back out to the office. Our driver and I began speaking to him. In German, I told the driver to ask him if we could get a pass from him to drive to the nearest town and use a telephone to make a call. It was like getting a hall pass in school. Reluctantly, and after a long argument in Arabic that seemed designed to remind us, not that we needed reminding, that he had power over us, he scribbled a note and handed it to us contemptuously. Armed with this safe-conduct pass, in case we were stopped by police and questioned about the taxi driver's expired license, we got in the Mercedes station wagon and drove wearily a few miles to a small border town. The only telephone we could find was an old-fashioned job like you see in ancient movies, a wooden box mounted to the wall, with no dial but a crank and a tube that you hold to your ear and a mouthpiece built into the wall unit with a flaring sleeve around it. Dean cranked the crank, held the earpiece to his ear, and said into the mouthpiece to a Jordanian operator that he wanted to be connected to a certain number, which was the home number of the press officer at the royal palace in Amman.

We waited.

At last Dean heard a voice at the other end. It was the press officer, who was just having breakfast. Dean explained our plight and begged him to get us out of it. After some more chat, Dean hung up the earpiece.

"He said to go back to the border."

Exhausted and hungry and not terribly hopeful, we drove back to the sorry excuse for a border outpost and went inside and sat on the hard bench. Nothing happened for a long time. The slovenly officer sat at his desk, eating breakfast and smoking a cigarette. Then something happened.

The phone rang.

Slowly, he reached for the phone and spoke into it. A startled look came over his face.

I turned to the crew.

"That's the palace," I said, with some satisfaction.

The officer listened to the voice at the other end for some time, saying little other than *"Aiwa"* (Yes), then at last hung up. He squinted at us and, without saying a word, made a dismissive motion with the back of his hand, as if brushing away flies that might have been buzzing around his head. That dismissive motion was the signal that we could go.

Finally we were free to cross the border. It was about 8 a.m. and already starting to get hot. We entered a no-man's-land between the borders of Jordan and Iraq, waited in a line of cars, waited more at an Iraqi border building, got Iraqi visas stamped in our passports (the Iraqi government wanted us journalists to come and cover their reaction to the Israeli bombing), and then, around noon, finally got on the four-lane highway to Baghdad and arrived, exhausted, in the early afternoon, just in time to check into our hotel and go to a press conference by the Iraqi foreign minister, who denounced Israel. I paid our Jordanian driver and he returned to Amman.

As was the case with all foreign journalists working in Iraq, we were assigned a minder, an employee of the Iraqi Information Ministry whose job was to escort us, keep an eye on us in case we might be spies, and to tell us what we could and could not do. Mostly he told us what we could not do. Needless to say, we asked to see the reactor and were told we would not be permitted to do that. No one was permitted to go there.

After contacting Western embassies and other journalists, I learned that the Osirak reactor, or what was left of it, was visible from a road that ran south from the capital and continued on to a tourist site. The day after our arrival, I told our minder that we wanted to do a feature story about tourism in Iraq, and asked if we could go to that tourist site. To my surprise, he agreed.

We all got into a taxi—me, the driver, Dean the cameraman, our sound man, and the minder from the Iraqi Information Ministry—and headed south. Some twelve miles out of Baghdad, we saw a seventy-foot-high dirt embankment set back from the road. Dean, in the front seat, cradled the camera in his arms, its lens pointed toward the side window, and acted nonchalant as he secretly video-taped the sight of the dirt embankment, all that was visible of the Osirak re-actor. Its high dome was gone. Because we had said we were doing a story on tourism, we were forced to continue on to the tourist site and pretend to get pictures there, but really we had what we wanted, a shot of the reactor that was dominating the news.

At the time we knew that it was risky to sneak the forbidden shot, but we did not know just how risky until later. It turned out that NBC reporter Neil Davis and producer David Philips had also driven to the area but were seized by secu-rity guards, blindfolded, taken to what they believed was a security headquar-ters, and interrogated by officials who accused them of spying for Israel and the United States. They were held in separate cells and were not released until a week later. They were lucky to escape alive. (Not so lucky was Farzad Bazoft, a journalist for the British *Observer* weekly newspaper. In 1990, after investi-gating an explosion at an Iraqi weapons factory, he was arrested, convicted of espionage, and hanged.)

Iraq continued to be a challenging story for journalists in the 1980s, what with the dictatorial regime of President Saddam Hussein and its tight grip on information. One of the important stories of the 1980s was the eight-year war between Iran and Iraq, a war begun by Saddam Hussein, which ultimately would take upward of five hundred thousand lives. No accurate estimate exists of the death toll. Some Western analysts say it could be 1.5 million. For journalists such as myself, finding out what was going on at the time was not easy. We had a glimpse into the difficulty of this during one trip we took to the front line.

It was during a lull in the fighting, a period of stalemate between the two sides, neither of which had been able to achieve any breakthrough, a situation similar to that of the trench warfare of Europe in World War I. The crew and I stayed at a hotel in Baghdad until the Iraqi Information Ministry organized a press tour of the Shatt al-Arab and Basra areas near the front, for us and other foreign reporters including Japanese journalists. The Iraqis took us in their bus southeast from Baghdad through the broad, flat plain of the Tigris and Euphrates rivers. I remember seeing heat waves rising from the flat land, and, at about noon, at the hottest time of the day, I saw a man baking bricks in an outdoor kiln, which I decided had to be one of the worst jobs in the world. The Iraqis insisted that we be the guests of an army general for lunch, at a reception building at a military base. Nothing notable happened, in terms of his answers, or non-answers, to our questions as to what was happening on the front, but on a more personal note I remember clumsily letting a piece of meat slip off my spoon into a bowl of beet soup, causing a red splash on my white shirt which looked for all the world like blood. To my horror I realized I would not be able to do an on-camera standup report at the front, unless I could get the red stain out or find some other solution to the problem.

After lunch they took us to an undisclosed part of the front line, probably near the Iraqi city of Basra, in a wedge of territory close to both the Kuwaiti and Iranian borders (so close, in fact, that the Iranians had been able to shell Basra from their own territory—we saw the ruins of buildings in Basra as testament to that). We drove past bleak, desolate stretches of concertina barbed wire. The Iraqis had a mixture of modern Soviet and antiquated American military equipment. At one point we saw an old U.S. Sherman tank lumbering along the road, and snuck a shot of it from the bus. We visiting journalists walked through a long trench reinforced by sandbags on both sides, walking about a mile until we came to a front-line observation post. Ahead of us was a minefield and rows of barbed wire across the flat, uninhabited, treeless terrain of beige and yellow ground or marshland, buffeted by strong winds that kicked up the dirt. The Iraqi troops posed cheerfully with their antiaircraft guns and binoculars. There was no sign of tension, yet we knew that over the past few years there had been suicidal assaults by troops of both sides and horrific casualties, in a war that eventually settled nothing.

After our crew had taken all the pictures and sound we needed, it was time for my fifteen-second on-camera "standup," only I could not do a report from the front line of a war wearing what looked like a bloodstained shirt, since the "blood" would be so distracting that no CNN viewer would pay any attention to whatever words I might say. In desperation I asked if I could borrow any other journalist's shirt, and one of the Japanese correspondents let me use his, literally giving me the shirt off his back in a generous act to rescue me from disaster. In turn, I lent him my stained shirt for protection against the sun while I did my standup about the harshness of the conditions at the front and the concerns of gulf states that the conflict might spread.

Back in Baghdad I made the rounds of Western embassies to try to get their input on what was happening at the front, but most of the diplomats I spoke to did not seem to know much more than the journalists. When I spoke to the British military attaché I was surprised that he asked me more questions than I asked him. He wanted to know what tanks and other military equipment we had seen at the front, and even asked if he could borrow our "outtakes" (unused videotape footage). This request created a dilemma. On the one hand he was implying that he would give me valuable information, perhaps a scoop, if I gave him something valuable, a chance to look at, and probably make copies of, our tapes of our trip to the front. On the other hand, he was presumably an agent of MI6, British intelligence, and I knew that my cooperating with him would compromise my integrity as an independent journalist. Not only would it be a serious violation of ethics (journalists need to keep an arms-length distance from government to maintain their credibility as impartial observers) but also it might have been dangerous to my life. Spies were executed, and I did not want the Iraqis mistakenly suspecting me of cooperating with foreign intelligence agents. I told the British military attaché I would be glad to give him a copy of our finished, edited story, which contained the same footage that every CNN viewer could see, but not the outtakes. He was not happy with that decision.

It was oppressive, reporting from Iraq in those days. The unavailability of Iraqi sources for interviews made coverage difficult, although we did do stories about an economic boom, an international conference of Gulf states, and the government propaganda campaign to try to build popular support for Saddam Hussein. (As we showed in our story, his picture seemed to be everywhere—on billboards, on money, even on a watch, like Mickey Mouse). Real stories were few and far between, and meanwhile we were harassed by our minders, who kept reminding us in no uncertain terms that when our visas expired we would be invited to leave, and if we failed to leave we would be in serious trouble. On the trip to Iraq to cover the Israeli bombing of the nuclear reactor, we had had a problem with our visas. Dean Vallos, the camera operator who had called the palace, had obtained an Iraqi *entry* visa with me and the sound technician at the border but for some reason had not obtained an Iraqi *exit* visa, and you needed both. We were booked on a flight leaving on a Saturday, and the day before we tried without success to find an Iraqi government office that could stamp an exit visa into his American passport.

Dealing with the bureaucracy was always a test of patience and an affront to reason. I remember one time I was in the office of an Iraqi official who granted press visas to foreign journalists and I noticed on his desk a foot-high pile of visa applications, a mound of papers that looked very old. Some of the applications were spilling out and falling over the edge of his desk onto the floor. An assistant brought in a fresh batch of applications and placed them on top of the pile, and he plucked one from the top to scrutinize, which meant, I assumed, that the ones at the bottom never got considered, even though they had arrived first, and instead they receded further and further toward oblivion.

It was difficult enough dealing with that type of mentality, but in the case of Dean Vallos we had another problem. The day before our scheduled flight was a Friday, and Friday is the sabbath in the Islamic world. Offices are closed. We ended up hectically rushing to a police office Saturday morning, then racing to the airport, accompanied by two glowering minders whose menacing expressions seemed to grow darker each minute. I had fears that these expressions reflected some kind of official displeasure at our reporting, perhaps at the forbidden shots of military equipment we had taken, and that the government might be seriously considering arresting us if there were any more problems with visas or other formalities at the airport, any excuse they could find. This was a government that had no problem torturing anyone it considered a threat, and there was an ominous tension in the air. When at last the plane's wheels were up and the runway dropped and shrank below us, I felt a relief I had rarely felt before in my life. We were free.

Me at my desk at the *Newsweek* bureau in London, 1978.

An AP interview with West German Chancellor Willy Brandt on East-West détente, Bonn, 1974. I am in the center, with Brandt in the foreground and an unidentified man on the left.

My interview with actress Claudia Cardinale in Moscow, for a story about her role in the film *The Red Tent,* 1969.

At the Rome trial of Bulgarians accused of plotting to assassinate the Pope.

At the Supreme Court, reporting a story for CNN.

Reporting a CNN story from a helicopter above the U.S.–Mexico border area.

Interviewing Skender Brame and his wife in Tripoli.

An interview with a Baghdad doctor during the Iran-Iraq War.

Near Basra during the Iran-Iraq War.

Chapter Seven

You Said That Yesterday

The man who shot the Pope stood in a cage in the courtroom. He was a bewildered-looking young Turk named Mehmet Ali Agca, thin and wiry with short black hair. He had already been convicted of attempted murder, after his 1981 assault with a pistol in St. Peter's Square. Now, in a separate trial in 1985, he was on hand as a witness against three Bulgarians accused of conspiracy in Agca's attempt on John Paul's life.

A group of reporters gathered in front of his cage, in a section of the Italian courtroom designed for use in cases involving terrorism, cases that required extraordinary security measures. There was a line of cages, or jail cells, along the right wall of the courtroom. Like animals in a zoo, the defendants were in two of them. Agca the witness was in the third. Before that day's hearing opened, we gathered in front of his cage, as we had done the day before. On that previous day, he had said, in Italian, *"Sono Gesù Cristo,"* meaning, "I am Jesus Christ." CNN and other American television networks had used that sound bite in their news reports on the opening of the so-called Bulgarian Connection trial, an informal title that journalists had given this trial in a play on the words of the film title *The French Connection.* I think that nickname for the trial also evolved from the fact that the prosecution's case sounded like something out of a terrorist thriller, and many thriller novels had titles that sounded similar, such as *The Eiger Sanction* or whatever. In fact, the Italian court did not find convincing evidence of official Bulgarian involvement in Agca's attack on the Pope. Despite the fact that many conservatives speculated that the KGB (the Soviet version of our CIA) must have been involved, that the KGB must have used Bulgarian proxies and that the Soviets wanted to remove a world figure who was stirring revolt in Poland, the trial would end in the acquittal of three Bulgarians and three Turks. Yet we journalists fell into the trap of treating this story as if it were a thriller plot.

Saying he was Jesus Christ was similar to Agca's behavior at his own trial, and the Italian press had speculated that this was the "crazy defense," a display of feigned insanity in hopes this would help him get a lighter sentence. In fact, he may really have been insane, or at the very least confused, based on my observation of his behavior in court. In any case, he had said he was Jesus Christ on the first day of the Bulgarians' trial, and now this was the second day and we were gathered in front of Agca's cage to see what he would say today.

He came forward to the bars of his cage.

We pressed forward, holding up our boom microphones and our television cameras and television lights and our notepads and pens.

Agca cleared his throat.

We leaned closer.

"Sono Gesù Cristo," he said.

A clearly disappointed producer for ABC said, "No, no. You said that yesterday."

The producer's words made it clear that Agca's sound bite was completely unsatisfactory, that he would have to try harder, that he would have to come up with something new and interesting. For television news, reality was not good enough. The reality this day was that Agca had said he was Jesus Christ, but we wanted something different. It was almost as if the producer would have to write out a script for Agca to make sure that he said something usable, because otherwise the producer might not get his story on the air that night. I began to wonder just how much we were interfering with reality and manipulating people's perceptions of events. We were treating a witness and historical figure as if he were some kind of actor in a thriller film who needed more training, more rehearsals, and a better script, so that we could keep our audience entertained.

The "thriller movie" frame for terrorism stories was an obstacle to the truth. So were the sensationalizing and oversimplifying of events, and the fact that both sides in the story (police and radicals) were highly secretive and released distorted bits of information or misinformation to achieve their aims through manipulating public opinion.

And at times the heightened security against terrorism made it not only more difficult for us to report the facts but also more dangerous. Take the time we were trying to do a story about the Christian Democrats and ended up in jail.

The Christian Democrats, known in Italian as *Democristiani* or DC, comprised Italy's longtime dominant political party. The DC had formed majorities in parliament and chosen prime ministers ever since the end of World War II. The party's strength stemmed partly from its close association with the Catholic Church and the church's opposition to the Italian Communist Party. Most

Italians were Catholic, of course, and many were opposed to communism, especially Soviet communism.

The DC held onto power for decades. Governments would rise and fall, but after each crisis one of the same four or five DC party leaders would end up as prime minister and the party would retain its grip. The DC was the establishment, and it became the target for radical groups, including extremely violent radical groups. One of these was the Red Brigades, a group of Italian Marxists that advocated violent revolution. In 1978 they kidnapped and murdered Aldo Moro, the Christian Democratic party leader and former prime minister, a man respected by many Italians for his moderate, conciliatory views. At the time of his capture Moro had been putting out feelers to the PCI, the Italian Communist Party, to see if there could be cooperation between the two main parties in Italy. Some political analysts speculated that the Red Brigades feared such cooperation would weaken the left. Aldo Moro was held for two months. The Red Brigades demanded the release of thirteen of its members, and the DC government refused, saying it would not give in to demands by terrorists.

Moro's body was dumped in a car parked symbolically between the headquarters of the DC and the PCI in the center of Rome. His death led to an outpouring of national grief and an intensified campaign against the Red Brigades by Italian police. By the time I arrived in Rome, in April 1981, the DC was no longer strong enough to lead the government, and instead was part of a coalition led by the Social Democrats, but the DC was still influential, and I thought it would be interesting to do a story about the party.

We drove to the DC headquarters in a small square called Piazza del Gesù—Jesus Place. We parked our car and picked a location for some shots of the ornate exterior of the old four-story building, and also for me to do a standup commentary. There was a blue and white car marked POLIZIA parked near the high doors of the building. Armed Italian police guarded the door. We set up our tripod. Immediately two police officers walked over to us and asked who we were and what we were doing there. I explained that we were CNN, American television, and were doing a story about the DC. The police said we needed permission and demanded to see some kind of authorization from the Italian government. Of course, we had none. Then, to my surprise, the police told us to get into our car and follow them in their car. I thought they were just going to have us fill in some forms so we could resume shooting, but instead they took us to a police station and locked us into separate holding cells while they tried to figure out what to do with us.

My jail cell was old and dirty, with the kind of steel bars and stone walls I had seen in movies. I sat on the plain bench in the cell and looked down.

On the floor was a dirty, bloody hypodermic needle.

The needle was similar to others I had seen discarded in vacant lots and alleys, reminders of Italy's heroin problem. To be in a cell that had once held an addict was a chilling experience. I felt violated and also angry and frustrated that we had been impeded in our work. Instead of being respected as journalists trying to do our job, we were treated as criminals. The Italians were overreacting, but I could see why. Police in Italy and elsewhere were under pressure. The continent was caught up in frightening experiences with the phenomenon of terrorism.

From the killings of Israeli athletes at the 1972 Munich Olympics to the bombings of tourist hotels in Spain, Europe in those years was the focus of attacks by a wide range of fanatics. Some, including Palestinians, Libyans, and the Moluccans of Southeast Asia, were foreign to Europe. Some were home-grown—including such separatists as the IRA in Northern Ireland and the Basque ETA in Spain, and such Marxist revolutionaries as the Red Brigades in Italy and the Baader-Meinhof group (called the "Baader-Meinhof gang" by police) in West Germany. It was difficult for journalists to cover this type of story for a number of reasons: the secrecy of both police and attackers, the hyperbole employed by both sides in their few public statements, the attempts by both sides to manipulate media to influence public opinion, and the temptation by journalists to overdramatize events and frame this story as a thriller narrative. Often what was missing from our coverage was a deep understanding of what was behind this phenomenon.

To get a better sense of the mentality of people who were willing to take the lives of civilians in the name of a political cause, in the late 1970s I had interviewed a minor member of the Baader-Meinhof group in a prison in Hamburg, when I was *Newsweek*'s Bonn bureau chief, prior to my joining CNN. The Baader-Meinhof group had kidnapped—and, in some cases, killed—members of the West German elite: a banker, industrialist, prosecutor, judge, diplomat, and leading politician.

I had contacted the Baader-Meinhof group member's defense attorney and obtained his agreement for the prisoner to do an interview for *Newsweek,* and I had contacted the prison and obtained permission to conduct the interview there. On a dull, overcast day I flew from Bonn to Hamburg and took a taxi to the prison. After a thorough body search, I was escorted to a visitors' room monitored by closed-circuit television. The door opened and he came in. I remember him as being stocky, muscular, and deadly serious behind his steel spectacles. I had hoped that through the process of question and answer I could get some sense of what made him tick, what led him to employ violence in a way designed to create publicity for a group that was calling for the overthrow of the state and the creation of a Communist dictatorship. I had written down a list of questions. To my surprise, I discovered that he had written something down, too—a prepared statement, beyond which he would not go, and instead of answering my first question, or any other question, for that matter, he began reading from his prepared statement in a monotone. It was full of jargon about the proletariat and the ruling capitalist classes. What was most amazing for me was how boring his statement was. No insights into what made him tick. No sense of personal grievance. No conversation about prison conditions or how he felt about people. No willingness to provide even the slightest chink of light into his soul. All I got was a speech.

As I sat there listening to him deliver his diatribe, I felt certain that he considered me to be a tool of the capitalist ruling classes who, he probably felt, used *Newsweek* as one of their ways to control the masses. So I was not to be trusted to be open, honest, fair, and impartial, not to be trusted as willing to try to see what was behind the Baader-Meinhof group, not to be trusted as a detached observer. In his eyes, I was the enemy. Under different circumstances, I was sure, he would have held me prisoner and used me to further his political cause and then, if it suited his purposes, either he would have released me in exchange for imprisoned members of his group or he would have simply executed me in the name of revolutionary justice and dumped my body in a car left by the side of the road.

So I did not obtain the insight into his soul that I had hoped to achieve, but what I did get was a greater awareness of how close-minded and determined these people were. They had taken politics to its extreme. Anything was justified in the name of their political goal.

It was difficult to come up with the right words to describe this phenomenon. For lack of a better word, we call it "terrorism." But that word and the way it is applied have always bothered me. Not that I have any sympathy for these people. On the contrary, they are repulsive. In fact, I can never forgive the members of one group who killed the teenaged daughter of a friend of mine. I have no desire to minimize the evil of their behavior or downplay the suffering they cause. But I do want to understand what they are doing and what police and other protectors of civil order are doing, so that ultimately society will make the right decisions on how to deal with this problem. We have to understand this phenomenon, and to understand it properly we have to avoid loaded words like "terrorism." It is imprecise and can easily be misused by one side or the other. For one thing, it's not really an "ism." It's not an economic and political system, such as communism or capitalism or socialism, or a system of belief, such as Islamic fundamentalism. It's an extreme means to achieve an end, and the end itself could be an ism.

It has been said that one person's terrorist is another person's freedom fighter. In Afghanistan during Soviet rule the United States indirectly armed the *mujahadeen,* the anti-Soviet guerrillas that Moscow considered to be terrorists.

Washington called them freedom fighters. Later, after the Soviets left, Osama bin Laden, who had fought alongside the guerrillas, turned against the United States and organized the attacks on the World Trade Center and the Pentagon, and the United States called him a terrorist. To be sure, when he was attacking Soviet military targets such as helicopters bin Laden was not engaged in terrorism in the normal sense of the word: intentionally using violence against ordinary people who are not military and not government officials in order to pursue a political objective. When he attacked the World Trade Center, he intended to kill women, children, and other people who had no direct connection to U.S. Government policy, in hopes that the general public would be terrified of his power and put pressure on Washington to give in to his demands for the U.S. military to withdraw from Saudi Arabia. But if that is an example of terrorism, then what was Hiroshima?

At Hiroshima in August 1945 the United States, exploding an atomic bomb, intentionally used violence against ordinary people who were not military personnel or government officials, and did this in order to pursue a political objective. On that single day the United States caused the deaths of more than a hundred and forty thousand people, most of them women, children, and other people who had no direct connection to Japanese government policy, in hopes that the Japanese public would be terrified of U.S. power and would put pressure on their government to give in to U.S. demands for unconditional surrender in World War II. One might argue that, technically, that was terrorism, but no U.S. history book will ever call Hiroshima an act of American terrorism. Some scholars might argue that terrorism is conducted only by nongovernmental groups. But then what about PanAm 103? Libya has officially accepted responsibility for the bomb that exploded over Lockerbie, Scotland, in 1988, killing 259 people on board and 11 people on the ground. There are times when governments do become involved in acts deemed "terroristic."

Sometimes a member of a violent nongovernmental group that kills civilians later becomes the leader of the government, and then is no longer deemed a terrorist. One example is Menachem Begin. During the 1940s in the British mandate of Palestine, Begin led Irgun Zvai Leumi, an armed Zionist group (described by the *New York Times* as an "underground terrorist faction"). The Irgun intentionally inflicted violence on targets such as the King David Hotel in Jerusalem in hopes that this would pressure the British to leave Palestine. The hotel was the British administration's headquarters in Palestine and might have been considered a political target, but among the ninety-one victims of a 1946 Irgun bombing of the hotel were civilians, including hotel staff. (Irgun also killed more than two hundred Arab men, women, and children in the village of Deir Yassin in April 1948.) Begin's name was on an official British list of terrorists. Eventually the British departed and Israel was created. Years later, in 1977,

Begin became Israeli prime minister and was treated with dignity and respect by Britain, and even received the Nobel Peace Prize. Conditions had changed.

This shows how the word "terrorist" is so loaded that it can be misleading. When a person uses this word to describe someone, what he or she really means is "someone I currently don't like who uses violence against civilians to achieve a political goal." The implication is that the rest of us should agree that this is a bad person and that extreme measures should be taken against this person. But this causes problems. Opponents of Israeli policy sometimes accuse the Israeli government of "terrorism" today but this wrongly implies that Palestinian civilians are *deliberately* targeted by the Israeli military, whereas in fact when such civilians are killed in Israeli attacks it is usually accidental, not intentional. It is simply too easy to throw around words such as "terrorist" to express opposition to what one side or the other is doing.

In the interest of journalistic objectivity (a fact-based approach in which the journalist tries to be as unemotional and nonjudgmental as is humanly possible) and in the interest of a more informed policy debate, it would be better if journalists could use more precise and neutral words such as "attackers" or "armed group" instead of "terrorists" to describe these people. In fact, the British news agency Reuters prefers the word "attackers" to describe the September 11 suicide hijackers, and when the British Broadcasting Corporation (BBC) uses the word "terrorists" to describe them it does so sparingly and often with attribution—for example, saying "Washington said the terrorists would strike again."

One of the dangers with using the word "terrorism" loosely is that it can touch off overreactions and be used to justify excessive government actions; for example, the United States conducted racial profiling of Arabs and Muslims and deprived them of civil liberties after 9/11. And, back in 1981, as I sat in that prison cell in Rome, I, too, was an example of the result of governmental overreaction against a falsely perceived threat of "terrorism," which in this case had been nothing more than a CNN correspondent and his two-man crew setting up a camera tripod outside a building.

After an hour or so, a Roman police officer came to my cell and escorted me upstairs to the office of a precinct official, where I found my crew. The official showed us a printout of a Telex message he had received from the West German Federal Criminal Police Office in Wiesbaden, indicating that we could be released. I glanced down at the sheet of paper on his desk. Our names were on a list, and next to each name was the German word NEIN, meaning "No." Apparently Italian police were relying on Interpol's terrorism information center in Wiesbaden for word as to whether we represented a threat.

By the time we were released it was too late to do our DC story. We had lost a day. The experience brought home to me how much the phenomenon of these attacks by armed groups dominated official thinking and the news in Europe.

We became swept up in a number of stories about this phenomenon. One of them was the kidnapping in Verona, Italy, of an American brigadier general, James Dozier, by the Red Brigades. Day after day the Italian carabinieri (national police) staged raids, mounted roadblocks, conducted house-to-house searches, and put on a public display of conducting a major search of cities in the north-central areas around Verona. Because CNN had such a small budget, we did not travel from Rome to the search area for our daily stories but instead made use of video footage provided to us at no charge by RAI (Italian state television) and supplemented this with our interviews in Rome of security experts or politicians (the few who spoke English) and the standups I did outside our bureau in our local square, Piazzale di Ponte Milvio. Eventually, after forty-two days, Dozier was rescued and we moved on to another story.

While the Dozier story received considerable attention in the United States because the kidnap victim was an American general, another story involving yet another attack by an armed group against Americans received far more attention, and that was because of the cruel treatment of the victims.

The *Achille Lauro* was an Italian cruise ship that took passengers on tours of the Mediterranean, calling at such ports as Alexandria. The name of the ship had been obscure prior to the event that thrust it into the news, but the image of the ship was already well known because it had been used for the opening aerial shots of the popular American television program, *Love Boat*. In fact, we used those aerial shots from the television show as one element in our news reports.

In October 1985, armed Palestinians hijacked the ship while it was sailing between the Egyptian cities of Alexandria and Port Said. They demanded the release of fifty Palestinian prisoners being held in Israel. Among the 413 passengers aboard the *Achille Lauro* was Leon Klinghoffer, a sixty-nine-year-old tourist from New York, who was confined to a wheelchair. One of the hijackers shot him dead and dumped his body into the water. This cruelty contributed to the notoriety of the hijacking and helped make it a story that dominated the news for days. It ended with Egypt holding and then releasing the hijackers in exchange for the release of the ship's passengers. The hijackers were put on a plane heading for Tunisia but U.S. Navy jets forced it to land in Italy, where the hijackers were put on trial.

Our CNN Rome bureau contributed stories about the background of the *Achille Lauro,* and we did a story when the ship returned to its home port of Genoa. CNN flew in another correspondent, an experienced reporter named Tom Mintier, who did a live shot as the ship slowly came to rest at its berth, amid music played over loudspeakers, an Italian song about sailing to a place far away. Later we did stories about the trial in Genoa of the Palestinian hijackers, who were placed in a courtroom cage the way Agca had been. They were

convicted of hijacking and related crimes and sentenced to prison terms ranging from fifteen to thirty years. I felt the excitement of involvement in a top
story in the world, but disappointment that we weren't really learning much
about the four young men behind the bars in the cage and the other hijackers
who were still at large. Just calling them "terrorists" did not shed much light.
We used the word "terrorists" reflexively without asking questions about its ap-
propriateness. We did not fully understand these stories or convey them properly to our audiences.

There were many attacks by Palestinians on American targets, as part of their
efforts to put pressure on the U.S. government to force Israel to be more ac-
commodating in talks with Palestinian leaders. One time we flew to Athens to
do a story on the aftermath of a bomb explosion that took place aboard TWA
Flight 840 at fifteen thousand feet above Argos, Greece, on a flight from Rome
to Athens. Four passengers including an eight-month-old girl were sucked out
of a hole in the plane and fell to their deaths. Their bodies were taken to a
morgue in Athens, where our camera crew shot footage not of the bodies but
of the room where they were held. It was gruesome and gloomy to be there. Not
only was it raining that day, but it happened to be the birthday of Jane Evans,
our camera operator. Not a very nice way to celebrate.

Of all the violent attacks by these armed groups, the one that hit closest to
home took place at Leonardo da Vinci Airport at Fiumicino, outside Rome, on
December 27, 1985. Among the passengers inside the terminal that day was
the family of Vic Simpson, an AP correspondent I knew. During my five years
in Rome he and I would chat while covering press conferences, and occasionally play tennis (he always beat me). Vic was there that day with his wife and
his eleven-year-old daughter Natasha and nine-year-old son Michael to check
in for a TWA flight to New York for their Christmas vacation. Four Palestinian
men entered the concourse of the terminal and made their way to the counter
of El Al, the Israeli airline, which was near the TWA counter. They pulled gre-
nades and AK-47 semi-automatic assault rifles out from under their coats and
attacked the line of passengers. Vic was wounded. His daughter Natasha was
killed, as were four other Americans.

When we received news of the attack, we drove from the CNN bureau in
Rome to the airport. Carabinieri kept us a distance from the terminal, and we
were able to get only a wide shot of the exterior of the building. The Italian state
television network RAI gave us footage of the interior and the aftermath of the
attack: spent cartridges and blood on the floor and police standing around. We
learned which hospital the wounded had been taken to, and there I conducted
one of the most painful interviews of my life. Vic was sitting up in his hospital
bed, a bandage on his right hand, a dazed look in his eyes. I told him how sorry
we were and gave him our condolences, but of course we were journalists and

we had to do this story even if it involved a friend, and I asked him if it would be all right for us to get a picture of him. Vic, as a journalist himself who had done stories about other attacks by similar armed groups, understood that we had no choice and that it was important for us to report as much as we could, within reason. He agreed to let us photograph him. Then I had to ask another question, and I dreaded it.

"I'm sorry, but you know I have to ask you if it's OK to interview you about what happened," I said.

He shook his head.

I said I understood, and we left. I hated having to ask that question. I felt conflicted. Part of me wanted to leave him alone and to protect him as my friend. But another part of me felt that it was important to include in our story any information he could provide about what exactly happened, if he felt comfortable talking about it. And it would not have been fair to other people I have interviewed after similar tragedies if I had treated a fellow journalist differently. I know that Vic understood and that he would have done the same if our roles had been reversed.

Natasha's funeral was held on a rainy day at the chapel of the North American College. My wife and I were among members of the American community who lined up to give their condolences to Vic and his wife at the entrance to the chapel. Inside, a Mass was celebrated. Later Natasha's white coffin was carried to the Prima Porta cemetery, not far from the Marymount International School where she had been a student.

The attacks on Americans were striking closer to home, and I think that many of us felt more vulnerable than before. In fact, each day now when our children arrived at the American school on the Via Cassia, they entered through a gate guarded by a carabinieri policeman wearing a helmet and bulletproof vest and carrying an assault rifle.

Chapter Eight

Two Endings

Clark Todd was a tall, cheery, gray-haired Canadian in his thirties who worked as a radio and television correspondent for NBC and CTV, the Canadian television network. His room was next to mine in a hotel in Belgrade, and that is how I met him in January 1980. We were there to cover the medical treatment of Yugoslav president Josip Broz Tito for a blood clot in his left leg, a major story at the time because Tito was seen as the main force holding the rival ethnicities of Yugoslavia together, and any health scare raised the possibility of the collapse of the federation he had put together.

Clark was thirty-five years old when I first met him in the corridor of the hotel, and I immediately liked him for his almost boyish enthusiasm for journalism and his friendliness and kindness to me. We stayed in touch later and got together socially one weekend, since both of us lived with our families in England. He and his wife, Anne, and two daughters, Anna and Alex, and son, Ben, lived in Hatfield, Hertfordshire, north of London. Clark was six years younger than I. We both had three young children we loved. We both were excited about being foreign correspondents, I as the London bureau chief of *Newsweek,* Clark as the London bureau chief of CTV. Earlier he had worked for NBC News overseas and before that he was a broadcaster in his native Saint John, New Brunswick, and later Quebec, in Canada.

Among the stories we both covered were the pro-democracy Solidarity movement in Poland, the aftermath in Egypt of the assassination of President Anwar Sadat, the Falkland Islands war (from London), and the conflict in Northern Ireland. He won an Overseas Press Club award in 1977 for his foreign news coverage. I admired him and assumed that he would continue with his successful career. But his story had a different ending.

In September 1983, a little over a year after the Israeli bombing of West Beirut and the PLO pullout, the United States was embroiled in the ethnic conflicts of the Lebanese. The Israeli army withdrew from the Lebanese capital to positions farther south in Lebanon, leaving a power vacuum in the Beirut area. To fill that vacuum, rival militias of the Islamic Druze sect and Maronite Christians, as well as the Lebanese army, attacked one another. Rockets and mortar fire hit largely Christian East Beirut, the Muslim southern suburbs and the mountains above the city, as the factions jockeyed for position. U.S. Marines were stationed near the Beirut airport as a peacekeeping force but came under mortar fire from Druze positions in the foothills of the mountains.

I read about the fighting while I was in Rome for CNN, and each day I would see the accounts on the roll of paper in our AP printer. On Tuesday, September 6, there were reports that on the preceding day two ABC-TV technicians were missing in the hills above Beirut and that a wounded Canadian correspondent who had been with them was stranded there because of heavy shelling.

The Canadian was identified as Clark Todd.

As soon as I read that name, I began to worry. I hoped he would somehow be taken to safety, be taken to a clinic for treatment, but I feared he might not.

A few days later Richard Roth had a long roll of AP paper in his hand and was reading it in our cramped Rome bureau. He knew that I was worried about Clark, and so he told me that he had come across a reference to Clark's name: a story that reported his death. I was stunned. I stopped working on a story. I felt dizzy.

He handed me the AP copy.

I studied the words but they did not seem to represent symbols of reality. They seemed to be the stuff of cheap paperback novels purchased at airport newsstands. A wounded man dying. A foreign war. What was the point? Later I found out more details of what had happened.

Clark had left the Commodore Hotel in Beirut on Sunday, September 4, along with an ABC television crew and driver. They had driven fifteen miles south, up into the hills overlooking Beirut International Airport, high ground where Syrian-backed Muslim Druze and Israeli-backed Maronite Christian Phalange militias with tanks and artillery were shelling and shooting at each other in a struggle for control of a key area now that the Israelis had pulled out. In part, the fighting was a resurgence of the sectarian and ethnic violence of the Lebanese civil war of the mid-1970s, and in part it reflected a larger power struggle between Israel and Syria for influence over parts of Lebanon. Clark and the ABC crew headed south, crossed a green valley with a view of snowy peaks, and drove up into the Aley mountains, making their way to the scene of heavy fighting, a Muslim Druze village called Kfar Matta.

What happened next in Kfar Matta at 10 a.m. that day is unclear because there are conflicting accounts from survivors. Clark's daughter Anna visited the village eighteen years later with her brother and sister and was told by a local man named Said that shrapnel from a shell had hit Clark in the top left of his chest, that he had been helped down to an arched cellar and was awaiting a local nurse when Phalange militiamen massacred everyone in the cellar. But another man named Quasim, who had been Clark's driver that day, told Anna that her father had been hit by a sniper's bullet, not by shrapnel, and that his crew had helped him to an empty house and put him on a bed and held padding to his chest wound. "He had blood dribbling from his mouth," Quasim told her. He said Clark had told his driver and crew that he was dying and that they should leave or they would be killed in the fighting. They had left him. Later they arrived at a UN peacekeeping headquarters and asked for help, and a UN car tried to get through to Kfar Matta but the fighting had been too intense, so no one had been able to rescue Clark, his daughter was told by a UN official.

Whatever exactly happened, Clark Todd's body was found a week later and was brought by a Red Cross team and Phalange militiamen to the Israeli-held southern Lebanese port of Sidon. Five months later, Druze militiamen recaptured Kfar Matta from the Phalange and discovered the bodies of more than a hundred village men who apparently had been massacred by the Phalange at about the time Clark was killed. A French television team that accompanied Druze forces reentering the village also found something else: a bloody pillow case on which Clark had scrawled the words *Please tell my family I love them.* Above those words was his address in Hatfield, England. A villager later sent the pillow case to Clark's family.

Clark Todd was inducted into the Canadian News Hall of Fame; his name is inscribed in a roll of honor at the Freedom Forum Journalists Memorial in the Newseum in Washington, D.C.; and there is now a Canadian television news award named after him. His daughter Anna continued in his footsteps, becoming a reporter for the BBC.

I was shocked by the news of his death, and I remembered his friendship and his eagerness to go out and cover the next story, whatever it was. In many ways I identified with him. Journalists in their tributes to him said that he had not died in vain, as the familiar phrase goes, but part of me wondered if that were true. Years later, how many people remembered the last story he had covered, the battle for Kfar Matta?

The story of Clark Todd had a terrible ending as he bled to death in that cellar. Elsewhere in Lebanon, the story of Jerry Levin had a different ending.

Jerry was the CNN bureau chief in Beirut in the early 1980s. On March 7, 1984, at the age of fifty-one, he was taken captive, apparently by a militant Islamic group, and spent eleven and a half months in solitary confinement somewhere in Lebanon, apparently near Baalbek in the Bekaa Valley. (After he was captured, CNN offered me the position of Beirut bureau chief to replace him. I declined on grounds that it was too dangerous and I did not want to put my family through that kind of worry.) In February 1985 Jerry made his way to freedom under circumstances that have never been fully clarified. Jerry has said he escaped by climbing down blankets tied together. Some U.S. and Syrian officials said Syria had persuaded his captors to let him go.

Whatever the circumstances, Jerry ended up making his way from Lebanon to Damascus, where for a while he received protection from the Syrian government. In fact, the Syrians insisted that Levin's first public appearance be at a press conference at the Syrian Foreign Ministry before he was whisked to the American ambassador's residence in Damascus. It was a big story at the time, and the way we covered it was interesting.

CNN headquarters in Atlanta was concerned that Jerry Levin be in good condition to return to a life in freedom, and I was asked to charter a plane from Rome, fly to Damascus, and bring him to Wiesbaden, West Germany, and to make sure before leaving Damascus that I was satisfied he was stable enough mentally and physically for the rigors of reentry into normal life.

We chartered a plane from Ciampino Airport, Rome, and flew to Damascus, and drove to the Syrian Foreign Ministry to await Jerry Levin's release. It was a Friday, the Muslim sabbath, and the foreign ministry building was empty. We were able to enter through the front door but when we got inside there was no one there. I was fully expecting security searches and diplomats and other government officials standing around, but not a soul was there. We sat in a reception room waiting area and waited. There were couches and stuffed chairs and an empty reception desk with a telephone.

The phone rang.

I looked around. No one came to answer the phone.

It rang again.

For some reason which I will never understand, I picked up the phone and said: "Syrian Foreign Ministry. Can I help you?"

Someone said something in Arabic. I apologized in English that I didn't understand and hung up. Afterward I realized that I had no business answering that phone, and that in fact it was wrong for an American journalist to play the role of a foreign government employee, because journalists should make sure they never cross the line separating them from the people they report on. They should not interfere with events. I should have just let it ring. I should have stayed out of it. The reason I include this incident in this book is that there was something eerie about it, something that seems to capture the oddness of being a journalist in a strange situation, waiting for an American hostage to be released and hearing a phone ring in a government building that should have been fully staffed and instead was oddly empty.

After a while there was a commotion outside and a motorcade pulled up in front of the Syrian Foreign Ministry. At last the building became staffed by Syrian diplomats, accompanied by security guards, and then another car pulled up and Jerry Levin stepped out, made a few comments to us and other journalists at the front door, then went inside where he took part in a formal press conference that included speeches by U.S. and Syrian diplomats. Then Jerry was taken to the American ambassador's residence. By prior arrangement, we were able to drive our car to the residence and go inside and be received by Ambassador William Eagleton, who briefed me on what was happening. He said that Jerry Levin was being debriefed by U.S. officials, who wanted to know how well he was holding up after almost a year of captivity and whatever information he might have about his captors. The U.S. government desperately needed information about them because there had been a number of kidnappings, and in fact the CIA station chief in Beirut, William Buckley, had been captured and the CIA had no idea where he was or how to rescue him. (As it turned out, Buckley was tortured and killed, apparently by the militant Islamic group Hezbollah. His colleagues at the CIA, despite all their efforts, were unable to help him.)

I asked the ambassador if Jerry was in condition to travel, because our plan was to fly from Damascus to Wiesbaden, West Germany, for a reunion with his wife, Sis, and a medical checkup at the U.S. military base, and the ambassador said that yes, he was well enough to travel. I asked if I could meet with Jerry to see for myself, and he agreed. The ambassador then asked me an odd question.

"Is it all right if somebody from our embassy accompanies you and Jerry on the plane?"

"Who?"

He gave me the name of a man on the embassy staff.

I asked: "What does he do here at the embassy?"

"He's . . . part of the mission."

The ambassador did not elaborate, but I could tell he was hinting that the man was a CIA agent. Buckley had been the CIA station chief in Beirut. The man the ambassador wanted aboard our plane was someone from the CIA who wanted information that might save Buckley.

I was conflicted.

On the one hand, I was uncomfortable about doing anything that smacked of CNN cooperating with the CIA, especially here in the Middle East, where, as I had seen when I was captured myself and suspected of being a spy, suspicious minds assumed that any American journalists must be spies. Anything I did that could be perceived as working with the CIA could place me and my crew in danger. There was also the question of journalistic ethics. Journalists are supposed to be independent, to take an adversary relationship toward anyone in power, especially the U.S. government, because one of our most important functions is as a check on abuses of power. It would compromise our independence if we cooperated with the CIA.

On the other hand, I knew why the ambassador wanted this CIA official aboard our plane. The CIA was concerned about the fate of Buckley, and needed any information it could acquire to help it try to find him and rescue him, and Jerry Levin might be the best hope. Although he had already been debriefed by embassy officials here, it was possible that during our plane ride Jerry might remember some detail that he had not mentioned earlier, some lead that the CIA could follow, some tiny bit of information that could help them find the hideout. As a human being, and as someone who had been held captive myself, I did not want to stand in the way of rescuing a fellow American.

"All right," I said.

Then I went to a guest bedroom, where Jerry had just taken a shower. We sat and chatted for a few minutes. Jerry, a thin, mustachioed man with thick-framed glasses, seemed all right, although I had to emphasize to him who I was and where we were going before he seemed to take it all in. He was slightly dazed, but seemed to me strong enough to make the trip, and I knew it was important to get him to that hospital in Wiesbaden as soon as possible.

We drove to the Damascus airport, to an isolated VIP terminal, and boarded our chartered plane. Our CNN crew got pictures of Jerry boarding the plane and getting settled, and the microphone picked up bits of "natural sound"—informal comments and chatter and background sounds of the plane's engines. Aboard the plane I met the CIA official. I will not give his name, as even today such secrecy needs to be maintained to protect him and to protect anyone who was ever seen talking to him. He was a short, middle-aged man with a round face and crew-cut gray hair, wearing a blue-and-white-striped seersucker suit. He had a small, spiral-bound steno pad, and he took extensive notes every time Jerry said anything.

We flew to the island of Rhodes in the eastern Mediterranean. On our way, I asked Jerry what items he would like to have, so that I could phone ahead to our Rome bureau and ask Richard Roth to get them. Jerry said he would like a newspaper, a watch, mouthwash, and pasta. He said these were among the things he had missed the most. They had taken his watch away, and he had missed having the familiar feeling of a watchstrap around his wrist, and now he wanted to have that feeling back. When we landed at Rhodes, I phoned ahead to Rome and gave Richard the wish list.

We took off on our next leg, from Rhodes to Rome, and during the flight I interviewed Jerry for our CNN camera and microphone, asking him what had happened and how he felt now. I remember he said some odd things. Being a journalist, he was of course interested in politics. He had been unable to follow the news while in captivity and had missed the entire 1984 presidential election. Since being released he had picked up a few highlights, in conversations. "I know Reagan won," he told me aboard the plane, "but who is vice president?"

I told him it was George H. W. Bush.

I asked Jerry how well he had been treated in captivity, and he said his captors had treated him fairly well, although they had kept him chained to a radiator. He said they had brought him a doctor one time when he was feeling ill.

"A doctor?" the CIA man said. He leaned closer.

He asked: "Can you describe the doctor? Anything you remember about him?"

Jerry described the doctor briefly. I realized that the CIA official planned to report this bit of information, in hopes that someone at the CIA would be able to figure out who the doctor was and possibly get a lead on which part of Lebanon held the hideout. As it turned out, however, the CIA was not able to locate the hideout in time and no one ever rescued Buckley.

Jerry said one of the things he had missed the most, in addition to the items he had mentioned, and in addition to missing his wife, Sis, of course, had been opera. He said it had been painful to be deprived of tapes of his favorite operas.

At Ciampino Airport, Rome, Richard was there to greet us, arms filled with items from the wish list: that day's copy of the *Rome Daily American*, a bowl of pasta, a bottle of mouthwash, and a cheap watch. Jerry eagerly strapped the watch to his wrist and sat down in the plane to read his paper and devour his pasta on the final leg of our journey, from Rome to Wiesbaden. When we arrived in the German city, our crew got a wonderful shot of Jerry being greeted by Sis, who had worked energetically for months to lobby the U.S. government and Arab governments for his release. Then the couple got into a U.S. Embassy car and went off to the military hospital. Using the phone in our Mercedes limousine I did a "beeper"—a live audio report for CNN, with the sound of my voice superimposed over screen images that included a map showing our route from Damascus to Wiesbaden and still photos of Jerry. I described the joyous reunion of husband and wife. For once I had a Middle East story with a happy ending.

Part II

Washington

Chapter Nine

Face Down in the Mud

Oliver North, jaw jutting, eyes glinting under dark brows, chest puffed out, medals on display, sat there ramrod straight in his Marine uniform. In many respects it should have been a solemn occasion, the televised testimony by this lieutenant colonel at a hearing in the Senate Caucus Room, a serious investigation into suspicions of lawbreaking, deceit, and diversion of funds by officials of the Reagan administration. Yet for all the trappings of solemnity, something about it struck me as funny. I don't know why. It might have been the preposterous lies that North told. It might have been the posturing by the senators and representatives who were supposed to be investigating him. Whatever it was, a photograph in *Time* the following week showed dozens of reporters at tables listening to North, and all but one of the journalists had serious looks on their faces. I recognized the one smiling reporter in the photo: me.

For me, the Oliver North scandal provided relief from the tedium of the usual daily news in Washington. Having covered wars, terrorism, repression, and other dramatic stories in Europe and the Middle East for twenty years, I returned to the United States in 1986 with my family to cover Washington for CNN for eleven years, and much of that time I covered tedious debates about policy proposals, canned statements and events, and political rituals. Words, words, words. Endless hot air. Thank-you speeches. (Politicians spent so much time thanking one another and thanking groups they gave speeches to that I once jokingly proposed a Federal Thank-You Tax that would wipe out the national debt.) I found many American politicians to be phony and provincial and predictable, and covering them was often boring. So when a big story came along, I jumped at it. The criminality of Oliver North was a big story, and it had the advantage of comic overtones.

Although many Washington officials were laughable in their pomposity, I found Oliver North especially ludicrous, what with his self-promotions and protestations of righteous indignation, wrapping himself in Old Glory and quoting

Scripture. One of my favorite Northisms came during the suspenseful period before he testified to Congress about the Iran-Contra scandal—a scandal that involved Reagan administration officials in secret and illegal U.S. arms sales to Iran, secret and illegal arms deliveries to anti-Communist guerrillas in Nicaragua, and a cover-up. The period was suspenseful because one overriding question loomed in the background: Would President Reagan be impeached?

When summoned to testify under oath before a special joint Senate-House investigating committee in the fall of 1986, Oliver North at first refused, citing his Fifth Amendment right not to testify against himself. In fact, this was a negotiating ploy. He knew that the congressional investigation needed his testimony. He wanted to pressure Congress into making a deal in which he would agree to testify only if Congress granted him legal immunity, meaning that nothing he said under oath to Congress could be used later by a prosecutor when, as seemed likely, he would be charged with Iran-Contra crimes. (As it turned out, he was convicted of three Iran-Contra felonies including obstructing Congress but won on appeal because an appeals court said prosecution witnesses had been improperly influenced by North's congressional testimony and that this violated his immunity deal.) For an ultraconservative anti-Communist like North to take the Fifth, the way suspected Communists had done in the past, was embarrassing. He had to dress it up as a patriotic and even religious act, to justify such stonewalling despite all the questions about his secret sales of Pentagon missiles to Iran at a time when his government was calling Iran a terrorist nation and imposing an arms embargo, questions about what appeared to be arms-for-hostages deals with terrorists when his government said it would never negotiate with terrorists, and questions about his skimming off the profits from arms sales to Iran, putting them into numbered Swiss bank accounts, and using the secret funds to smuggle guns into Nicaragua for local anti-Communist guerrillas (known as the Contras) despite a law forbidding U.S. military supplies to them. President Reagan's wife, Nancy, had joined the chorus of those demanding that North answer all these questions.

On Thursday, December 18, 1986, shortly after 6 a.m., North was leaving his Great Falls, Virginia, home when a CBS News television crew approached and asked what he would say to Nancy Reagan. North replied: "There have been a number of people who have suggested that I abandon my individual rights under the Constitution of the United States. The president has not asked that I do that. I don't believe the president really wants me to abandon my individual rights under the Constitution. People have died face down in the mud all over the world defending those individual rights."

If these maudlin words about people dying face down in the mud did not move the television audience to tearful support then surely, he must have thought, his next words would. Told that CBS understood the president had already spoken with him and asked him to come forth, North said, "I have, over the last twenty-three days, found myself abandoned by former friends and so-called friends and colleagues. I continue to place my trust in the Lord. I would refer you to Psalm 7, Verse 1." (Journalists had to scurry to their Bibles to learn that this verse said: "O Lord my God, in Thee do I take refuge; save me from all my pursuers, and deliver me.")

Whether or not through divine intervention, North would indeed be saved from all his pursuers in the end when the appeals court overturned his three Iran-Contra felony convictions. And although we journalists thought we were serving the public good by giving so much coverage to this scandal, it was the massive coverage we gave to North's testimony that helped him avoid punishment for his crimes. After his trial, the appeals court would rule that his televised testimony had been seen by so many people that Independent Counsel Lawrence Walsh could not possibly guarantee that prosecution witnesses had not been influenced by it.

While I don't agree that Walsh had failed to avoid the use of witnesses tainted by exposure to North's testimony (I interviewed Walsh and found him to be an honorable man), it was true that North's testimony dominated the news at the time. We journalists had no choice but to give saturation coverage. Public interest was high. No one knew whether this scandal would become big enough to bring down Reagan. CNN was the only all-news cable channel in those days, and we provided blanket coverage, and I was one part of that. Each day, throughout the morning and afternoon of North's testimony, correspondent Linda Taira, a smart, hard-working journalist, would do live shots outside the Russell Senate Office Building while I did the day's wrapup story to air on the news in the evening.

The first day that North testified, the story was so big that the CNN brass decided my "daywrap" package would not be the usual two minutes but instead would be eight minutes long. I immediately began worrying whether we could pull this off. Normally it takes about one hour to edit each minute of news package, but we didn't have eight hours to edit my eight-minute package. We would have only about three hours in late afternoon, so the decision was made to have not one but two videotape editors work on it—simultaneously. Linda Lashendock would edit the first four minutes and Sheila Kanzler would edit the second four minutes. I didn't see how we could get it finished in time, but I was told by Linda and Sheila not to worry, that they would make it happen. That was a typical CNN attitude, which I loved: we'll make it happen. Still, I had my doubts.

The two editors began working on their front and back halves of my story. I had a yellow legal pad filled with notes as to what North had said in his testimony, and at what point during his testimony he had said it, so I could help Linda and Sheila cue up the tapes and find the relevant sound bites to insert into the package. In between sound bites they inserted "b-roll," pictures illustrating what this story was about: Reagan, Iranian leaders, obscure arms dealers, TOW antitank missiles, hostages in Lebanon, Swiss banks, the CIA, the White House, and the Contra guerrillas in the jungles of Nicaragua. As I shuttled back and forth between Linda's edit bay and Sheila's edit bay next door, answering their questions as to which sound bite went where and helping them identify people in file tapes, we were told that we were coming up to our deadline. The eight-minute package had to be on the air in a few minutes. Linda said she was almost done. Sheila still had a ways to go and would not be ready in time. The network producers were so eager to get this package on the air that they made an amazing decision: As soon as Linda finished editing her first half of the package, CNN would begin airing it. Meanwhile, Sheila would keep editing her back half of the package, and we would begin rolling her edited tape when Linda's edited tape ended. My nervousness grew worse.

I was sure this would be a disaster. Sheila was still far from being done. To my dismay, and despite my protests, CNN stuck to this insane plan. Linda finished editing the front half, ran into the control room, popped the tape into the deck, and "hot-rolled" it (played it directly for broadcast from the Washington bureau, rather than following the usual procedure of feeding it to Atlanta where it would be recorded and saved for use from there after producers had a chance to review it). As I sat next to Sheila, my face drenched in sweat, I could see on the monitor and hear on the loudspeaker my daywrap report on the air on CNN. The first minute of it went by, and Sheila was still editing. The second minute went by.

Sheila was still editing and a third minute went by.

"Come on," I begged her. "We're running out of time."

"I need one more tape. Where is it?"

She began rummaging through teetering piles of Sony Beta-format videotapes in their thick gray boxes.

"Sheila! We're into the fourth minute!"

I watched on the monitor as the first half neared its end, and still Sheila fiddled with the buttons and dials of her editing machine. Nervous producers crowded the doorway of her edit bay. There was the air of some terrible disaster about to happen, a Hindenburg hovering overhead. Producers, writers, and correspondents looked stricken, me most of all.

At last, with seconds to go, Sheila rewound the tape and pushed the EJECT button. The tape slowly emerged. She grabbed it, ran past the rows of facing edit bays into the control room, slammed it into a tape machine, and hit PLAY.

On television screens around the world, what audiences saw was a seamless continuation of the CNN edited taped report of the first day of testimony by Oliver North, with not one second of gap. Not one second of "dead air" or the dreaded "going to black" that we all had feared. Seamless.

The newsroom burst into applause.

I sank back into a chair, exhausted. Linda and Sheila had pulled off a miracle. Of course, they and all the other videotape editors at CNN pulled off miracles every day, and I was amazed at their skill, especially given the soul-crushing pressure of the news business. The pressure produced its share of profanity (I once witnessed a screaming fight between a producer and an editor whose exchange of words consisted of nothing other than "F—— you" endlessly repeated) but somehow, day after day, they got the news out. They pulled it off. They made it happen, and the pressure bonded us like a family. Now, when I go back to visit the DC bureau, there are hugs and even a few tears, and it feels like a family reunion.

Our CNN team won a National Headliner Award for our Iran-Contra coverage, and many other journalists did outstanding jobs covering the story. But the coverage was not perfect, and some angles were never thoroughly explored. At one point in North's testimony a congressman tried to ask him about a *Miami Herald* story quoting unnamed sources as claiming North had once helped draft a plan to suspend the Constitution in the event of a national crisis, but North's lawyer and the congressional committee chairman cut him off, so North never commented. A documentary called *Cover Up* later repeated this allegation, without proof, but I never saw any major newspaper or magazine look into this in depth. Although I was intrigued, I was too busy with day-to-day coverage of Iran-Contra to ever check up on the *Herald*'s allegations. Was there a contingency plan to suspend the Constitution? Some reputable news organization should have tried harder to find out.

During the Iran-Contra scandal, one thing I found amusing was the epidemic of amnesia that swept through officialdom when North and fellow White House officials were asked about their involvement in criminality. "Doesn't ring a bell," his boss, Robert McFarlane, a key player in the scandal, repeatedly replied to investigators.

The players either developed amnesia or they split hairs, anything to avoid telling the truth, anything to deceive while technically not lying. On November 13, 1986, McFarlane, who had been Reagan's national security adviser, was asked by Ted Koppel, moderator of the ABC News program *Nightline*, if it were true, as had been reported, that he and North had taken a chocolate cake on a secret flight to Iran earlier that year to present as a gift that would smooth the way to the arms sales. McFarlane replied: "That's not the way I do business." That seemed to end the cake story. But later reports insisted

McFarlane and North had, indeed, brought a cake with them. Koppel interviewed McFarlane a second time, on January 20, 1987, and asked whether he had missed a nuance during the first interview. This time McFarlane admitted that there had been a cake, and he gave a tortuous, weasel-wording explanation as to why he had deceived Koppel and the American public the first time about the cake:

"I didn't buy it, bake it, cook it, eat it, present it or otherwise get involved with it. Apparently, I am told, the cake was the product of a spontaneous idea of Col. North. . . . I didn't get involved with it, and that's not the way I do business."

This explanation, which I found hilarious, gave a real insight into the kind of lying and deception that goes on all the time in Washington.

There were more lies to come. When North was put on trial, he told an obvious lie to the prosecutor from the Independent Counsel's office, John W. Keker, himself a former Marine. It was a lie that may have blown his chances for acquittal.

Each morning that North was testifying Keker would begin by saying, "Good morning, Colonel North," and North would glare back at him in silence. One morning, after this ritual good morning/silence exchange, Keker sought to impeach North's credibility, since several of the charges dealt with alleged lying to Congress (and Keker in his summation would compare North to Pinocchio with a long nose), so the prosecutor raised an issue that was not part of the indictment: North's use of $8,000 in cash to buy a used GMC Suburban van for himself. Keker asked North to describe what happened on the day he bought the vehicle. Reluctantly, under prodding, North said he looked at the vehicle at a dealer's lot in Tysons Corner, northern Virginia, put $5,000 down, then went to the office in Vienna, northern Virginia, of retired U.S. Air Force general Richard Secord, a fellow Iran-Contra figure who kept cash withdrawn from the secret Swiss bank accounts in his office. Then North told of returning to the car dealer's lot three days later and paying $3,000 to complete the purchase.

Up until this point the jury of ordinary Washington residents may have had trouble understanding the complexities of the Iran-Contra case with its arcane intelligence agency procedures and documents, legal niceties of the Boland amendment (forbidding arms sales to the Contras), bewildering meetings, titles of obscure officials, unpronounceable names of Israeli, Iranian, and other weapons dealers and government figures, and nuances of State Department policies. But as I sat in the courthouse that day I was sure that the jury had no trouble understanding what we were talking about now. It was about someone with access to Swiss bank accounts paying $8,000 in cash for a van. I saw the jurors watching with rapt attention. For once they had some idea of what was going on, and the question in their minds, surely, was the next question Keker asked North on the stand:

"Where did you get the cash?"

North glared at Keker and said something along these lines: "Every day when I come home from work I empty loose change from my pockets. I put the coins in a little metal box in our closet. And over the years, it adds up." Over twenty years, he said, it had added up to a total of $15,000.

Keker asked if he was saying that he had saved up the $8,000 for the vehicle from loose coins from his pockets, and North, indignant that anyone would even question his veracity, insisted this was the case.

Some of the jurors had looks of amazement and incredulity on their faces. I had the impression that earlier they might have been divided on some issues but not on this one. They seemed united in their belief that North had used some of the diverted arms sales profits for his personal use—and lied about it.

Or take the case of the Contras who amazingly morphed into helicopters.

Donald Gregg, national security adviser to then vice president George H. W. Bush, helped set up a 1986 Bush meeting with a North operative at a time when the Contras were trying to get more arms from the Reagan administration. Congress wanted to find out if this meeting was designed to achieve resupply of the Contras, which would have been illegal and would have implicated Bush in a crime. A Bush office scheduling memo was produced, and on it a secretary had written down the purpose of the meeting: *resupply of the Contras.* Clearly embarrassed, Bush's people and Gregg's people tried to come up with a plausible explanation. At last they thought they had found it: Gregg testified to Congress under oath that his secretary may have made a spelling error, and that what she had really meant to write down as the topic for the meeting was: *resupply of the copters.*

I remember laughing out loud when I heard Gregg try to persuade doubting congressional investigators that it was "copters," not "Contras," that the VP knew about. (A prosecutor later investigated Gregg on suspicion of false testimony but was unable to prove it beyond a reasonable doubt and did not bring criminal charges.)

There were more amusing lies and obfuscations to come. When it became clear that Vice President Bush's name was listed as among those officially attending a White House meeting where arms-for-hostages deals were discussed (and, according to one senior official, Bush had not only attended but had been among those favoring the deals), this created a public relations and legal problem, because Bush earlier had claimed that he had been "out of the loop" and had not attended any meetings where arms-for-hostages deals were discussed. Faced with this conflict between reality and Bush's lie, his people had to come up with an explanation, and their solution was to say that yes, he did attend *part* of the meeting but that he *arrived late* and missed the part where they discussed making deals with terrorists.

All these lies and alibis I found amusing, and during the trial of Oliver North I often had trouble suppressing a laugh but forced myself to keep silent. I did not want to get into trouble with Judge Gerhard Gesell, for whom the word "curmudgeon" surely had been invented. Judge Gesell was such a curmudgeon, so crusty and cranky, that he cowed even the most abrasive attorneys and witnesses.

One day there was a flurry of excitement when the glamorous Fawn Hall swept into the courtroom. She had been North's secretary and was the daughter of McFarlane's secretary. Although this scandal had no hint of sex, her sensational looks added some spice to the trial. She testified about shredding some documents and smuggling others out of the White House hidden under her clothes. And she had earned a bizarre footnote in history because, due to an apparent typing error, she had transposed two digits in the number of one of the Swiss bank accounts, causing $10 million from the Sultan of Brunei to be deposited into the wrong bank account (which, again, I found to be hilarious). In interviews and in court, Fawn Hall was ferociously loyal to North and indignant that he was being put on trial. I had the impression, watching her testify, that she was accustomed to getting her way, possibly because of her good looks. But she wasn't able to get her way with Judge Gesell. At one point she was up on the witness stand and the judge was addressing the courtroom. Fawn Hall interrupted him to correct something he had said. Judge Gesell leaned down toward her and said: "Miss Hall, when I am speaking, please keep your mouth shut." Her shocked look was one of the highlights of the trial for me.

At the end of North's trial, as the jury deliberated, we journalists waited in the press room on the fourth floor of the U.S. District Court for the District of Columbia . . . and waited . . . and waited. There was nothing to do but wait for someone from the judge's office to come and tell us to return to the courtroom to hear the verdict. While we waited, we killed time writing satirical ditties about the trial.

But finally the jokes ended and we had serious work to do. After twelve days of jury deliberation, a clerk from Judge Gesell's office passed word to us that the jury was returning to the courtroom. From the press room at the courthouse I called supervising producer Rob Reynolds at the nearby DC office of CNN and told him to stand by. We had another producer keep the phone line open at the press room while I was downstairs in the courtroom. I sat in the press area on the left side of the spectator portion of the room, with its pew-like benches. The jury was sitting in its area directly in front of us. The prosecution and defense attorneys were at their tables. Judge Gesell came in and sat down. It was quiet for a moment. There was a real sense of history about to be made.

Then we got the news: guilty on three counts. Although all of us journalists felt an urge to race from the room, we were under judge's orders to remain seated until the end of the session. Then it ended and we did run, up the stairs to the press room, where I grabbed the open phone and told Rob *guilty on three counts.* Being a good journalist, he insisted I repeat it, and he said he wanted to make sure he understood me correctly as to which counts these were: obstruction of Congress, mutilating government documents, and taking an illegal gratuity. It took only a few seconds, but his insistence on guarding against mistakes was the right thing to do. We both knew that this story would dominate the day's news, and that many people, including other journalists, would be influenced by the way CNN first reported it. Satisfied, he gave the information to an anchor who broke the news to the audience, and we were off and running. Gene Randall did live shots outside the courthouse while I did the daywrap.

All the lies and preposterous claims made by North and other Washington officeholders kept us journalists laughing for months, and I enjoyed it, but I also felt it my duty to expose how untruthful these politicians were, that the duty of a journalist is to do everything humanly possible to see that the truth gets through, to expose pretense, to say that the emperor has no clothes. Of course, an objective reporter writing a straight news report (as opposed to a commentary) can't say "he's lying," but what the reporter *can* do is balance an official's claim with a quote from a reputable source who can cast doubt on this claim and show how unlikely it is, and let readers draw their own conclusions. Doing this is an important part of the press's adversarial relationship toward those in power, a check on their power, a safeguard against abuse.

The worst abuse of power that I heard about was Watergate, and one of the worst abusers was John Mitchell, President Nixon's attorney general. As an employee of *Newsweek,* owned by the Washington Post Company, I was proud of the *Washington Post* for investigating him and the others. I felt related to a family that was giving American journalism its finest hour.

The *Post,* and subsequent prosecutions, revealed that Mitchell had approved the break-in and bugging of the Democratic National Committee headquarters and that he knew about the subsequent cover-up. He did not hide his disdain for the *Post* and its publisher, Katharine Graham. When reporter Carl Bernstein phoned Mitchell to get his reaction to a *Post* story that Mitchell had controlled a secret GOP slush fund, Mitchell said: "Katie Graham's gonna get her tit caught in a big fat wringer if that's published." But if this was meant as a threat, it didn't work. With Kay Graham's encouragement, the *Post* kept digging for the truth. Mitchell and Nixon's other top men were convicted of conspiracy, perjury, and obstruction of justice.

On June 22, 1977, John Mitchell, former attorney general of the United States, checked into a prison in Montgomery, Alabama. On that same day, in London, Kay Graham was checking into Claridge's, a luxury hotel near the American Embassy. As London bureau chief of *Newsweek,* it was my protocol duty to accompany her on her arrival from Washington, and I couldn't help noticing the irony of the situation. As we stood at the reception desk, I looked down at the Reuters teletype and saw that the machine was typing out a report on Mitchell's arrival at the prison. He was quoted as saying, "It's always great to be in Alabama." I thought to myself: *I'm standing next to the person who helped put him there.* A tall, thin, elegant woman who was both aristocratic and down-to-earth, Kay Graham, for me, was the embodiment of the highest ideals of journalism. At that moment, I believed that if journalists pursued the truth diligently enough they could hold the powerful accountable.

But nine years later, when I covered the Iran-Contra scandal for CNN, I saw that the world was not quite that simple.

Despite the press revelations, Reagan was never impeached, Bush was elected president, and the top officials in the Reagan government who either had been convicted of Iran-Contra crimes or had faced possible indictment avoided punishment. Either their convictions were overturned by an appeals court or they received pardons from George H. W. Bush later when he became president. There was some political fallout, however. When Bush ran for reelection, Bill Clinton defeated him, and some political analysts said Bush had been hurt in the election by later revelations from a prosecutor that Bush had been implicated in the Iran-Contra scandal. North later ran for U.S. senator from Virginia and lost. But Bush's son won election as president, and some Reagan-era officials implicated in the Iran-Contra crimes became part of his secretive administration. Even the best journalists could not always hold the powerful accountable.

Chapter Ten

All the Earmarks

One spring day I was sitting in the courtroom of the Supreme Court, listening to arguments in a case about racial patterns of voting in Louisiana, when I noticed that, one by one, all of my colleagues were being pulled out of the room. Someone would enter from the rear left of the room, make his or her way to the press section at the front left, tap a journalist on the shoulder or wave to catch the reporter's attention, and beckon the reporter to leave. What was going on? I knew it had to be something of great importance, but there was no way to know what it was. No beepers, pagers, or other electronic devices were allowed inside the courtroom, and we were cut off from the outside world.

An intern from the CNN Washington office suddenly appeared and tapped me on the shoulder, motioning for me to follow him out of the courtroom. As soon as we were outside in the high-ceilinged marble hallway I asked: "What is it?"

"There was an explosion in Oklahoma City. You're supposed to go straight to the Justice Department and do a live shot." He handed me a printout from the AP newswire but it had few details: an explosion was heard this morning, a federal building damaged, no indication if it was a gas main.

My first thoughts were questions: *Was it a bomb? How do we know for sure? Who could I talk to to get details? Who else is working on this story? What resources will CNN make available?*

From the fact that I and other reporters were being pulled out of the Supreme Court I could tell that, whatever had happened, it would dominate the news for days or weeks, and I knew that these first reports had to be done carefully and cautiously because they would carry consequences for the public's perception later of what had happened and what needed to be done. With news events of this magnitude there are public policy implications, and the press has a responsibility to provide an accurate account based on verifiable facts, to avoid panicking the public and pressuring law enforcement officers into over-reacting. As I was soon to see, there were some in the press who failed to meet that responsibility.

It was Wednesday, April 19, 1995, about 10:30 a.m. Washington time. The explosion had taken place at 10:03 a.m. our time (9:03 a.m. in Oklahoma City) and already CNN and other news organizations were clearing the decks for massive news coverage. The intern and I entered a waiting car and raced to the Justice Department, on Pennsylvania Avenue, and on the way we listened to WTOP, the all-news Washington radio station. Still no word whether it was a bomb, and, if it was a bomb, who might have done it. *Be cautious,* I thought.

CNN had a desk in the small press room on the ground floor of the Justice Department, and producer Terry Frieden was there, on the phone as usual. "They want you to do a live shot right now," he said.

"What do we know?"

"Not much. The FBI is on it."

I went out into the hallway and ran into John Russell, one of the press officers. He was a quirky, slightly rumpled figure in a long-sleeved pink shirt, tie loose, a slim, middle-aged man with gray hair, a man who was sometimes cranky but often helpful and, occasionally, refreshingly honest.

"Was it a bomb?" I asked.

"We're investigating."

"Is it possible it was a gas explosion? An accident?"

John looked at me, dead serious. "We're treating it as terrorism."

I was startled. This was new. No one in the government had used the word "terrorism" until now. I hurried back into the press room and told Terry, who quickly passed word to the supervising producers, so that CNN anchors could use this information in their updates. Meanwhile, I prepared for the first of what would be many live shots outside the Justice Department. In fact, for the next two weeks my life was a blur of live shots every day, from six in the morning until midnight.

In each live shot, as I stood on Pennsylvania Avenue and faced the camera, with the tall gray monolithic building of the Justice Department behind me and the J. Edgar Hoover Building of the FBI across the street behind the camera, I summarized the few facts that I knew for sure to be true and, at the same time, I tried to resist the temptation to speculate. In the beginning, those few facts were that it was a powerful bomb, the FBI was investigating, and a Justice Department spokesperson had said the government was treating the incident as terrorism.

Later, when suspect Timothy McVeigh was arrested, I reported what Justice had to say about him, and, still later, when the FBI released an artist's sketch of "John Doe #2," a man believed to have been with McVeigh, I reported only what I knew for certain and resisted the anchors' attempts to have me specu-late on why the sketch was released or what its release meant. The truth was, I simply didn't know anything more than what FBI and Justice officials were saying, and my job was to report, accurately, the fact that they had said this, and to put it into the larger context of the investigation. Meanwhile, the CNN producer at Justice, Terry Frieden, was pushing hard for more facts, more in-terviews, more pictures, and he was quick to alert CNN, and bulldoze his way to getting CNN to free up an extra camera crew, when the local FBI field office permitted cameras to show telephone operators receiving tips from the public over a hot line.

My live shots supplemented more substantive on-scene live shots from Okla-homa City by Tony Clark, Bonnie Anderson, and other CNN reporters, as well as still other live shots by correspondents at the White House and Capitol Hill. The pace was intensive, relentless, one live shot after another, and Terry and I were getting little sleep yet trying to stay clearheaded enough to avoid journal-istic mistakes and pitfalls.

Most of us at CNN were being careful, but the same could not be said of some other news organizations. Take CBS. In one of its first live cut-ins into regular morning programming, CBS network news carried a report that a senior Clinton administration official had said the explosion "bears all the earmarks of Middle Eastern terrorism." As soon as I heard this, I asked my-self: *How would he know?* Other than the fact that the collapsed Murrah Fed-eral Building now resembled the collapsed apartment buildings I had seen in Beirut after bombings, what other evidence was there to make such a sensa-tional and ominous statement? CBS seemed to be straining for some exclu-sive angle and did not treat the source's statement with the proper amount of caution and skepticism. Its script should have included a line saying some-thing like "The source did not say what he based his statement on, and federal investigators have not said whether or not there is evidence the bombing was the work of foreign or domestic terrorists."

But what did the "senior official" actually say to CBS? The network did not give the full context of the interview. Sometimes in situations like this a jour-nalist might raise a possibility and ask for an official's reaction. The journal-ist might ask, "Was it Middle East terrorism?" The Washington official might reply, "We're not sure," or "We're leaving every possibility open," which is the most likely comment by any responsible, knowledgeable official. I'm not saying that CBS made up or exaggerated the comment, but I do feel that even if the of-ficial had volunteered this comment without being prompted by the reporter, CBS should have provided more context and caution.

Even worse, sometimes in situations like this it's not a government official but a *former* government official now working as a consultant to the news organization who says something to a reporter, and the reporter then takes that person's speculation and asks an actual current government official if he agrees with it, and receives a noncommittal reply such as "anything is possible." That is a typical sequence of events in the news business, and it sometimes leads to hyperbole in which the reporter combines a consultant's wild speculation with a government official's careful ambiguity and comes up with "a senior administration official says it bears all the earmarks of Middle Eastern terrorism." In Washington, as a rule of thumb I found that the more sensational the statement, the less informed the speaker.

Television overuses "experts" who often know little more than what's in the *Washington Post* that day. Television producers permit their idle chatter and irresponsible speculation to misinform and misguide the public. They blur the distinction between actual reporting and mere guessing by someone who doesn't have anything new to say but who wants to be on television to promote himself and say what the network producers want to hear: something sensational and dramatic that is exclusive to their channel. Gatekeepers need to be more cautious in choosing live guests. The producers need to have the anchor question the guest closely to clarify whether he has some new information or is merely speculating. Anchors also need to keep reminding viewers that this guest is speculating and has no direct knowledge of the course of the investigation. The problem is that news organizations, especially television news, don't like to tear down the credibility of their live guests. In some cases, before the show went on the air the producers had had to compete with rival networks to win the guest's agreement to appear on their show and so after all that hard work, they want to show the guest off as a trophy, a great "get," even if he or she has nothing new to say. In other cases, the guest is a paid consultant of the network itself, and, again, the network doesn't want to undermine his or her credibility by pointing out that he doesn't really know what he's talking about.

Here's an example of how this speculation and hype feeds on itself and gets circulated to a mass audience: At 12:07 p.m. Eastern time on April 19, 1995, only some two hours after the explosion, David McCurdy, a former congressman from Oklahoma, was already on CNN's air saying:

> Well, my first reaction when I heard of the explosion was that there could be a very real connection to some of the Islamic fundamentalist groups that have, actually, been operating out of Oklahoma City. They've had recent meetings— even a convention—where terrorists from the Middle East that were connected directly to Hamas and Hezbollah participated.

To her credit, anchor Natalie Allen immediately pressed McCurdy to say what his source was for saying Middle Eastern terrorists had attended a convention in Oklahoma City. It turned out he based this on having seen a television documentary, "Jihad in America." So an uninformed ex-legislator speculates it could have been the work of Islamic fundamentalists with Middle Eastern connections, based on an earlier television show he saw. The CNN anchor did a good job of forcing him to admit that he had no firsthand knowledge of this, and that in fact his information came from a documentary, but the harm was done: viewers were left with the general impression that somehow Middle Eastern— meaning Arab—terrorists were to blame. This shows the worst side of our news media at work.

I feel very strongly about this, because initial reports carry such weight and contribute powerfully to overall impressions. And any speculation about Middle Eastern involvement carries with it the potential for harm to innocent individuals, as Abrahim Ahmad found out.

On April 19, the day of the bombing, Ahmad, thirty-two, a Jordanian-American who had lived for thirteen years in Oklahoma, happened to be traveling from Oklahoma City to Amman, Jordan, to visit relatives. He had nothing to do with the bombing but was guilty of being an Arab in the wrong place at the wrong time.

That morning Ahmad flew from Oklahoma City to Chicago, and that evening he checked into O'Hare International Airport in Chicago for a flight to Amman. Before he could board his flight in Chicago, FBI agents pulled him aside and questioned him because he fit a general profile issued to police and airport authorities around the world: young men traveling alone to destinations such as the Middle East. And he was wearing a jogging suit similar to one that a witness had reported seen worn by a man at the scene of the explosion. He was questioned for hours, causing him to miss his flight. FBI agents released him, doubting he was a suspect, but his luggage was already on the plane and went on without him. When Italian police opened it in Rome they said they found items such as spools of electric wire, tape, silicone, pliers, and photos of military weapons. They told U.S. investigators, who decided they wanted to question Ahmad again.

Meanwhile, Ahmad had caught a flight from Chicago to London, where he intended to make a connection to Rome and Amman, but British authorities detained him as he disembarked from the transatlantic flight at Heathrow Airport, outside London. The British authorities handcuffed the hapless man and put him on a flight back across the Atlantic to the United States, this time to Dulles Airport, outside Washington, because the FBI had deemed him a "possible witness." The news coverage of his detention was massive. He may have been officially called a *possible witness,* but the blanket news coverage carried with it a subtext: *possible Arab terrorist.* The coverage was so intense, in fact, that CNN even sent a correspondent to Dulles Airport for a live shot in which he merely noted the fact that the flight carrying Ahmad back from London had landed. That was all. Everything else in the live shot was a rehash of the few known facts. The producers who decided to have the correspondent go live from Dulles were guilty of overreacting, hyping the story and, albeit unintentionally, reinforcing the racially stereotypical subtext.

It's understandable in a dramatic story like a bombing investigation that the public wants to know all the latest information including who is being questioned, but a detainee in this country still has a presumption of innocence, even when we as a nation are threatened by terrorists and especially when there is no credible evidence connecting the detainee with the crime. That presumption of innocence is one of our strengths, one of our greatest protections against government abuse of power. When journalists focus too much attention on someone being questioned, they distort reality, hurt the innocent, and contribute to a mob mentality. During the three days Ahmad was held before finally being released, his wife was spat upon and trash was dumped on his front lawn in Oklahoma City because of public anger whipped up by irresponsible coverage.

My producer Terry Frieden and I tried to avoid that type of coverage and made efforts to be careful and cautious in our reporting from the Justice Department on the investigation into the Oklahoma City bombing. Sometimes our cautious approach put us in conflict with CNN executives, as we saw in the case of a mysterious fax.

News leaked out on Sunday, April 23, that, on the previous Wednesday, the day of the bombing, the Washington office of Representative Steve Stockman, R-Texas, had received by fax an anonymous, handwritten message, time-stamped on the fax machine more than an hour before the bombing, with cryptic wording that seemed to include references to the Oklahoma City attack: *Seven to 10 floors only. Military people on the scene. BATF/FBI. Bomb threat received last week. Perpetrator unknown at this time. Oklahoma.* Surely, whoever had sent that fax *before the bombing* must have known the bombing was coming and probably was either one of the perpetrators or someone close to them. Not only that, but the word *Wolverine* was also on the fax, and that suggested Michigan, the state of origin of the two main suspects in custody, Timothy McVeigh and Terry Nichols. Had the sender of the fax tried to tip off authorities? Or had the sender of the fax wanted to boast of foreknowledge?

The AP ran a story saying that federal investigators had received the fax and were studying it. One oddity is that first reports said Stockman's office had given the fax to the NRA, which in turn had passed it on to the Bureau of Alcohol, Tobacco and Firearms, which in turn had passed it on to the FBI. That was very odd indeed. But our Justice Department and FBI sources steered us away from any speculation that this fax might be an important clue. Instead, they said that it was one of many items that had been sent to the FBI to look into but at this stage there was no indication that it was or was not of any value for the investigation. They gave us this caution because rumors were flying that someone in the Michigan Militia, a right-wing extremist group led by Mark Koernke, had sent the fax and might be one of the terrorist conspirators.

I was assigned to prepare a wrapup of the day's events from the Washington end of the investigation (as a companion piece to a similar "daywrap" from one of the CNN reporters in Oklahoma City). As I sifted through the various elements to use in this wrapup story, I decided that the mysterious fax was worth mentioning briefly, probably down near the bottom of the piece. I considered not including it at all, since there was no way of knowing whether it was of any value to the investigation, but I decided to mention it at least briefly because it involved a congressman and the NRA, and there might later be questions about why Stockman had gone first to the NRA and not directly to the FBI, if in fact that had happened. It was theoretically possible that there might later be accusations that he had delayed the investigation, although I could not know this for sure.

When I told supervising producers in the CNN Washington bureau about my planned structure for the daywrap story, they said a senior CNN executive wanted me to lead my piece with the fax and to make that the main focus of my story.

"But the FBI says they don't know if it's of any value," I complained. "What if it's a hoax? The work of a crank? Something totally unrelated to the bombing?"

"Just do it," I was told.

The senior executive then contacted me and said that he had spoken to the FBI director, Louis Freeh, whom he knew personally, and that Freeh had told him, on background, that the FBI was taking this seriously. At the time I found that hard to believe, and, now that I look back on it, years later, I doubt very much that that is what Freeh said. I think it's very likely he said something along the lines of, "We're looking at everything," without giving this fax any special significance. But the CNN executive, who was eager to play up the fact that he had spoken to Freeh when no other journalist apparently had done this, ordered me to lead with the fax angle and insert a line saying sources told CNN the FBI was taking this seriously.

I was in a quandary. My gut told me it was wrong to build my entire story around a fax that might have been of no significance. But I was under orders to play up the fax angle, apparently as a way for CNN to boast that it had a mini-scoop from the FBI and to give this CNN executive bragging rights. I argued and argued, but it was late in the day and we needed to get my story on the air by 5 p.m., which meant the video editor needed to get my script soon, which meant the supervising producers had to approve the script in the next few minutes. There was no time to do the additional reporting that might have provided better guidance for us on whether the fax was a big deal or irrelevant. I caved in, feeling terrible. I led with the fax. My only consolation was that I was able to insert a line into the story noting that the FBI was pursuing many leads and this was only one of them, and that there was no suggestion of a direct link with the bombing. But I'm sure any viewer that evening would have received the impression that this fax was some kind of breakthrough in the investigation.

To be sure, I kept downplaying its importance. Here's an exchange, during my 7:09 a.m. live shot from the Justice Department, Monday, April 24, between me and anchor Bob Cain:

> BOB CAIN: Anthony, what is the perceived significance of the fax having been sent, if that's when it was—an hour after the bombing? It would seem there might have been a number of faxes sent within that time frame.
>
> ANTHONY COLLINGS: Yes, investigators are not quite sure of the significance. As one of them told CNN, this doesn't necessarily prove anything but we are very interested and we want to follow up on it.

Later, we found out what really had happened. It was a comedy of errors. Olivia (Libby) Molley, who was an associate of Koernke in Michigan and a former campaign worker for Stockman in Texas, said she had received a fax from a militia supporter in Oklahoma City who apparently had been listening to radio and television news reports *after* the Oklahoma City bombing and had jotted down a few words from these reports, including *Bldg 7 to 10 floors only* and *BATF/FBI* and *bomb threat* and *Oklahoma.* For some reason, she had decided to fax the handwritten notes of what he had heard on the news to Representative Stockman. The time stamp on the fax machine in Stockman's office was set incorrectly, Stockman later said.

In other words, someone in Oklahoma, listening to the same news reports that millions of other people were listening to, sent a fax that was of no value whatsoever to the investigation, yet CNN wound up leading its wrapup of the day's major developments with this worthless item, and print and broadcast outlets around the world cited the CNN story. The moral of the story: err on the side of caution, avoid hype, be careful to quote investigators as precisely and as literally as possible, and don't let a network's desire to promote itself, or an executive's desire to promote himself, get in the way of the truth.

There were some other problems with our coverage, including an occasional bending of the two-source rule. Ever since the *Washington Post*'s great reporting of Watergate, many news organizations had adopted the rule of thumb that, when investigative pieces depend on sources who choose not to be identified, each major fact in that report should not be based entirely on just one anonymous source. Every effort should be made to find a second source to confirm the report. This is obviously needed to avoid overreliance on a single source who may have some personal interest in misleading the public or who may simply have misunderstood something. While CNN generally kept to this two-source rule in its Oklahoma City bombing coverage, there were a few instances in which the second source didn't fully confirm the first source's tidbit of information, for example as to what type of chemical traces were linked to McVeigh, and a supervising producer had to make a close call: do we go with the story anyway or do we hold it and keep trying for a full instead of only partial confirmation from the second source? Sometimes the call that was made was: go with it, because we're under pressure from other networks. (The pressure is even greater today, now that CNN as a cable network has real-time competition from Fox News and MSNBC, not to mention competition online from many news organizations.)

Despite these occasional lapses, our CNN team did an outstanding job with its coverage of the Oklahoma City bombing, the investigation, and the aftermath. I felt proud to be part of this team, and it was one of the highlights of my life as a reporter when our team won an Emmy, the highest award for television journalism. All that work, the long hours, the care to get the facts right and to avoid hype—it all had been worth it.

Chapter Eleven

Scoop

In addition to the misery that reporters experience when getting a story wrong, one of the worst feelings is to be on the receiving end of a "rocket"—a complaint by your editor or producer that you've been beaten by the competition. Many journalists get these rockets, especially in Washington, where the competition for scoops is intense and where the government often favors certain news organizations, such as the *Washington Post* or *New York Times,* for its leaks. You're sitting in the press area of the State Department and suddenly your phone rings, as do the phones of all your colleagues except the smiling reporter who had the scoop, and the voice at the other end of the phone is your boss telling you that you've failed to get the top story and you've let yourself be beaten by a rival, and you are in deep trouble. I was on the receiving end of rockets more times than I care to remember, but on one happy occasion in Washington I was the reporter who was smiling.

It was in 1987. I was covering the State Department for CNN. The Soviet foreign minister, Eduard Shevardnadze, was visiting Washington, and his talks with Secretary of State George Shultz dealt with intermediate-range nuclear forces (INF) in Europe. If Shevardnadze and Shultz could find a way to agree on steps toward reduction of U.S. and Soviet INF missiles, then plans could go ahead for Soviet leader Mikhail Gorbachev to visit Washington for a summit with President Reagan. But we journalists had no way of knowing how the Shultz-Shevardnadze talks were going. All the State Department spokesperson would say each day was that the two had met and that they had had a useful exchange of views. Total secrecy reigned as to whether they were making any progress.

We had video of Shevardnadze arriving at the State Department, video of him and Shultz shaking hands, video of them making small talk for the cameras, and video of Shevardnadze leaving the State Department at the end of that day of talks. We had sound bites from interviews with Soviet affairs experts at think tanks, who didn't know any more than we did how the talks were going. We had file footage of the missiles in question and a map showing Europe and which countries were in the NATO and Warsaw Pact alliances confronting one another. But what we did not have was the crucial piece of information that many people were waiting to learn: was there any progress in the INF talks, and if so was it enough to clear the way for a summit?

I had a list of the participants in the talks. One of the American participants was an expert on arms control issues. It was a long shot, but I decided to call him and see if he would talk. (I will not identify him further, even all these years later, because he agreed to speak to me on background—meaning that I could use general information he gave me but I could not use a direct quote or identify the source. This is one of the ground rules often used for interviews, especially in Washington. Usually the ground rules are worked out after a verbal tussle. Journalists try to win agreement that they can give the source's name and title, in order to maximize the truth and help the reader see what bias the source might have, but the source tries to win agreement that he or she is not identified by name or title and can speak freely and not be held accountable for his or her words. Once the ground rules are agreed upon, they are strictly adhered to. This makes it possible for journalists to obtain more information, and for government officials to leak their version of reality without fear of retribution by their bosses. Journalists, of course, then have to try for confirmation from other sources and to use common sense to minimize the danger of being manipulated by the source.)

I called the office of this official and expected to be given the usual runaround by his gatekeeper, but to my surprise my call was transferred into the official's office. I decided to play a trick. One of the devices used sometimes by journalists, and also by police interrogators, is to pretend that you know more than you do, so that the person being questioned doesn't feel that he is revealing something new but is merely elaborating on information the questioner already has.

I asked him: "What time are they going to announce that INF agreement?"

Of course, no one had said anything about any INF agreement. I was just guessing that they'd reached agreement.

I expected him to laugh and say "Nice try," but to my amazement he replied: "One p.m. tomorrow."

I could hardly believe what I was hearing. Here was a high government official with direct knowledge of the negotiations revealing to me that the United States and the Soviet Union had reached agreement on missile reductions.

To avoid any misunderstanding, I asked him: "Just to make sure I've got this right, Shultz and Shevardnadze have reached agreement on reduction of INF missiles, and this clears the way for a summit, and this will be announced tomorrow at one p.m., right?"

"One p.m. Washington time, simultaneously in Washington and Moscow."

"And I can go with that?"

"Yes."

I thanked him and hung up quickly, before he had time to change his mind. In all my eleven years in Washington, this was the one and only time that I knew for sure I had a world-exclusive major story, a guaranteed surefire home run.

I called the Washington bureau of CNN and spoke to a supervising producer, who told me to get ready to do a live shot from the State Department briefing room. As I was preparing my script for the live shot, my phone rang. It was Pam Benson, the executive news producer of the Washington bureau, and she had a good question: "I need to know this, Tony, before you can go live: Who is your source?"

I told her, and she agreed that this made the story solid, especially since I would attribute the information to a knowledgeable source, not by name but as "a senior administration official." Pam was right to ask me that question, because CNN needed to be sure that the source was truly reliable, knowledgeable, and authoritative. Otherwise CNN could have egg on its face.

"Go for it," she said.

I went to the briefing room and stood facing the camera. A sound technician put a clip-on mike on my tie. Lights were adjusted. An earpiece was inserted into my ear. I could hear a producer telling me to stand by. Then I heard the voice of anchor Bernie Shaw.

"I'll try to read this as calmly as possible," Bernie told the audience, causing me to pray that I had the story right, since he was building it up into something momentous. Then he summarized my scoop: the United States and the Soviet Union had achieved a breakthrough agreement on INF missiles, according to a senior administration official who spoke to Tony Collings. Then he threw to me. In my live shot, I gave the details: the official, who spoke on condition of anonymity, told CNN that an announcement on an INF agreement would be made at 1 p.m. tomorrow, and this clears the way for a summit.

When I returned to the CNN booth in the press area, I heard the sweetest sound any journalist can ever hear: phones ringing at all the other desks.

The rockets.

But my triumphant mood did not last long. Soon the other journalists were going down the same list of participants and calling them up. Somebody reached my source, who issued an angry statement, on the record, denying that any agreement had been reached and denouncing CNN for irresponsible journalism.

My heart sank. CNN producers called me and asked if we were still OK. Was I sure I got it right? Had we made a mistake? I said I had heard the official confirm it to me, and I had it in my notes, and he may be now trying to cover himself against criticism from on high that he had deprived the White House of the opportunity to break the news itself, and that we should hold our ground. But deep inside I had doubts. Had I misunderstood the official in our brief phone conversation? Was he talking about some other announcement scheduled for the next day? This whole scoop started to look shaky to me.

That night I had trouble sleeping. The press of much of the world had picked up my CNN story and if I got it wrong CNN would be seriously damaged, and I might have to kiss my job good-bye.

The next day at 1 p.m. the White House and the Kremlin simultaneously announced agreement on INF missiles and preparations for a summit. All I felt was relief.

For a brief two days, I had learned what it's like to have that rarest of all Washington stories: a real scoop. By definition, only one journalist at a time gets the scoop. All the others get the angry phone calls from their producers and editors. And in fact, to tell the truth, I never had another scoop as big as that one.

Prior to that, the closest I had ever come to a major exclusive was in 1983 in Rome. It came while I was having lunch with an American priest who worked in the bureaucracy of the Vatican. Over pasta and wine at a restaurant on a side street in Rome just outside the Vatican, we chatted about a controversy in Michigan involving a Catholic nun, Sister Agnes Mary Mansour. She was the director of Michigan's Department of Social Services, a post that involved funding abortions. The nun was refusing a church demand that she publicly oppose abortion, and the church had to decide what action to take. The story was gaining national and international attention. The priest revealed to me that a decision had been made by the Vatican to force her to resign from her religious order. When he told me that, I knew that at that moment I possessed information that no other journalist had, and my thoughts began racing as to how I would do the story. I had a scoop, and it felt wonderful.

Regrettably, I did not clarify the ground rules for our conversation. I assumed that he was speaking on background, meaning the information, but not the identity of its source, could be reported, whereas he assumed he was speaking off the record, meaning none of the information could be reported or used by me in any way. The misunderstanding was my fault, not his, because instead of assuming I should have asked him whether this was on background. I did the story, and CNN played it up as a world exclusive. Later the priest complained privately to me and he was right to complain. I was sorry that the story disturbed him, although I was glad that he had not been personally harmed since he had not been identified as the source.

The journalistic obsession with trying for exclusive stories is beautifully satirized in the comic novel *Scoop* by the British author Evelyn Waugh. In the novel, confusion reigns at the *Daily Beast,* a tabloid owned by a pompous publisher named Lord Copper. Due to a name mix-up, the *Beast* sends the wrong person, its gardening correspondent William Boot, to cover a war in Africa. Boot is told by other journalists what to do, including spy on fellow journalists and invent stories. There's something juvenile about the behavior of these hacks, like English schoolboys suddenly entrusted with expense accounts, put in hotel rooms in Africa, and told they were expected to produce miraculous front-page exclusives. Some of my favorite parts of the book are when all the other reporters dash off to what they think is a rebel press conference in what they think is a city called Laku. There is no press conference—and the city doesn't even exist. Years earlier when the country was being colonized, British explorers had put the word "Laku" on their map because they had pointed to a hill and asked their translator what it was and he had said "laku," which means "I don't know" in his language. I love the wordy, expensive, and useless cables the hero sends back from the African country to his increasingly frustrated editors in London, cables in which he chats about the weather; in one of them he says not much is happening other than the president of the country being kidnapped. And there is the wonderful scene where another reporter, Jakes, assigned to cover a revolution, falls asleep on a train, misses his stop, gets off in the wrong country where there is no revolution, and invents one anyway, and because of his story the country's stock market collapses, setting off panic, unrest—and finally a real revolution.

William Boot, the hero of Waugh's novel, eventually stumbles onto an actual scoop: all the other reporters go off to the nonexistent rebel press conference in the nonexistent city of Laku, and Boot, who wants to be with his girlfriend, stays behind in the capital, where a coup takes place and he alone has the story. The story of Boot of the *Beast* has become a legend among real-life journalists, especially the British, and you might hear them quoting from it as they have a drink at a hotel bar after a day of war coverage. (A famous line from the book, often quoted by journalists, is, "Up to a point, Lord Copper," the wording used by Lord Copper's foreign editor when he's trying to tell the boss he is wrong.)

As the title of Waugh's novel indicates, the mania to beat the competition with a momentous exclusive remains one of the great driving forces of Anglo-American journalism today. Competing to get exclusive stories has its good side, as journalists dig deeper for the truth, but it also may lead to journalistic disasters. Journalists are so hungry for scoops that con men are sometimes able to trick them. *Newsweek* once published a cover story boasting exclusive excerpts from Hitler's diary and enjoyed its triumph over its rival, *Time*, until the diary turned out to be a hoax.

A far greater disaster befell CBS and Dan Rather because of the journalistic mania for scoops. In 2004, CBS producer Mary Mapes learned that a man in Texas named Bill Burkett had what he said were documents about George W.

Bush's service in the Texas Air National Guard during the Vietnam War. Among them was an alleged memorandum in which the late Lieutenant Colonel Jerry B. Killian, Commander of the 111th Fighter Interceptor Squadron, said that then-lieutenant Bush failed to meet Guard standards and failed to take a physical. Another alleged memo by Killian said that officers were under pressure to "sugar coat" Bush's officer evaluation. If true, these documents would seem to provide damaging evidence, in the middle of the 2004 presidential election campaign, that Bush had shirked his military duty at home at a time when his opponent, Senator John Kerry, had risked his life in Vietnam. The documents, again if true, could have played a role in the outcome of the 2004 election. And, of course, all of this seemed to amount to a great journalistic coup—a CBS scoop—if the documents were true.

If true. That was the crucial question. As a later independent investigation of CBS's blunders made clear, Mapes and other CBS producers failed to obtain clear authentication of the documents and failed to scrutinize the background of Burkett, a former Texas National Guard officer who was a known opponent of Bush. Burkett later admitted he had lied when he had told Mapes that he had received the documents from another former Army National Guardsman. As for the alleged documents themselves, they used a kind of typewriter font that apparently had not existed for most typewriters at the time of the Vietnam War—a discrepancy that probably would have been caught if CBS had had an independent expert properly examine the documents. Obviously, if the type font was wrong, the alleged documents could be forgeries. Even more damaging, these alleged documents were not originals but copies, and copies are notoriously hard to authenticate because to do a proper authentication the experts need to examine the original paper and ink. And there was no way to obtain independent confirmation of the documents by the alleged author, Killian, who was dead. All of these facts meant that it would be extremely difficult if not impossible to authenticate the documents. What Mapes should have done was tell her bosses at CBS that they could not go ahead with the story.

But Mapes heard footsteps—the journalistic term for learning that rival news organizations are pursuing the same story and may get it first. Convinced that she had a great scoop, and hurrying to get the story on the air on *60 Minutes II* before any rival news organization did the story, Mapes arranged to have four experts quickly look at the alleged documents. The experts later maintained that they warned her they could not vouch for the authenticity of the documents. One of the experts said only that Killian's signature appeared authentic, but that did not mean that the documents themselves were authentic. In the final story that appeared on air, CBS ignored these warnings and told millions of viewers that an expert "believes the material is authentic"—wording that was highly misleading, implying that the documents themselves were authentic.

The segment was presented by CBS as a report by anchor Dan Rather, although in fact the reporting was largely the work of Mapes. Rather himself had been busy with two other stories—the Republican national convention in New York and a hurricane in Florida—and was brought into the Bush/National Guard story only at the last minute.

After the story aired on September 8, 2004, bloggers quickly raised questions about its veracity. The bloggers, many of them conservative Republicans, claimed that the inaccuracy of the story proved CBS's alleged anti-Republican and pro-liberal bias. Not only bloggers but also some of the mainstream national news media, including ABC News and the *Washington Post,* raised questions about the accuracy of the CBS report. Instead of taking the criticisms seriously, CBS management insisted their story was true and adamantly stood by it for twelve days. Meanwhile, the criticism grew larger day by day. CBS's credibility and integrity suffered more and more damage. Finally, on September 20, CBS admitted that it could not authenticate the documents and said it regretted the mistake. CBS appointed an independent panel to investigate what went wrong. The panel consisted of former attorney general Dick Thornburgh, a Republican, and Lou Boccardi, a respected journalist who was the former CEO and president of the Associated Press.

The Thornburgh-Boccardi report on what went wrong amounts to a kind of textbook case study of a major violation of journalistic ethics, especially the haste with which CBS prepared the story because of its desire to have a scoop. The report said the CBS report and the failure to correct it quickly afterward violated the two core principles of the network's own code of ethics: accuracy and fairness. It concluded: "These problems were caused primarily by a myopic zeal to be the first news organization to broadcast what was believed to be a new story about President Bush's TexANG [Texas Air National Guard] service" and CBS's "rigid and blind" defense of the story after it was broadcast. Thornburgh and Boccardi recommended a number of steps CBS should take in the future, including the creation of a new executive position to enforce the network's ethical standards. As to the obsession with scoops, Thornburgh and Boccardi recommended that CBS News's leadership "make clear to all personnel that competitive pressures cannot be allowed to prompt the airing of a story before it is ready. It would have been better to 'lose' the story on the Killian documents to a competitor than to air it short of investigating and vetting to the highest standards of fairness and accuracy."

CBS management implemented the recommendations, and also meted out punishment for those involved in the fiasco. Mapes was fired. A vice president and two senior producers were asked to resign. The most prominent journalist at CBS, Dan Rather, was forced to retire as anchor earlier than planned, then was relegated to relatively minor reporting duties. Finally, in a humiliating denouement, his contract was not renewed. The downfall of Rather and others at CBS is a dramatic example of the price that journalists pay when they let the "myopic zeal to be the first" get in the way of journalistic ethics.

I know what Thornburgh and Boccardi mean when they speak of the zeal to be first, because I experienced that emotion often as a journalist, and my few scoops were indeed exciting for me, although, other than my report of the breakthrough in U.S.-Soviet INF negotiations, the stories themselves were hardly momentous. More often it was a tidbit of information here or there that took the story a bit further.

Take the case of the 1980 Iranian embassy siege in London. After six armed men seized twenty-six hostages at the embassy and killed one hostage, British SAS commandoes stormed the building, killed five of the gunmen, and rescued the remaining hostages. The problem for me and my colleague Lea Donosky as *Newsweek* journalists working the story was that the SAS raid was shown live on television in Britain—and in the United States, where our editors could see it. Furthermore, this happened on a Monday, which meant that all of that week there would be many reports on every possible angle. What could we possibly add that would be of any interest by the following Monday, when the next issue of *Newsweek* would finally appear? The answer, I realized, was an exclusive interview with one of the rescued hostages, but none of them was talking to journalists. I went down the list of rescued hostages and found telephone numbers for some of them, but the ones I reached refused to talk. No other news organization had any interview with any of them, either. I knew that my editors would not accept that as an excuse for my not obtaining an exclusive interview with a rescued hostage.

I went down the list again, and tried one more time with one of the people who had been held in the embassy, a short, wiry, soft-spoken man named Muhammad Hashir Faruqi, who was a British journalist of Pakistani extraction. He was the editor of an obscure magazine and worked in a tiny office in north London. I asked if I could visit him at his office so that he could tell me about the magazine. He agreed. I felt somewhat relieved: at least I could get a foot in the door. But he remained reluctant to talk about his ordeal at the embassy, and I had doubts that my visit would lead to anything useful. For an hour he showed me around his office and talked about the stories he edited for his magazine. Slowly he began to talk about the fact that he had planned to visit Iran to gather material for an article for his magazine and had gone to the embassy to apply for a visa on the day that the embassy was taken over by armed members of an Iranian Arab minority group. I looked at him and wondered: Would he finally talk about what happened? Slowly, gradually, he began to talk about it. I did not take notes for fear that this would scare him off. Instead, I concentrated on remembering what he said, as best I could, and wrote it down as soon as I left his office.

The most compelling part of his account was his description of the moment that the SAS stormed the embassy:

> An SAS man lifted his mask and asked, "Who are the terrorists?" There was confusion, and the SAS man asked again, "Who are the terrorists?" Some Iranians pointed to two terrorists, who were trying to hide. The SAS shot them dead.

As soon as he said that, I could see it in print in *Newsweek,* and in fact that quote did appear in the final story.

Another exclusive, a minor one, came in Bonn in May 1974 when Willy Brandt was forced to resign as West German chancellor in a spy scandal. A close aide was revealed as an East German agent. *Newsweek* planned a cover story, and I was able to get confirmation from Brandt's press secretary of something that up until then had been only a rumor: that Brandt was a womanizer and vulnerable to blackmail.

But exclusive tidbits like that were hard to find during my career as a journalist, especially in Washington, where there are so many reporters chasing after each day's big story. I spent much of my time in Washington trying to play catch-up with *Washington Post* or *New York Times* exclusives and, like other journalists, finding myself reprimanded by my bosses for getting beaten on stories. It's all part of the pressure of reporting from Washington, some of the most intense pressure in all of journalism (although not as intense as war correspondence).

The pressure makes for a very long day for the typical correspondent. After going to bed at midnight, you rise early and turn on the local all-news radio station WTOP and the all-news cable television channels CNN, MSNBC, and Fox News Channel. Over breakfast you read the *Washington Post* and *New York Times,* and if either paper has a scoop on a story on your news beat you know that you will spend the rest of the morning trying to match it.

You also surf the Net, and check for e-mail messages and internal memos on your news organization's intranet, and you call your assignment desk to see what your tentative assignment is that day and what events you are expected to keep an eye on. In addition, you call some of your sources, including press officers at government agencies on your beat (in my case, at various times the State Department or the Justice Department), to see what's new, and you might send a message to your producers updating them on developing stories and suggesting coverage angles. Then you dress and fight your way through horrific Washington traffic, listening to WTOP and NPR on your car radio the whole way in to work.

At CNN, on First Street, NE, near Union Station and not far from Capitol Hill, you check in again with the assignment desk, look for more e-mails, scan the Web sites of the *New York Times* and other major news organizations, and then either propose a story idea for that day or carry out your assignment. Often your assignment is to match a story in the *Washington Post* so that CNN anchors will not have to keep mentioning the *Post* all morning as the attribution for a news report. You do that by going to the source for the *Post* story and trying to get that person to say the same thing to you, so that CNN anchors can now say, "CNN has learned." All of this is because one news organization hates to give free publicity to another news organization, in the intensely competitive atmosphere of DC. Not only do you try to get rid of the *Post* attribution, but you also try to advance the story with some new angle, and again there is pressure on you to come up somehow with a scoop. This is all frustrating, because sometimes the *Post*'s source is anonymous, and it's not always possible to guess who it is. Even if you can guess who it is, you may not be able to reach that person, often a senior official or a deputy to the senior official, in the White House, the Pentagon, or State or Justice.

Sometimes you will go to a late-morning news conference, which CNN may or may not carry live, in total or in part. If it is live, you need to be ready to do a quick live shot at the end of it, summarizing the main news development, and then quickly gather the other elements needed for a "package"—an edited, taped report. This package will be used by producers for one of the afternoon or evening shows. When I was there, CNN used more packages than it does now. Today, CNN relies more heavily on "talking heads"—journalists and live guests who are on camera, speaking about a news event or policy issue or general situation. The reasons for this change are simple: it is easier and cheaper than producing a news package. You don't need a news team that has to go out and find video to shoot, and then select key shots and edit them down into a report. But when I was there we had to produce these packages, dashing across DC (or perhaps crawling across DC in traffic) under terrible time pressure. Sometimes the package wasn't completed yet by airtime, so you did a "donut"—a combination of live and tape, with you live at the top of the report, then as much of the edited package as was ready, and then you live again at the bottom, with possibly a question-and-answer with the anchor afterward.

One of the most memorable question-and-answers occurred when I did a donut about an investigation into President Reagan's attorney general, Ed Meese. Meese was investigated several times, and in this particular probe Independent Counsel James McKay investigated alleged bribery and other misconduct. At the end of the investigation, the independent counsel did not indict Meese but prepared a secret, 830-page report about Meese's conduct and filed it under seal with the U.S. Court of Appeals for the District of Columbia. That day's story was simply the special prosecutor's announcement that he had submitted the secret report to a three-judge panel for review. There was no announcement as to the actual contents of his report, and no lawyer or other source involved in the case knew or was talking about the contents. I tried every way I could think of to get a scoop and find out what was in the sealed report, but no one would tell me.

In my live-shot donut, I repeatedly stressed that the contents were secret, that no one outside the independent counsel's office or the court panel knew what was in it, and that the report was sealed and would not be made public until the court panel decided what to do with it.

The anchor in Atlanta, a handsome, silver-haired man who probably had been doing something else while I was talking (possibly reading the script for his next news item), then asked me:

"So, Tony, what's in that report?"

I was dumbfounded. I felt like saying, *I just said no one is telling us!* But instead I bit my tongue and said, "Well, it's being kept secret, so we'll just have to wait until it's made public."

As I soon learned, anchors don't always pay attention to what the correspondent is saying during a live shot. Often the correspondent or his or her producer writes out a question in advance for the anchor to ask, but sometimes the anchor ignores the prepared question and asks one that stuns the reporter, which is what happened in the Meese case.

In the Washington correspondent's typical long day, after the donut version of the package you spend more time on it until it is complete and then the package in its full form airs on a late-afternoon show, on both CNN and Headline News (HN). Sometimes HN would trim it to make it shorter, as that sister network needed to cram all of the day's news into half-hour segments, and after sports, business and entertainment items, and commercials, there was really only about fifteen minutes of general news.

On CNN, you may be asked to do a live debrief with an anchor of one of the evening shows, before or after your package airs on that show. This consists of you answering questions from the anchor. The anchor is on the set, and you may be sitting next to him or her or you may be at a remote location. In addition to the live debrief, you may be asked to do a longer version of your package if it is the top story of the day, so that you might use two sound bites instead of only one from each of the two or three people interviewed by you or a field producer for your package. This longer version, sometimes lasting four minutes, is likely to be more complete, likely to cover more angles and provide a more subtle, nuanced report on the reality of the story, rather than just the usual two minutes, or less, of once-over-lightly.

The usual short versions of packages are so brief that the viewer is left with a simplified impression of a subject that may not be simple at all. For example, the 1993 Clinton health-care plan was never really properly explained by most television news reports, and instead was kissed off simply as a "controversial, complex plan." As James Fallows notes in his book *Breaking the News,* television news failed to provide the fuller understanding that people needed so that the public could have a useful debate, and instead opponents of the health-care plan exploited public ignorance and influenced opinion with such things as simple-minded television ads showing actors playing an imaginary couple, "Harry and Louise," who expressed concern over the plan's cost, complexity, and alleged violation of personal freedom.

There were many Washington policy issues that required lengthier treatment by television news but never got them, other than by the reports of *Nightline* or the *Lehrer NewsHour.* This is one of the frustrations of Washington television news correspondents and producers: there isn't enough air time given to serious policy stories. Instead, air time is given to stories that are more visual or have more easily understood elements such as conflict or sex (such as the Chandra Levy missing-intern story). Television is beholden to pictures, and it's almost impossible to tell the news story on air if there are no good pictures. (In one of the few exceptions, I once did an entire package about an Iran-Contra figure of whom we could find no pictures. We had to use an artist's silhouette outline of a man's head and shoulders, with a question mark inside the outline.) Pictures work well as story elements for news items such as war, but not for complex policy stories. Pictures alone cannot convey context, perspective, complexity, or subtlety. For that you need print or Internet text. But the television news programs need stories, and producers favor the packages with the strongest visual elements. And, of course, they favor scoops.

After your package begins airing on the various CNN news hours, and HN half hours, your day is still not done. You need to watch the main evening news programs of the noncable networks, primarily CBS, NBC, and ABC, to see if their correspondents have a scoop, to see if they have beaten you on some angle in your story, and if so you need to go back to your sources and try to match the competition. There may be a satellite feed coming in from another city that evening with an interview that you need to see so that you can insert a fifteen-second sound bite into your package to update it. Or there may be a late-night debate in Congress that might provide material for an update. Even if there is not, you still need to meet with supervising producers to begin planning tomorrow's coverage: is there a press conference scheduled tomorrow morning, or an interview lined up, or a report due to be released? If there's no hard news likely, is there a feature story you can work on? And, underscoring all of this, there is the constant pressure to beat the odds and somehow, some way, find a scoop.

You leave the news bureau at seven or eight or nine or ten p.m. and drive home exhausted, listening to WTOP and NPR on the way, eat something, watch more news, check news Web sites, cram more information into your brain, watch the ten and eleven p.m. local Washington news reports, and finally collapse into bed dead-tired, having failed to produce a scoop, only to start it all again early next morning.

These long days, and the relentless pursuit of exclusive bits of information, do serve the public interest in some ways, as they sometimes result in valuable glimpses behind the closed doors of those who have power in Washington. The rare exclusive report may, indeed, advance the public's understanding of a situation that requires a policy decision. But the pressure for scoops is so intense that it also may lead to mistakes, ethical shortcuts, and distortions of the truth. What is needed is leadership, by news executives and teachers at journalism schools, to make clear to young journalists that it's more important to get it right than to get it first. These leaders need to provide constant reminders of that principle. They need to hold violators accountable. They need to schedule training sessions to discuss case histories of these violations, and encourage discussions of better ways to handle the pressure for exclusives. Instead of a culture of scoops, journalism needs a culture of truth. That is the highest value.

Part III

What's Wrong

In parts 1 and 2, I presented highlights from my life as a reporter. Now, in part 3, I explore some of the issues that troubled me as a reporter and that continue to bedevil journalism today. I begin my critique with an incident from my days with *Newsweek* in the 1970s . . .

Chapter Twelve

Dead Baby

I made my way in the bitter November cold to the village of Muradiye, where bodies of the dead lay on the ground covered with straw. The chubby hand of what looked like a doll stuck out of one pile of hay. The baby's hand was blue-gray with death, its skin the texture of rubber.

The child's mother, also dead, lay nearby.

After interviewing survivors of the earthquake in this eastern Turkish village in 1976, and talking to rescue workers in several towns and villages, I returned to the provincial capital of Van to try to catch the last flight back to Ankara to file my story, and almost didn't make it. Chaos reigned at the dingy airport, and after an hour of delay and confusion, passengers were not given boarding passes but simply were released from the terminal building like cattle and allowed to stampede toward the only plane on the tarmac. After a mad dash we fought our way up the stairs and into the door at the rear of the plane, and those who got there first got seats and those who got there later did not, the airline apparently believing in a kind of musical chairs approach to boarding. I wrote my earthquake story, "Villages of the Dead," during the flight, struggling to decipher my notes and in some cases having to guess at the spelling of names, and in Ankara I sent the story to *Newsweek* editors in New York from the office of my hotel, where I had to use a Turkish Telex machine with a keyboard that lacked the usual "qwerty" arrangement of letters on Western keyboards, so that it took me hours to hunt and peck my way through the transmission. But the story finally got through, and *Newsweek* devoted a full page to it that week in November 1976.

It was an important story, the human tragedy of the earthquake and the death and injury and homelessness of those impoverished peasant families in Turkey. My emotional news report might have done some good—for example, in moving Americans to donate money or food, clothing, and tents to the International Red Cross to help these suffering people. But did the full truth get through? Did my subjectivity and bias get in the way?

Years later in Washington, having been a *Newsweek* correspondent and then a CNN correspondent, I thought back to the emotion I had felt earlier abroad covering stories such as the Muradiye earthquake, and I felt conflicted. Empathy and sadness were powerful forces driving me to write a story that might move readers to help the suffering villagers. But these emotions also distorted the truth. What was I to do?

Just as hype bends the truth in such stories as the Oklahoma City bombing, emotionalism and subjectivity also distort reality. As a journalist at home and abroad, I tried to be as objective as possible, knowing that, of course, achieving total objectivity is impossible because only a cold, inhuman machine can achieve that state. Objectivity is more of an aspiration. Author David Mindich quotes one unnamed reporter as comparing journalistic objectivity to the North Star. The implication is that reporters will never reach it but by orienting themselves toward it they can find the right way.

Journalistic objectivity is important because stories often have policy implications. A reporter presents facts to the public, and the public then forms an opinion. That public opinion then pressures the government to take action. The hard-news reporter's job is to select and present facts in such a way that the public can make a fair, reasonable judgment after being fully informed.

The value of minimizing subjectivity in straight-news reporting, at least within the Western model of journalism, is that of reducing the risk of error in presenting all the relevant facts to the reader or viewer. Get too emotional and you become blinded by anger or sorrow and don't see the complete picture. We've all seen this when we become angry at someone and make sweeping, unfair generalizations ("You always . . ." or "You never . . ."). Later, when we're calmer and more rational, we see that reality is more complex, and to describe it correctly and fairly we know we must try to be careful, exact, precise ("You sometimes . . .").

A journalist is supposed to be detached and professional, like a doctor, so that emotion does not get in the way of the facts, but sometimes you can't help caring so much that it might distort the reporting.

The dead baby in Muradiye evoked many emotions in me: shock, pity, sorrow, compassion, a sense of injustice (if these villagers had not been so poor they might have been able to afford sturdy, earthquake-resistant buildings instead of mud-brick homes), and a desire to help. These altruistic emotions, of course, were mixed with my more selfish ones: anxiety that I might not be able to get this story to New York in time, exhilaration to be covering an important story, and the adrenalin surge of competition with other reporters to get the best details. Having been an AP correspondent in Moscow, London, and Bonn, I was now trying to make my name as a *Newsweek* correspondent based in Bonn, and this story might help me. That was part of the selfish side.

There is no question that the sight of that baby motivated me to write an even more emotional story than I might have otherwise. It felt like the right thing to do, and yet it flew in the face of objectivity. The issue here is whether that kind of subjectivity in this particular story was an obstacle to truth, distorted reality, placed too much emphasis on one thing and not enough on another, and created a misleading overall picture. In this particular case I don't believe it did, because the main point of the story was to tell the public how much the people were suffering because of this disaster. But someone might argue that focusing so heavily on that tiny corpse might imply that rescue and relief workers were doing a bad job, failing to remove the dead quickly enough, permitting unsanitary conditions, and so on.

It becomes more of a problem if the story is more political and closer to home. If the story is not human suffering but a controversy over how effectively a state governor responded to an emergency, for example, then dwelling on one particular detail cited as evidence by supporters of one side of the controversy to the exclusion of details cited by the other side would be unfair. That type of subjectivity is much more harmful, because it deprives the public (and ultimately voters) of all the facts they need to make up their minds as to whether the governor did a good job. It is a real obstacle to truth.

In wartime, often each side in a conflict will try to use news media to generate sympathy for its cause. One side will take journalists to villages that it claims were bombed by the other side, and show journalists what this side claims are civilian victims of the bombing. Knowing how moved I was by the sight of the dead baby, I could see how journalists might become emotional at the sight of alleged bombing victims and jump to the conclusion that these people really are what that one side claims they are, innocent victims of the other side's cruel bombing—even though the journalists might not have enough facts to know for sure that that is true. After all, unless they see the villagers being hit by the bombs at the time of the bombing, and can identify the nationality of the bombers, how do the journalists know what really happened? It could have been an accidental bombing by the very side that is making the attempt to blame its enemy.

In the case of the earthquake in Turkey, I feel conflicted. On the one hand, I violated the principle of objectivity. On the other hand, I expressed an emotion that most people in the world would share, in a story that was not really about a controversy, and I wrote a story that might have done some good if it generated charitable support for the victims.

A similar conflict, but one that *did* involve a controversy, arose back in Bonn for *Newsweek* when I felt so moved by another story that I took sides in a conflict and wrote a story that turned out to be, of all the thousands of stories I covered in my life, the one I feel best about today—the story of a divided family.

After coming back from Turkey, I was reading through German newspapers and magazines, including the ones that covered what I considered to be the most fascinating stories, human-interest stories that related to larger themes in current history. In that year, 1976, one of the larger themes was the Cold War, the tension between the Soviet bloc and the U.S.-led Western bloc, and it took many forms, one of them being the story of divided families. In such papers as the *Süddeutsche Zeitung* and magazines such as *Der Spiegel* there were many stories of these families divided by the borders between East and West, whether the Berlin Wall or the minefield and barbed-wire border between West Germany and the country then known as Czechoslovakia. The story of one divided family seized my attention.

Karel Zaveta, thirty-six, and his wife, Anna, both Czech exiles, lived in Frankfurt, West Germany, but their seven-year-old son, Karel, and their two daughters, Sonja, thirteen, and Jolana, eleven, were still back in Czechoslovakia. The parents had defected to the West in 1969 while on a visit and said they thought that the Communist government in Prague would let their children join them later, but the government refused, and was in effect using the children as hostages in an attempt to force the parents to return to the East. I visited the parents in their apartment in a drab gray building in a working-class district of Frankfurt. Anna had become blind while in exile, but that had not moved the Czech government. She and Karel told me the story of their efforts to win the release of their children, and the cold bureaucratic replies they received (complete with postage-due notices). They showed me the two spare bedrooms with their beds neatly made up, dolls arranged on the pillows in one room for the girls, waiting for children who apparently would never live there.

The sight of those empty bedrooms stayed with me on the drive back to Bonn. I felt angered that a Communist government—or any government, for that matter—might deprive children of their parents because of politics. The divided families had dominated the news in West Germany but not in the United States, and their stories were compelling, so I knew that if I suggested it to my editors in New York they would be interested.

I acted out of a variety of motives, including the selfish desire to get a story into the domestic edition of *Newsweek*. (Most of my stories, and those of other *Newsweek* foreign correspondents, appeared only in the international editions, as there was little room in the domestic edition for foreign news.) But another of my motives was a desire to help these families, a hope that adding to the pressure on the Communist governments would force them to release the children and reunite the families. In addition, the subject of families was a sensitive one for me because my own family felt the stress of my absences on journalistic assignments. Too often we lost precious days that we could have been together. To this day I regret that loss in my own case, and I could see how other families could suffer as well when they were not together.

In terms of strict journalistic objectivity, it was wrong for me to let myself be swayed by emotion, and I was guilty, perhaps, not only of subjectivity but also of a lack of balance and fairness. By doing a story that put the Communist governments in a bad light, did that make me a Cold Warrior? Did I play into the hands of the military-industrial complex in the West that vilified and demonized governments of Eastern Europe so that Western governments would spend more on defense? Was I adding to the heated rhetoric of anti-Communist propaganda? Did I fail to give the Prague government enough of a chance to present its side of the story, which might have included an argument that it needed to protect its borders and enforce its laws, and that the United States had divided similar families? These are all legitimate questions, but the injustice was so blatant in these cases of divided families that I couldn't help feeling strong emotions and taking their side.

My story, "Czechoslovakia: The Child Hostages," ran in the March 15, 1976, edition. Seven months later I was happy to learn that the two Czech girls and their young brother would be released. I did a follow-up story at the train station at Aschaffenburg, southeast of Frankfurt. I was there with a freelance photographer I had hired. The parents stood on the dimly lit platform of the station on an evening in October, their breath misting in the cold. At last the train from Prague pulled into the station and slowly came to a stop. Karel and Anna Zaveta made their way to a railway car near the end as their daughters stepped off the train. The photograph that appeared in the European edition of *Newsweek* showed the moment I had hoped for, the moment when the mother and her daughters embraced again after so many years, tears in their eyes. Yes, it was corny, but I felt a surge of happiness, a feeling that, for once, something good had happened.

Years later in Washington, covering the U.S. Supreme Court for CNN, I stumbled across yet another story of a divided family. Once again I gave in to emotion.

In late summer 1991 the Court was preparing to hear a case called *U.S. v. Fordice,* a dispute over whether Mississippi had fully desegregated its higher education system including "Ole Miss," the University of Mississippi. I realized that I would need to travel to get an on-scene feel for the story and for its historical context, set against the background of the great 1954 Supreme Court decision, *Brown v. Board of Education,* which ruled that school segregation was unconstitutional. When I flew from Washington, D.C., to Jackson, Mississippi, and drove to Oxford, home of the University of Mississippi, I had no idea that I would be returning with not only the desegregation story itself but also an unrelated story that was bizarre and disturbing.

As I did with most stories I covered from Washington, while in Oxford I requested interviews through the press officer of the University of Mississippi, who set them up. One interview was with the chancellor of the university.

Another was with a historian. Another was with students. I also had my television crew shoot pictures of campus scenes, from band practice for a football game (they still played "Dixie") to the graceful columns of the main buildings, which suggested the antebellum South. I interviewed people from both sides of the dispute: those who said Ole Miss and the other largely white universities had done everything they needed to do to remove vestiges of segregation, by making themselves open to applicants of all races, and those who said these universities still had not done enough because they had higher minimum test scores and received more state funding than the state's largely black universities. I did a standup on the campus summarizing this key issue that the Supreme Court would be deciding.

The surprising thing that happened while I was there occurred when the press officer of Ole Miss introduced me to his secretary, Alice, a stunningly beautiful young woman who told a story that could have been the plot of a soap opera. Her face constricted with pain, she told me that earlier that year, in July, her estranged husband, Hassan, a Lebanese citizen, had taken their daughters Sara, aged nine, and Megan, five, to Canada, with her permission, and then on to Sidon, in southern Lebanon, without her permission, and refused to bring them back. She said the girls had been abducted and were now being held against their will in Lebanon.

This was not the story I had come to Mississippi for, but it was intriguing, and I thought it might make a separate feature story for CNN, especially if I could broaden it to a larger theme. At her home in Oxford, Alice showed me a taunting videotape that her husband had sent her. On the tape, the girls could be seen at a house, presumably somewhere in Lebanon and, addressing the camera, they stated that they were happy there and did not want to return to their mother. Alice said her daughters had been forced to say those hurtful words. I asked for a copy of the videotape. I interviewed Alice on camera. When I returned to Washington I broadened the story with information from the State Department. I learned that there were at least a thousand international parental abductions of children from the United States each year, and that State Department officials listed as a top priority their efforts to assist American parents in the return of abducted children being held abroad, but critics accused U.S. diplomats of only half-hearted efforts, noting that most abducted children never come back. So there was a public policy component to this story, and a controversy, and, of course, the compelling human-interest elements of abducted children and anguished parents.

I pushed hard for CNN to do the story. Why I pushed that hard, I am not sure, but I think it may have been for reasons similar to my emotional involvement in the story of the divided Czech family in Germany. Something about divided families touched a nerve in me. And, somewhere deep inside, I may have hoped that my doing this story would put pressure on the U.S. govern-ment to make more of an effort to help Alice. In any case, I did a selling job on CNN, and succeeded in persuading producers that this story was newsworthy. They agreed to broadcast it. Did it do any good? I have no evidence of that, but perhaps it added to the pressures on the government, and in any case I was glad to learn later that in July 2000—nine years after their abduction—the girls, now teenagers, were returned to the United States and made their way back to their mother.

Because I was emotionally involved, I took Alice's side, and assumed that her version of what happened was correct. To be sure, I quoted her, so I was not saying that this all really happened, but instead that she said it did. Still, the implication was that her story was credible. But what if it later turned out that her version was not the full truth? So often what journalists report is not necessarily what really happened, but what someone *says* happened. The journalist wasn't there at the time of the alleged event. The journalist is there afterward, when someone gives his or her account of what happened. That person's account could be distorted by a failure of memory, or by misspeak-ing. In some cases the person could be lying. To guard against that, good journalists quote a second source who might disagree as to what happened, and they are skeptical of all sources. But you can't be skeptical if your heart goes out to someone in pain.

The dilemma is that there is both a bad side and a good side to being emo-tional about a news story, and it's difficult to know how to reconcile the two. Over the years, at home and abroad, I found that some of the most compelling stories were the ones steeped in emotion. When I cared more about human suf-fering, I made more of an effort to tell the story, and that improved the chances that an editor would be moved to publish it.

While reporting for *Newsweek* from Bonn in the 1970s, I decided to find out how present-day Germans felt about their past and whether the horrors of their history made any difference to them now in their shining cities filled with abundant consumer goods. I interviewed German historians. I talked to German writers, one of whom, Golo Mann, son of the novelist Thomas Mann, told me the guilt was so overwhelming that "I taste ashes in my mouth every day." I read a German high school history book and was surprised to see that it went into great detail about the Holocaust, even including excerpts from Anne Frank's diary. I visited the former concentration camps of Buchenwald and Dachau, now museums, and studied the comments that modern-day Ger-man visitors wrote in the museum guest books. The visitors seemed divided. Some Germans wrote that they were horrified and ashamed, and that despite all of West Germany's prosperity these crimes should never be forgotten. Oth-ers wrote that yes, these terrible things did happen, but that that was the past and we shouldn't dwell on it, that we need to get on with our lives and not be crippled by shame.

I sat down to write my story for *Newsweek,* late one evening, alone in the magazine's Bonn bureau on Winston-Churchill-Strasse, one block from the Bundestag parliament building. I inserted a sheet of paper into my typewriter and studied my notes and thought about the past, the nightmares of Buchenwald and Dachau and Auschwitz, the cattle cars bringing Jews to their deaths in this country, the starvation, filth, cruelty, seemingly never ending, children murdered, families destroyed. I tried to write. My fingers seemed paralyzed. I felt suffocated, buried, overwhelmed by depression. It was not until later in the evening in that office that I could compose myself, wipe away the tears, and at last begin writing.

A few years later in Northern Ireland something similar happened, and again it was because of the overwhelming sadness of human suffering. In Belfast three children were crushed to death by an IRA gunman's getaway car. (The gunman was dead at the wheel, having been shot by British troops.) In the aftermath there arose a briefly hopeful phenomenon known as the Peace People, and I couldn't help getting caught up in the optimism of the moment. I felt a strong personal connection to Ireland. After all, my mother was the daughter of Irish immigrants who had come to Wilmington, Delaware, where she was born. My mother's maiden name was Monigle, and one time when I was a boy she had taken me to her father's village in the far north of the Irish republic, about twenty miles north of the Northern Ireland city of Londonderry. My grandfather's village was called Ballygorman, near the town of Malin, and when we visited it we stopped by the local post office. My mother asked the postmistress, "Is there anyone here who is named Monigle?" The postmistress joked: "Is there anyone here who *isn't?*"

Yet although I may have felt a strong personal connection to Ireland, as a journalist I was always an outsider, a stranger, and in Belfast it was especially hard to identify with people so steeped in hatred. I found myself trying, often without much luck, to explain how and why two sectarian groups, the Irish Protestants and the Irish Catholics, could perpetuate such ancient hatreds even in the modern day, even in one of the supposedly advanced nations of the world. There were events that were difficult for me as an outsider to understand, such as the annual drum-beating marches in August by Protestants gloating over a victory over Catholics in the Battle of the Boyne—a battle that had taken place back in the year 1690. In one of the grim jokes journalists used to tell, an airline pilot on a flight from London announces to his passengers: "We are about to land at Belfast Airport. Due to the time change, please set your watches back three hundred years."

Humor helped us cope with the horror of those times in Northern Ireland, but beneath the humor lay sadness. And that sadness drove me to pursue the story about the three children crushed to death and the movement that grew out of that tragedy, the Peace People. The aunt of the three children, Mairead Corrigan, joined with another Catholic woman in Belfast, Betty Williams, to found the movement in hopes that if enough people shared their revulsion at the violence and death there could be peace in Northern Ireland. Although later they had a falling-out and split up, and the movement disintegrated, at its height the movement had thousands of followers, and the two women won a Nobel Peace Prize.

During that hopeful period I found myself losing my professional effort to be as objective as possible and instead let myself become emotionally involved. I interviewed the women and their supporters (and their opponents, fellow members of the Catholic minority who suspected that anyone trying to bring about peace was a traitor). Later I inserted a sheet of paper into my typewriter. All I could do was stare at it. I thought about the children who had died. I thought about their funeral. As with the Holocaust story, I had no choice but to let the tears flow for a while until I could think clearly enough to write.

You might think it's a good thing for a journalist to show a caring side, and to some extent that's true, but it's also dangerous. Where do you draw the line between the journalist's caring about human suffering and the journalist's misleading the public?

Instead, the journalist's main job is to tell us what happened today (the French word, *jour,* meaning "day," is the root of the word "journalism"), selecting the most important facts out of the multitude of events of the day, and doing so guided by the journalistic consensus as to what is news: the unusual, the important, the interesting, the new, the useful. The journalist is further guided by such criteria as the policy implications of certain facts, the likelihood that publication of these facts will have an impact on public opinion, which in turn will have an impact on government.

Just as earlier journalists saw what they thought was reality through a Cold War prism, many journalists today see what they perceive as the truth through the prism of a so-called war on terror. It is dangerous. Better to discard the light-bending prism in favor of a clear windowpane. While some of my own reporting may have been helped by emotions of compassion and sadness, as a rule it is better for journalists to avoid emotion as much as possible and stick to the facts.

Chapter Thirteen

Down, Down

"As he whistled southeastward out of Oakland, Calif. in his T-33 jet one day last May, Air Force Lieut. David Steeves, like any pilot, could survey the earth beneath him . . ."

So begins a stirring account in *Time* magazine in July 1957. It told the story of what sounded like an amazing adventure that was experienced by an Air Force pilot.

"Suddenly Steeves felt a sharp explosion. The cockpit filled with smoke. . . . [H]e jettisoned his canopy, blew himself out by the ejection rig, pulled the cord on his parachute. Down, down he swayed toward the Sierra's peaks. Up, up they came in sharpness, ruggedness, meanness."

In a novel this might be considered good if pulpy writing but in a news magazine it's dreadful. It is purple prose that creates the impression of reality without the slightest bit of journalistic caution or detachment or uncertainty as to whether any of this really happened. There is no attribution, no statement to the reader as to who says this happened. Since the *Time* writer had not been in the cockpit with the pilot, the writer is getting these alleged details from an interview with Steeves or from a version handed out by Air Force public relations officers. Some parts of the story sound like embellishments based on the writer's ability to imagine what it was like.

The gushing *Time* account goes on to describe Steeves, crippled by sprained ankles, surviving on fish, snakes, and deer for fifty-four days in the wilderness. *Time* ends up calling him "a hero returned from the dead." A photo of him with his wife is captioned, "Life with courage." All of this might cause a reader to feel a lump in the throat and almost be on the verge of tears, so inspiring and patriotic is this story.

There is only one problem. A month later, Steeves's account of his crash and miraculous survival, relayed through Air Force press officers to the nation's print and television media, seemed not to be true. The *Saturday Evening Post* magazine, having offered him ten thousand dollars for his exclusive story, canceled the contract when its writer found "discrepancies." Air Force colleagues said they believed that Steeves had faked the survival story. There were rumors that he had sold his plane to the Communists. The Air Force investigated him. His wife left him. *Time* was forced to do a follow-up story that used remarkably less credulous prose:

"Air Force Lieut. David Steeves got considerable mileage out of his dramatic story of a bail-out from his T-33 jet over California's Sierra Nevada range and the ensuing 54 days during which he claims to have trekked (on sprained ankles) precariously through the wilderness."

Note the new word "claims." Now *Time* is being careful to attribute anything that it cannot independently verify, something it should have done in the first place.

Time goes on to write in its more cautious follow-up story: *"Returning to civilization sporting a handsome beard (TIME, July 15), Steeves, 23, was taken in tow by Air Force press agents . . ."* Now we learn that much of the earlier hype had been encouraged by Pentagon p.r., a fact that was missing from the first story. *Time* goes on to recount apparent discrepancies in Steeves's story (*"his boots seemed to be in remarkably good shape"*) and, most damaging of all, *"Air Force investigators could not find remnants of the jet plane that Lieutenant Steeves said he had abandoned at 33,000 ft."* Here is a key difference in wording compared to the first story. Now we are told that Steeves *said* he had abandoned the plane. Earlier *Time* had assumed that his claim was true, and did not bother to attribute any of his statements to him.

This was at the height of the Cold War, and the Air Force, presumably eager to win more congressional appropriations for military spending, encouraged a hero cult of pilots. *Time* got swept along in the patriotic pride until the story soured. (Ironically, as it turned out much later, it's possible that at least part of Steeves's claim was true. What may have been his plane's cockpit canopy was found twenty years later in the mountains. But at the time there was no evidence to back up his claim, and *Time* should never have let itself be manipulated by the Pentagon into writing such prose.)

I read that original *Time* story and its sheepish follow-up in the summer of 1957 between my college freshman and sophomore years, when I was an intern at *Newsweek* in New York. What struck me at the time was how absurd the original story was, with its naïve adulation of the military hero, and how sobering the follow-up story was, as *Time* got closer to the truth. It was a warning to me as a budding journalist: Be careful. It's so easy to be spun. Guard against bullshit.

You might say that *Time*'s account was a product of the Cold War, before Vietnam and Watergate and the skepticism toward government claims that resulted from them, and that it could never happen now. But is the *Time* story of 1957 so different from a *Washington Post* story of 2003 about Private Jessica Lynch? She was an attractive, nineteen-year-old U.S. Army soldier who was held captive and later rescued during the American invasion of Iraq. The *Post* quoted an unnamed U.S. official as saying that, despite being wounded by gunshots and stabbings, Private Lynch kept firing her weapon and shot several enemy soldiers. The April 3, 2003, front-page headline proclaimed:

"She Was Fighting to the Death"; Details Emerging of W. Va. Soldier's Capture and Rescue

She became a national hero. It later turned out that Jessica Lynch was not shot or stabbed, and she did not fight to the death. In fact, she never fired her weapon. While the *Post* had been careful to attribute the "fighting to the death" quotes to a U.S. official and also had added a cautionary note about unreliable Iraqi sources, it still failed to clarify what exactly it was that the U.S. official was basing his or her comments on. Was it the unreliable Iraqi sources? Was it rumor? Speculation? The paper failed to take a skeptical enough attitude toward the overall impression created by these selective quotes, even though they were attributed. By playing up the sensational claims of Lynch's alleged heroism, and playing down the uncertainty of what really happened, the *Post* created the false impression that what U.S. officials *said* was true *was* in fact true.

You might argue that adulating Private Lynch was a regrettable but harmless lapse, but it was part of a larger and more dangerous trend. Throughout the Bush administration's 2002 buildup to the invasion of Iraq, most of the American press let itself be swept along by the war bandwagon, rarely if ever questioning the government's insistence that Iraq's leader had terrifying weapons of mass destruction. Later it turned out that there were no such weapons. Later, news organizations such as the *New York Times* and *Washington Post* conducted postmortems on their failed scrutiny. They wouldn't have had this problem in the first place if they had made more of an effort to avoid taking sides.

Whether it's an Air Force p.r. officer's claim of a pilot's heroic survival, or an army p.r. officer's claim of a private fighting to the death, it's all too easy to get suckered into believing these stories. Because these stories arouse such pride and patriotism, it's difficult for news organizations to be skeptical without appearing to be unpatriotic. So they buy into the government's spin without taking a closer look. In effect, by furthering the government's spin they take sides and abandon their implied promise to the public to be impartial. They would be much better off sticking to the facts.

There are some journalists and academics who feel that reporters should do more than stick to the facts. They support a proposal known as civic journalism or public journalism, a proposal that journalists become better connected to their communities and help them take constructive social action, that they listen to citizens discuss their problems and what the citizens see as solutions, and then be guided by that in writing news stories. Under this type of journalism, reporters and news organizations would help mobilize the public to take action to solve society's problems.

Supporters of civic or public journalism admit that it's a bit difficult to define. Jay Rosen, one of the proponents of this approach, once referred to "an ethic of care, in which the press tried to strengthen the community's resources for coming to grips with public problems." (He was approvingly paraphrasing the words of James K. Batten, president of the Knight-Ridder newspaper chain.)

One of the best definitions came from Davis "Buzz" Merritt, professor of journalism at Kansas University: "Public journalism is a set of values about the craft that recognizes and acts upon the interdependence between journalism and democracy. It values the concerns of citizens over the needs of the media and political actors, and conceives of citizens as stakeholders in the democratic process rather than as merely victims, spectators or inevitable adversaries. As inherent participants in the process, we should do our work in ways that aid in the resolution of public problems by fostering broad citizen engagement . . ."

The good side of this proposal is that it might help news organizations reconnect with the public and overcome some of the public's distrust of them. It might remind journalists of their duty to serve society. In an election campaign story, for example, it would encourage reporters to avoid the horserace frame (Which politician is ahead?) and instead focus on voter concerns (Whose policies address issues people care about?). And it might encourage a news organization to provide a forum for airing all sides of a public policy issue. That's fine, as far as it goes, but there's a problem when it goes further and gets into actually helping mobilize the public: It's not journalism. It's social activism.

I don't think it's the job of journalists to organize town meetings to try to solve society's problems. I think it's the job of journalists to provide the public with as much information as possible so that citizens can make informed decisions. Once you start organizing meetings and taking the lead in trying to solve social problems, you become an activist. It comes dangerously close to advocacy journalism. You get far away from being a neutral, detached, and reliable observer. To take an obvious example, if you help organize a meeting and one of your co-organizers of the meeting is the leader of a citizen's group advocating a certain cause, what will you do when that leader becomes the subject of a news report and perhaps even the subject of controversy? Will you report fully and accurately and let the chips fall where they may, or will you pull your punches because you don't want to hurt the cause? The journalist's first duty is to the public and the public good, but that does not mean the journalist should withhold information that might embarrass and weaken a political figure whose policies the journalist feels are best for society. You have to trust the public to make the right decisions, once the public has a full range of information.

Take the case of Winnie Mandela.

Back in the 1960s and 1970s she was the wife of Nelson Mandela, the imprisoned antiapartheid leader in South Africa. Many American, British, and other foreign journalists, as well as antiapartheid local journalists, befriended her, not only as a news source but also as someone they looked up to because of her involvement in the courageous fight against the crimes and human rights violations of the white minority regime. The journalists wrote stories about her protests against the regime. But there was a problem. There were other stories they could have written—and didn't.

The journalists knew that there were allegations that Winnie Mandela had committed abuses herself including kidnapping, and there were even allegations that she had been involved in murder. The journalists faced a dilemma. On the one hand, this definitely qualified as a story: the wife of an imprisoned civil rights leader is suspected of crimes. On the other hand, that type of bad publicity would hurt the antiapartheid, pro–civil rights movement which these same journalists personally supported. They cared about the suffering of the South African people. They had to choose, and they chose silence. Her alleged crimes were kept from the public. As Peter Godwin, one foreign journalist, later wrote: "In fact, muted by the constraints of political correctness, we had all been reporting less than we knew about Winnie, her bodyguards and their reign of terror in Soweto."

You might argue that the journalists did the right thing. They helped a good cause, the human rights campaign of the antiapartheid movement. That movement eventually triumphed. Nelson Mandela was freed from prison and became the first president of a multiracial, more democratic South Africa. But I would argue that the journalist's job is not to help one cause or another, not to help one political movement or another, no matter how righteous it may be and no matter how much the reporter cares personally about the people on one side of an issue.

I'm not saying that news organizations shouldn't engage in limited, selective support of certain obvious good causes that virtually everyone in society supports, such as disaster relief or election turnout. But when they do these things, they need to be careful. It could be a slippery slope leading to support of causes that do not enjoy a consensus. It's one thing to support the Red Cross. It's another to support the Palestinian equivalent, the Red Crescent Society, when it is headed by Arafat's brother.

The argument might be made: What's wrong with advocacy journalism? Isn't that what patriots like Tom Paine and muckrakers like Upton Sinclair practiced? The answer is: Yes, they did expose injustice and wrongdoing, but they did it through commentary, not through hard-news reporting. I have nothing against commentary as long as it is clearly identified as commentary. A columnist provides a vital social function by gathering certain facts and using them to argue a viewpoint that might move public opinion to corrective action. But that's not the same thing as seeking the truth.

The type of journalism I write about in this book is hard-news reporting. It really is "just the facts." I focus on it because I know how difficult it is to get the facts right, to get to the truth, and I worry that advocating a cause, no matter how worthy, distorts the truth. I am mindful of the fact that supporters of advocacy journalism feel that, done properly, it can be quite respectful of the truth. I understand their viewpoint—but I disagree. There is too great a danger that what may start out as advocacy journalism could degenerate into propaganda.

Even when journalists try to avoid the advocacy approach and try to remain neutral in a controversy, bias sometimes creeps in. Take the issue of gun control. It's difficult to find any news report that is sympathetic to the gun lobby, the National Rifle Association. It's equally difficult to find any news report that is hostile to the gun control lobby. But there is no shortage of news reports sympathetic to gun control and hostile to the NRA. News reports will say the NRA "claimed" something, but that gun control advocates "said" something. That's not just my subjective impression. It has been documented in good, solid content-analysis research by Brian Patrick, a former graduate student in my department, Communication Studies, at the University of Michigan. In his book, *The National Rifle Association and the Media: The Motivating Force of Negative Coverage,* he shows how mainstream news reports use negative words about the NRA and more neutral or positive words about Handgun Control. (And he says this actually helps the NRA recruit media-hating members.)

To be sure, journalists' attitudes toward the NRA and Handgun Control are partly influenced by attitudes toward journalists by the two sides. When I was covering stories involving the issue of whether to have gun control, I received nothing but friendly cooperation from the lobbying group called Handgun Control and I got nothing but stonewalling and hostility from the NRA, even on the pettiest of issues such as what time to schedule an interview and where it could take place. The NRA headquarters was out in Fairfax, Virginia, a good thirty-to-forty-minute drive from DC, so we blew several hours round trip just to get a fifteen-second sound bite, but they wouldn't send a spokesperson into DC to help us. That deepened my own personal bias against the NRA. To be sure, I worked hard to keep any evidence of that bias out of my CNN stories, and I believe that if you look at my stories today you won't be able to tell how I feel about the two sides, but it is true that I do have feelings about them, and I am not a supporter of the NRA. So if I were to practice advocacy journalism (which I will not), I would advocate support of Handgun Control, and I would distort the truth to present a one-sided view furthering that support. If you like Handgun Control, you might be happy to see such one-sided coverage, but if you want the full truth, you will be unhappy.

I'm not saying that news organizations shouldn't go beyond just the facts in a few cases. For example, I agree that journalists should create a forum for discussion of the great issues of the day. They should lay out the positions of the various sides in a major policy debate, especially on such issues as war and peace. For example, at a time when a government is trying to mobilize public opinion in favor of going to war, it's legitimate for a news organization to do a feature story saying here is what pro-war forces say and here is what anti-war forces say, and to do this in depth and in the larger context of history, so that it is not just a once-over glimpse of the controversy. And they can do this without fear of being called unpatriotic by the government that wants to go to war. In fact, it's more patriotic to resist a war bandwagon and make sure the public has enough time and facts to make an informed decision about such life-and-death matters. The *New York Times* and the *Washington Post* failed to do that before the 2003 U.S. invasion and occupation of Iraq, as the *Times* and the *Post* later admitted. While they offered many explanations, including being overwhelmed by events, it seems clear to me that they were swayed by emotions: fear of new attacks, whether by terrorists or the Iraqi regime of Saddam Hussein, after 9/11; a desire to be seen as patriotic; the glory of scoops (fed to the *Times* by an administration clever at stroking egotistical journalists); the arrogance of being Washington insiders; and the belief that this was a just war. All of these are emotions that distort the truth.

The idea that journalists should create a forum for discussion goes back many years. In 1947 the Hutchins Commission, a blue-ribbon panel of scholars headed by the president of the University of Chicago, said that a forum for exchanging comment and criticism was one of the five requirements of a free and responsible press. (The others: accuracy, diversity, clarifying social values, and wide distribution of news.) These five requirements were seen as part of the social responsibility of the press.

That's fine up to a point. But it's one thing to have social responsibility. It's quite another to have a bias that distorts reality. I would support journalists helping create a forum if the purpose is to enlighten the public but not if the purpose is to come up with an action plan under the auspices of the news organization, because an action plan fostered by a news organization could result in the journalists being seen as taking sides in policy debates and could undermine their credibility as independent observers. It's a question of degree.

Journalists should be primarily observers, not participants, except in a few rare cases such as helping raise money for disaster relief.

What about investigative journalism? Doesn't that take sides, by investigating wrongdoers? This is a closer call, but I still believe that it can be done as objectively as possible. For one thing, journalists often do their investigative reporting based on tips they receive from interest groups that suspect wrongdoing by a company or political group or other entity. So the journalists can quote the interest groups in the investigative piece. For example, the journalist could write: *"Citizens for Corporate Ethics accuses Exxon Mobil of human rights violations in Brazil. An investigation by our newspaper into these allegations turned up these facts."* And then the journalist can report what he or she found, and can be sure to give Exxon Mobil a chance to respond. Critics of this approach would say it gives a "false balance" by quoting both sides, but if the investigation turns up damaging facts they will speak for themselves, and readers can decide whether the corporation's denials are credible. Not quoting the company would be unfair and would deprive readers of a chance to see the issue from all sides. There could be some truth in the company's position. Why not permit as many bits of truth to be aired as possible?

Some investigative reporting is done because the journalist senses that there might be wrongdoing, without having been tipped by a source. One obvious example is Watergate. Bob Woodward was covering an arraignment in a burglary case when he realized that there was something odd about the burglars. His curiosity led him to keep asking questions until he and fellow reporter Carl Bernstein found a White House connection.

While their reporting had an implied suggestion of action—that the White House should be held accountable by Congress and the courts—their investigative reporting itself was not civic journalism or advocacy journalism. All the investigative facts were carefully attributed to sources, and editors made sure that there were at least two sources if the reporters used anonymous sources. The reporters were not guided by the need to respond to citizens' concerns or to seek sources outside the establishment, nor were they guided by any need to help organize society to take action or to encourage civic engagement or to be participants in social action, so it was not civic journalism in that sense. And the reporters were not explicitly taking a position and calling for action, so it was not advocacy journalism. They did not come out and say that the political corruption and criminality they uncovered should be punished, although one could argue that that may have been implied by the prominence given to their reports on the front pages of the *Washington Post.*

While I understand and respect those who support civic journalism or advocacy journalism, I oppose those forms of reporting because they involve too much bias—and therefore too much distortion of the truth.

Bias is damaging, even if it's merely the *appearance* of bias.

As I noted in chapter 11, "Scoop," CBS News stumbled badly on the Bush/National Guard story. In the earlier chapter I discussed that journalistic disaster as an example of errors caused by the rush to get a scoop. But that same CBS incident is also an example of the harm caused by an appearance of bias.

In that incident, according to the independent investigation afterward, CBS producer Mary Mapes created the appearance of a pro-Democratic bias during the 2004 election. She put Bill Burkett, an anti-Bush source, in touch with a senior advisor to Democratic presidential candidate Senator John Kerry. Burkett had demanded this as his price for handing over what he had claimed were documents proving Bush got preferential treatment in the Guard. Mapes called Joe Lockhart, a media adviser to Kerry, and asked him to call Burkett, which Lockhart did. This was a terrible mistake by the CBS producer. It was, in the words of the independent investigation into the debacle that followed, "a clear conflict of interest—that created the appearance of a political bias."

Not only did the producer let a source dictate unreasonable terms for cooperating on a story, but she created the perception of bias, and perception is everything. It was unprofessional on her part. She should have moved heaven and earth to make sure that nothing she or CBS did put them in league with one campaign or the other, or even gave the appearance of taking sides.

One of the most harmful new developments is the rise of Fox News Channel, which perhaps ought to be called Faux News Channel because of the fact that at least part of what it foists upon the viewer is not real news but false news. Fox regularly distorts the elements of news reports, inflating anything that makes Republicans look good and Democrats look bad, and minimizing to the point of near-invisibility anything that makes Republicans look bad and Democrats look good. To give just one example, I heard an anchor refer to "Marin County [California], which many people feel is too liberal." The "news" network is even headed by a former Republic Party strategist and political operative. It is depressing to see such blatant Republican Party propaganda masquerade as news.

Many journalists who care about quality news are sickened by all this. I know one good correspondent, a former intern of mine at CNN, who has quit Fox because of the constant distortions of the truth in favor of one political party.

That channel also goes for cheap jokes at the expense of good taste. During its excessive coverage of the disappearance and suspected death of congressional intern Chandra Levy, who was later found murdered, Fox had as one of its countless unnecessary live guests a so-called psychic who claimed to be in touch with the dead woman, and the words on the screen said CHANNELING CHANDRA. Clever and cute, but trivializing a young woman's death.

Even if Fox News Channel were more responsible, there would still be a problem. Three general-news cable channels—CNN, Fox, and MSNBC—are on twenty-four hours a day, and when there is little or no news they have to fill the void with something, so they replace reporting with commentary. The cable networks might argue that newspapers have columnists and op-eds, so why can't television? The difference is that on television everything looks the same. With a newspaper, the editorial page looks different from the news page and is located in a different part of the newspaper. With television (and the Internet), it's just another image on the screen, and commentary can easily be confused with an on-air news report. What makes it even worse is that some of the pundits offering their personal opinions are reporters. Reporters should report. Period. They shouldn't offer their personal opinions on any subject. (Perhaps they could comment on the state of journalism, but that's all.) Why? Because we the audience will trust them more if we don't know their personal views. We won't have the suspicion in the backs of our minds that the next time this person claims to be reporting the news he or she might be misleading us in order to win our support for that person's agenda. Most journalists I know do not intentionally distort the news, but the audience doesn't know that, and if the audience perceives bias, rightly or wrongly, that is just as bad as actual bias.

I believe so strongly in the need for journalists to keep their opinions to themselves that during the Vietnam War, when I was at the AP in New York, I refused to take part in anti-war protests even though I supported them. My wife pushed a pram decked out with diapers on which she had written NAPALM KILLS BABIES, and my heart was with her, but I did not march with her. Even though it was unlikely that any spectator on the street would know that I was an AP staffer who edited Vietnam stories that came in to New York from Saigon, I still felt that the principle was important enough for me to stay on the sidelines.

Taking this principle even further, I know of a former top editor at the *Washington Post* who doesn't even vote in elections, for the same reason, even though no one other than him will ever know how he voted. That may be an extreme position, but the principle is a good one. A lot of the public's distrust of journalists stems from punditry, and this has been shown by research such as the studies in the book *Warp Speed* about the coverage of the Clinton-Lewinsky scandal. These studies show that the more news organizations stick to reporting just the facts, the more the public trusts them, and the more they mix in commentary with facts, the less the public trusts them.

Even some of our best newspapers have contributed to this problem. The *New York Times* regularly publishes front-page items that look like news but are labeled "News Analysis." Basically they're a mixture of fact and opinion. Supporters of news analysis see it as a strength, helping readers understand the import of events. I don't see it that way. I feel that news analyses don't belong on the front page—or on any news page, for that matter. The reader has almost no way of separating fact from opinion, as they're jumbled together. For an example, take a page-one item from August 29, 2005. The context is a controversy whether democracy and stability in Iraq were improving or deteriorating. The Bush administration said a draft constitution was evidence of progress, while critics said things were getting worse. A good newspaper would report what each side claimed, and let the reader come to his or her own conclusion. Instead, the *New York Times* "news analysis" began this way:

> As Iraq's draft constitution was presented to its National Assembly and honored at a brief ceremony largely boycotted by Sunnis, President Bush joined with others in his administration on Sunday in praising the charter as a milestone in the transition to democracy and the battle against insurgents.
>
> But in the disarray in Baghdad that was becoming evident, with Sunnis and some Shiites vowing to defeat the constitution and others angrily predicting a surge in anti-government violence, statements by the president and others in his administration had the air of making a case that the situation was not as bad as it looked.

The factual part of this excerpt includes the fact that a draft constitution was presented at a ceremony, and the fact that statements were made by the Bush administration and Iraqi Sunnis and some Shiites. The opinion part of this excerpt includes the words "disarray," "becoming evident," "angrily," "had the air of" and "as bad as it looked." When a journalist writes that something is "becoming evident" he often means "it is evident to me"—in other words, that is his *opinion,* not an objective fact. Not only individual words but also the overall story structure implies comment. The juxtaposition of the first paragraph with a second paragraph beginning with the word "but" implies that Bush's claim of a milestone is false. The overall approach is to stack the deck against the administration.

If the same story had quoted reputable analysts from both sides of the controversy, it would have been far more objective and fair. The story could have said, "Analysts differed as to whether the administration was right. Mary Smith from the liberal think tank Center for American Progress said, 'In the disarray in Baghdad, the administration seems to be trying to make a case that things are not as bad as they really are.' John Jones from the conservative study group American Enterprise Institute said, 'While we haven't made as much progress as we'd like, drafting a constitution is still a tremendous step forward and shows that things are actually much better than they seem.'" The journalist could then conclude this section of the story with a neutral factual statement, for example: "Most experts agreed that the next six months could determine which view is correct." Using this approach, the same information is conveyed but in a way that leaves the reader free to decide what to make of the facts without being manipulated by the journalist. Otherwise the reader could end up basing an opinion on a version of the facts that might turn out to be wrong. If the dire predictions of Iraqi chaos didn't come true later then the *New York Times* article would have grossly misled the public and been unfair to the administration.

So I feel that the article should have been recast as a controversy story, with the journalist carefully not taking sides. The only other way to deal with this problem would be to leave the article written in the slanted way it was but move it to an opinion page. While that might deal with the issue of subjectivity, it would still leave another problem: readers who happened to pay attention to the name of the author would, in the future, have less trust in the objectivity and fairness of any article by him that appeared on a news page. Most readers probably don't pay attention to individual bylines, but they do receive an overall impression of a newspaper's objectivity, and the use of news analysis on news pages is damaging the credibility of the *New York Times*.

To be sure, the public seems to like commentary, especially if it coincides with the public's own opinions, as seen by the popularity of talk shows on cable, yet at the same time the public has less trust in a reporter who spouts personal views. I don't think cable shows will ever give up commentary, as it makes money for them, so perhaps the best that we can hope for is that they make a clearer, sharper delineation between news and opinion. They can make sure that no reporter is ever asked to give his or her opinion on air. And they can use graphics and other visual cues, such as a different colored border around the screen, and the word COMMENTARY kept onscreen throughout the segment, to distinguish commentary shows from news reports.

It's not only cable that is hurting journalistic quality. There is also the Internet.

Reliable detached journalism is all the more needed in our new age of multiple media outlets including blog sites. When people Google, their search produces a bewildering range of items, from carefully researched, written, and edited mainstream news media pieces to the ravings of some rumor-monger who has got his facts wrong. On the Internet, as with television, sometimes it's difficult to tell fact from opinion, especially if the Web site item is a video clip. It all looks the same. That's part of the problem. In the print edition of a newspaper, you have physical cues as to what is news and what is opinion; opinion is what is on the opinion page. But in the online version of a newspaper, often it all looks the same, and there is no way of telling what is what. For example, the *Washington Post* had an opinion writer whose column, until 2007, was entitled, "White House Briefing," but many people may not have known that this was an opinion column. If you did a Google search for the phrase "white house briefing," you might get official transcripts of press briefings at the White House but you also might get the *Washington Post* opinion columns of that same name. A careful look and some good guessing might sort out which was which, but there were bound to be readers who were confused. After complaints by the paper's ombudsman, the title was changed to "White House Watch."

I have students who tell me, when I ask them how they know that something is true, "I read it on the Internet." But what exactly did they read? A blog? How does the student know for sure that every word in the blog is carefully checked for accuracy? I joke with students that they should think of a Web site as a bathroom wall that some stranger has scribbled on; why would they assume that every word on it is true?

Adding commentary to a factual report may make it livelier and more readable or watchable, but the danger is just too great that it will reduce the reporter's credibility, and that the reporter might actually get it wrong. If *Time* had kept commentary out of its Air Force "hero" story with its gushing prose (*"Down, down he swayed toward the Sierra's peaks"*), it might have spared itself embarrassment later.

Chapter Fourteen

Firewall

As part of their culture, journalists respect what they call "the firewall"—an inviolable separation between the business side and the editorial side of a news organization. Reporters are not supposed to tell the circulation and advertising managers how to do their work, and the people who sell the papers, market the cable distribution, sell the advertising, or handle other business matters are not supposed to tell the journalists how to cover the news. That's to avoid any conflict of interest—even the *appearance* of a conflict of interest—by the news organization. The reports that the public reads and sees and hears should not be tainted by any business consideration, by any desire to sell them something. All of this is so that the public will trust the news organization to be as unbiased and independent as is humanly possible. It's one of the sacred rules of journalism.

In my thirty-four years as a journalist, I found that the firewall protecting reporters from commercial taint remained intact most of the time, but on a few occasions it was weakened by cracks in the structure.

One day in Washington in early July 1986 there was a story in the news about two U.S. Army boxers who wanted to compete in a new international sports event in Moscow but were forbidden by the Pentagon. They said they were determined to go ahead anyway and risk Pentagon punishment. The sports event was the Goodwill Games, sponsored jointly by the Soviet government and Ted Turner and held in Moscow. Turner conceived the sports event after the United States boycotted the Moscow Olympics in 1980 to protest the Soviet invasion of Afghanistan and the Soviets retaliated by boycotting the Los Angeles Olympics in 1984. Based on everything I know about him, I believe that Turner had mixed motives for investing in the Goodwill Games: making money, gaining publicity for himself, and helping world peace.

Whatever Turner's motives, the project was not going well. Public interest was not high (the games would later deliver low television ratings and a $26 million loss for Turner Broadcasting), Turner's board was not happy, the International

Olympic Committee objected to the Goodwill Games, and the Reagan White House, with its firm stance against Soviet communism, was against the sports event. Two days before the Goodwill Games opened in Moscow, the Pentagon banned all U.S. military personnel from taking part and that included eleven boxers. Turner said he was in contact with U.S. officials in an effort to persuade them to reverse the ban. It was in this context that I received a strange request.

Working in the Washington bureau of CNN, I began planning which elements to use for my spot news story that day in early July, checking to see which video clips we had of the two defiant U.S. Army athletes and which sound bites our producers were gathering. In the middle of my preparations, one of the supervising producers in our Washington bureau told me that CNN's Atlanta headquarters had called to say that the producers there wanted me to include in my story a line noting that President Reagan had once said, months earlier that year, that it was good for the United States and the Soviet Union to compete in sports.

"Why should I include that?" I asked. "It has nothing to do with today's story—two guys fighting the Pentagon."

"Doesn't matter. You've got to include it."

"But it sounds like editorial comment. You know, 'Look what a hypocrite Reagan is, saying we should compete and then not letting our athletes compete.'"

"I know."

"And," I said, still uncomfortable, "I don't have room for it. It's extraneous. I've only got room for today's developments and a brief bit of background."

"Tony," the producer said, "Atlanta wants it in, and it's going to be in."

In all my sixteen years as a bureau chief and correspondent of Cable News Network that was the only time that I saw the naked hand of commercialism controlling one element, albeit a minor one, of a CNN news report. It disturbed me. Probably no one in the audience was bothered by it, but I was. Here we were, trying to tell the truth in an honest, detached manner, and we were forced by someone on the business side of Turner Communications to include a self-serving line designed to put pressure on the government to back down and remove an obstacle to Turner's making himself even richer than he already was. It was shameful. (As it turned out, none of the boxers banned by the Pentagon took part in the games.)

Critics of American news media sometimes say that the editorial content is dictated entirely by the owners of the news organizations. I found that rarely to be true at CNN in any overt sense. The Goodwill Games incident was one of those rare exceptions. Another one was the time that Ted Turner did the CNN on-air editorial in which he foolishly commented that the producers of the film *Taxi Driver* should be put on trial for the shooting of President Reagan. But, to its credit, CNN balanced Turner's commentary with a separate on-air commentary by the respected journalist Daniel Schorr rejecting Turner's nonsense. To our relief at CNN, Turner never did another on-air editorial. One other example I can think of regarding Turner's direct influence was his order that the word "foreign" was never to be used by us correspondents.

But these are all petty exceptions to the rule of editorial independence. When CNN merged with Time Warner, and later with AOL, CNN to its credit did stories that included quotes from critics saying the mergers would not succeed. CNN producers did so not just to try to look independent of their corporate owners but also because their knowledge of the American journalistic culture, the value system in which they work, told them that coverage of any controversial event needed to include quotes from both sides, for fairness. It is the journalistic culture, not ownership, which often dictates specific content in hard-news stories.

To be sure, some newspapers are pressured to publish non-news items about the doings of their publisher. The Hearst chain regularly ran stories on the travels and statements of their publisher, William Randolph Hearst, even if they had no news value. The same was true of the *Chicago Tribune* and its right-wing owner, Colonel Robert R. McCormick. The liberalism of the owners of the *New York Times* spills over into some shaping of "news analysis" stories that include opinion. But if, as some critics say, media owners decide what is newsworthy and how to write and edit hard-news stories, I never saw it in my experience as a reporter at the *Wall Street Journal,* AP, *Newsweek,* and CNN. What I saw was that the news culture was the deciding factor. And the firewall protecting editorial independence is a fundamental element in that culture.

In the case of the Goodwill Games story I failed to prevent a breach of the firewall, but in an earlier case I did manage to maintain the protective barrier. Back in the 1970s, when I was in Bonn for *Newsweek,* I received a phone call from the head of *Newsweek*'s advertising bureau in Frankfurt, a charming, urbane man who sported a trim gray beard and well-tailored suits. His job was to encourage German companies to buy advertising space in the Atlantic edition of the magazine. He told me that he had an idea.

"We're going to be publishing a special advertising section for Ford of Germany next month," he said. "Why don't you do a feature story on Ford of Germany? You could focus on their new models and their increased sales."

I wondered whether I might have misunderstood him. Was he really suggesting I tailor my reporting to promote an advertiser in *Newsweek*? Or was he tipping me off about a possible news story in my neighborhood? Ford's German operation was based in Cologne, only fifteen miles from Bonn. Perhaps he was just doing me a favor.

"Is there some new development at Ford?" I asked.

"No. I just thought the timing would be good, to have your story run in the same issue as the special advertising section. It would help promote the special section."

I was unpleasantly surprised. He was indeed placing a figurative dynamite charge next to the firewall. From his position on the business side of *Newsweek* he was suggesting that I, on the editorial side, invent some reason for doing a feature story on an automobile manufacturer even though there was no legitimate, newsworthy development to justify a story about the company. There was no justification in terms of editorial content. The only justification would have been to attract reader interest in an advertising section designed to benefit Ford and the business side of *Newsweek.* I would be betraying the reader's trust, breaking the implied promise to the reader that, whenever I did my job as a reporter, I was attempting to serve the interest of the public, not help some corporation. It was something I felt deeply, the need to avoid being tainted by commercial motives, to distance myself as far as possible from the corrupting influence of money. There was already too much distrust of news media by the general public, and any appearance of a conflict of interest, any suggestion that a news story was intended primarily to help company stockholders fatten their wallets, would only deepen that distrust. Of course, *Newsweek* itself was a company and, like all companies, it wanted to make a profit, but the way it did so was to attract readers to stories that were interesting and important and, most of all, *credible*—credible because of the magazine's journalistic integrity and independence. You can't have integrity and independence if your primary motive is to please a car company.

"Sorry," I told the advertising manager in Frankfurt. "I can't do it."

And *Newsweek* did not run a story about Ford in that issue. In the annals of journalistic ethics, this may not have been a major victory in defense of the firewall, but at least this one time the wall remained standing.

For journalists at the *Los Angeles Times,* however, the firewall that was supposed to protect their independence was badly breached in the Staples Center incident of 1999, a disaster that happened because a *Times* executive set about intentionally to tear down the wall.

Prior to the incident, the *Times* had built a reputation for integrity under the leadership of its publisher, Otis Chandler. He raised its journalistic standards, rejecting its previously one-sided pro-Republican political coverage and establishing a more neutral and detached stance. After his retirement, the newspaper continued for a while to enjoy nationwide journalistic respect for its independence, as well as respect from the business community for its healthy circulation growth, revenues, and profits. But by 1995 the business side of the paper had turned sour. The board, in desperation, appointed a new chief executive who did not come from the newspaper world. He was Mark H. Willes, former vice chairman of cereal maker General Mills.

His gaze firmly fixed on the bottom line, Willes not only laid off more than twenty-two hundred employees of the paper's parent company and subsidiaries but also decided to eliminate the traditional barrier between advertising and journalism. As he put it: "I'll use a bazooka, if necessary." As part of Willes's wall-demolition effort, a Willes associate made a secret deal to devote an entire edition of the newspaper's Sunday magazine to the opening of the Staples Center, a basketball and hockey arena, which would generate lucrative revenues from advertisements in the magazine. The *Times* agreed to share the ad revenues with the arena's owners, who got $300,000 out of the deal. Sharing the advertising revenues with the arena meant that both the newspaper and the subject of the magazine's articles benefited financially from the editorial decision to devote that issue to the arena. That clearly cast doubt on the integrity of the editorial decision. As a further indication of how far the wall had fallen, a *Times* advertising executive was allowed to see advance page proofs of the magazine's editorial content, something that is forbidden at most newspapers.

When *Times* journalists found out about the secret revenue-sharing deal, they were understandably outraged. The paper's media reporter, David Shaw, described the reaction as "open revolt." Otis Chandler, the retired publisher, wrote an open letter to the staff saying the management's "unbelievably stupid and unprofessional" behavior threatened to destroy the *Times*'s reputation for independent journalism. Chandler was so upset that he later welcomed the decision by his family members a year later to sell the paper to the Chicago-based Tribune Company. Top executives were forced out, including the editor, Michael Parks, who later admitted: "I underestimated the impact of the Staples arrangement on our credibility, on the journalistic ethos that we foster, on our standing in the community and the profession. And for all those things I have profound regret."

Any time the business and editorial sides of a news organization are mentioned in the same breath, journalists become suspicious. When Turner Communications merged with Time Warner in 1996, a CNN vice president met with the DC bureau staff and told us that the merger would be good for CNN because we could draw upon the resources of Time, Inc., and that there would be a synergy between journalists from the two corporations. He encouraged us at CNN to continue to do a great job breaking stories that beat the competition. He said that by working hard we would be able to enhance CNN's reputation for quality journalism and serve our viewers.

"And," he said, "it'll be good for stockholders."

That struck me as an odd thing to say, although I'm sure he meant it in the sense that helping our business to survive was a good thing for us to do. Obviously, if the business did not survive we could not work as CNN journalists and we could not provide the quality journalism that we believed in. He was just doing his job to remind us of the business context for our work. That's fine. But what bothered me was that someone might interpret his words as meaning that when we do our reporting we should be mindful of the fact that part of our mission was to help boost the price of Time Warner Turner stock. I was concerned that if we did that we might breach the firewall.

Fortunately, I know of no instance in which any CNN journalist violated this sacred rule after the merger. One indirect problem that did result, however, was that, in 1998, CNN producers came under pressure from management to show how merger synergy pays off, and they were told to come up with blockbuster investigative pieces for a new show that would combine the talents of *Time* and CNN. Under that pressure, CNN made the disastrous decision to air the unsubstantiated "Tailwind" report alleging that U.S. Special Forces had used nerve gas during the Vietnam War.

Not only news organizations but also individual journalists need to avoid any kind of financial arrangement that casts doubt on their independence. Paul Krugman, a Princeton economics professor and *New York Times* columnist who writes about economic and business matters, among other subjects, agreed to be paid $50,000 in 1999 from the Enron corporation for being on its advisory committee. (Krugman says he was actually paid $37,500. He had agreed to be paid a total of $50,000 but, later in 1999, when he accepted an offer to write for the *Times,* he resigned from the Enron panel and thus did not receive his last quarterly payment from Enron.) Krugman said later in his defense that he took the Enron money only before he became a *Times* columnist (but after becoming a columnist for *Fortune*) and that he severed his ties with Enron when he joined the *Times* so that he could comply with the newspaper's strict rules against conflict of interest. Krugman also said that he told readers about his relationship with Enron the first time he mentioned Enron in both *Fortune* and the *Times.* But some ethicists said he should have disclosed the Enron payments earlier, and more fully, since even general comments about business could benefit Enron.

One of Krugman's arguments in his defense is that the Enron money did not buy favorable publicity, although he did write positively about Enron in *Fortune,* and that, on the contrary, as he later wrote in a blog, "I have been giving Enron a hard time since that first *NY Times* column, on Jan. 24, 2001—a time when Enron was riding high." But that's no defense. Taking money from a company and then criticizing it does not get the journalist off the hook. There is still no way of knowing what the journalist would have written about the company had he not been paid by it. Would he have been even more critical? Would he have been *less* critical, since he would not have felt the need to try to prove his independence and instead could have given a more honest opinion? Either way the money could distort the truth.

Krugman revealed his Enron connection in his first *Times* column that mentioned the company. In the column he said he was making a "full disclosure," but it wasn't quite full. He said only that he served on an Enron advisory board—with no mention of being paid. (His first *Fortune* column about Enron also mentioned only his joining the board, not the money it earned him.) And it was not entirely true that he had been "giving Enron a hard time" since that first *Times* column. In fact, in the first column Krugman, while making some critical comments about Enron, also said that he presumed that Enron chairman Kenneth Lay was "an honorable man" and that Lay "has a point" in some of his support of electricity deregulation. Although Krugman did disclose his connection in that first column, he was silent about it later in other columns in which he denounced "cronyism and corruption" linking the Bush administration with Enron, at a time when readers needed to be reminded that Krugman himself had been financially linked with the disgraced company. Months after his first Enron column, the *Times* itself revealed that the amount of money Krugman had agreed to receive was $50,000.

Krugman's Enron connection was denounced by another journalist, Andrew Sullivan, a columnist for the *Atlantic* and a contributing writer to the *New York Times Magazine*. Sullivan demanded Krugman return the money to Enron (Krugman did not) and accused him of failing to make a full disclosure. ("Don't you think that someone who bemoans cronyism and corruption might, after this scandal broke, acknowledge in his own column that he himself was an Enron crony?") Sullivan also helped reveal the fact that Krugman wasn't alone. For example, William Kristol, editor of the *Weekly Standard,* was forced to admit he had accepted $100,000 from Enron. But while Sullivan performed a valuable service by getting this information out into the light of day, his own ethics came into question. Sullivan's critics pointed out that Sullivan himself had accepted $7,500 in sponsorship for his Web site from a drug industry trade group. Critics called this a conflict since Sullivan had written articles about the drug industry. At first Sullivan defended his acceptance of the money but later gave it back.

All of this shows the corrosive effect of money on journalistic integrity. The safest thing for journalists to do is make sure that any payments and benefits they receive come only from their own news organizations or publications. The minute they begin to receive anything of value from outside organizations, especially organizations that are in the news, their integrity suffers.

By the same token, journalists should not pay their sources for interviews, because once again money corrupts the relationship. When I was in London for CNN, covering the Falklands war, I called up Winston S. Churchill III, a member of Parliament and grandson of the revered Winston, to request an interview. I was shocked to hear him ask me how much I would pay him. I told him he would receive nothing. He did the interview anyway.

Chapter Fifteen

Only Time Will Tell

Almost every summer ominous reports emerge from Texas telling of a swarm of deadly insects heading north. These creatures are portrayed as marauders who invade peaceful towns in the Lone Star State looking for helpless women, children, and old people to slaughter before moving on to other conquests farther north, the murderous insects spreading an ever-expanding swath of death that threatens the American population. These are the dreaded "killer bees," like monsters from a horror movie. They help sell newspapers and lift ratings during the slow news period of late summer. They may be known as killer bees to journalists, but to scientists they are simply Africanized honey bees, and, while they will react aggressively if threatened, they don't really look for victims to attack. In any given year, very few if any people die of their stings.

The killer bees story is an example of a cliché, a news report that is done over and over again, assumed to be true without scrutiny, and based on a simplistic generalization and stereotype that ignores reality. (The words "cliché" and "stereotype" derive from French words having to do with printing, "stereotype" being a metal printing plate and "cliché" being the sound made when the plate is created. Both words refer to a device for repeating a preconceived concept.) Often these stories exploit assumptions, fears, archetypes, perhaps even the collective unconscious. They are similar to urban myths, and, like them, their claim to truth is no less powerful for being unproven and possibly spurious.

One scorching August day in the 1990s during a nationwide heat wave my assignment in the CNN Washington bureau was to do a weather story. I knew that the standard opening scene for a TV news story about a heat wave was the sight and sound of little boys splashing in water, usually in a big-city fountain or fire hydrant. I resolved to come up with something different, something more original, to beat the cliché. A producer sent a memo to all CNN domestic bureaus to gather interesting, compelling shots of people coping with the hot weather. Meanwhile, one of the DC crews drove around in a van, looking for

heat-wave shots. When the DC crew returned, and when the other CNN bureaus fed their video shots by satellite, I went through all the tapes, hoping to
find something fresh. But there was only one shot that worked really well for
telling this story. When my CNN report appeared on air, it began with a shot of
boys splashing in the fountain on the west lawn of Capitol Hill. The cliché had
won again.

On a bitter cold Thanksgiving in Washington in 1995 I went with a camera
crew to a homeless shelter. My assignment was to do a story about the feeding of turkey dinners to the homeless on Thanksgiving Day. None of us in the
CNN Washington bureau stopped to question the premise of the story or to ask
why we did it every year. It was a journalistic tradition to focus on the homeless
at Thanksgiving. I suppose if anyone had asked us why we always did the same
story we would have said it was so that viewers would feel kindness and compassion toward those "less fortunate," or so that viewers would feel that they
were not the only ones gorging themselves that day, or so that viewers would
have a warm, patriotic feeling that on this very American holiday all of us were
united in our eating of turkey, or perhaps so that viewers would be reminded
that not everyone had something to be thankful for and so the viewers should
realize how lucky they were.

Whatever the reason, I was there in the dining room of the shelter, wearing
my blue blazer and blue shirt and red tie and gray slacks, observing sullen souls
as they chewed on food dished out by volunteers from among the ranks of
Washington's cheerfully altruistic middle-class women. Needing the inevitable
sound bite, I asked one stubble-chinned old man in soiled shirt and jeans how
was the food. His reply: "You're CIA."

His comment created a dilemma. On the one hand, I was there to report the
truth, and the truth is that he had really said that. On the other hand, I couldn't
use what he had said. He was clearly disoriented and possibly mentally ill. He
genuinely believed that I and the crew and the charitable Washington ladies
dishing out the turkey were secret operatives of the Central Intelligence Agency. The sound bite made no sense. More important, it didn't fit into the heart-
warming cliché story of the grateful homeless being treated nicely one day of
the year. He didn't say what was expected of him by the rest of us: *This food is so
good and I'm so thankful that someone thought of me.* The cliché got in the way
of the truth. I didn't use the CIA sound bite. I found someone else to interview,
and that person said something less offbeat, something that fit better into the
preconception, and viewers once again saw the familiar story of the grateful
homeless being fed on Thanksgiving. What they didn't see was the messy, confusing truth.

In Rome one hot day in July 1981 I was in the cramped CNN office looking around for a story. It was during the early days of CNN and at that time

all bureaus were expected to provide at least one story a day, whether any-thing newsworthy was happening or not. A feature would do if there were no breaking news stories. I combed through *La Repubblica* and the other Italian newspapers. I watched the news on RAI, the state-owned television channel. Nothing. Finally I decided that the crew and I would just go to the Rome zoo and get some hot-weather pictures of the polar bear. Now *that's* a real cliché. In this case, however, I did end up with something different in the final story.

When we arrived at the zoo I discovered a fight between two female seals over a baby seal, the two adults thrashing in the water in a tug of war and the hapless baby being yanked back and forth. We got pictures of that vicious dispute in-stead of the standard friendly shot of a polar bear cooling off. The foreign editor later told me that viewers complained that the images were too disturbing. The audience would have been happier with the familiar and comfortable, the hot-weather polar bear story, than something a little too close to reality.

One of the cliché stories I did often was the "Man on the Street" story, known in the trade as MOS. (Actually, that's a sexist term. It should be Person on the Street, or POS, but for some reason it's still known as MOS.) The idea is that if you go outside and stop people on the sidewalk and ask them their opinion of something, you'll get vox populi, a sense of what the public is really thinking, the pulse of the nation. That's the theory. But the reality is that often what you get is incoherence. I have stopped pedestrians in Washington outside the CNN building and asked them what they thought of the president's gun-control policy and been told in reply, "I trust in Jesus." Now what does *that* mean?

Sometimes there's a further cliché within the main cliché. When I stopped people on the street to ask their reactions to the death of some famous person, almost all of them said exactly the same thing: "I was shocked. I couldn't believe it." Another example of a cliché within the cliché is the standard reaction to news of the arrest of someone's neighbor who is charged with murder. Almost invari-ably, the neighbor will say: "He was a quiet man. He kept to himself."

Sometimes MOS stories produce surprises. When Soviet leader Leonid Brezh-nev died in November 1982, a CNN crew and I happened to be in Warsaw to cover an unrelated story (the release of pro-democracy advocates from intern-ment). I decided to get the reactions of people on a street called Nowy Swiat. Speaking through a translator, I told one diminutive old woman that Brezhnev had died. She immediately began sobbing and weeping. I thought that that was odd, since the Soviets were despised by many Poles, but then the translator in-formed me: "She's weeping for joy."

One day in Rome I stopped passers-by on the Via Nazionale, a busy main street, and asked them how they felt about Soviet rejection of a Reagan ad-ministration proposal on nuclear arms control. The reactions I got some-times didn't make sense or were ill informed, and to make it worse most of the people did not speak English. I got a lot of on-camera comments in Italian, which I figured we could use with an English translation spoken by Doug Mason, the sound engineer, but voiceover translations are never as effective as the real thing. I wanted an MOS quote that would not require any translation. I continued to stop people and ask them for a comment in English. No luck. Finally, just as we were about to leave, a burly, balding, middle-aged Italian man in a short-sleeved khaki shirt informed me that he spoke English. But his reaction to this complex development in the arms control talks was limited to the following quote, which I reluctantly used: "Reagan good, Brezhnev no good."

The one time that doing MOS made sense was when I did a story about the Mafia. We were in Palermo, the capital of Sicily, for a trial of organized crime leaders, a trial that took place in a specially built, gray concrete maximum-security courthouse with separate jail cells, for defendants and state's-evidence witnesses, built right into the courtroom. For my story setting the scene before the trial, I wanted to find out how ordinary Sicilians felt about the Mafia. Did they fear the secret society with its *omertà*, its oath of silence? Did they respect the Mafia? Did they despise it?

I went out with a camera crew onto a main street of the city to stop passers-by. I noticed how elegant and luxurious the shops and restaurants were, and I wondered if this affluence could be the result of heroin money. With the camera crew standing behind me on the sidewalk, I stopped a middle-aged woman who was bustling along carrying shopping bags. I explained, in Italian, that I was a correspondent of the American television news company CNN, that I was doing a story about the Mafia—

Before I could say another word the woman brushed past me and continued down the street. I stopped an elderly man and asked what he thought of the Mafia. He shook his head to indicate unwillingness to comment and walked away. I stopped two well-dressed young women and asked how they felt about the Mafia. They kept on walking.

After numerous additional refusals to comment, I felt discouraged. I had failed to get any MOS, and my story would be incomplete. To be sure, earlier I had obtained sound bites during formal sit-down interviews with government officials and analysts and experts, but nothing this day from ordinary people. Then, driving in the van back to our hotel to edit the field tapes into a finished report, a thought occurred to me: *Why don't we show people not answering? How better to show the fear and anxiety?* I wrote one element of the script to include a montage of people refusing to comment, one non-answer after another in rapid succession on this main street in Palermo. It was more powerful than any sound bite.

That was a variation on the cliché of MOS, but more often than not there is no variation, no originality. And when it comes to the concluding remarks of

TV correspondents, in the part of the report known as the "standup closer," the cliché is even more fully entrenched. Here are two examples:

"Whether that will happen remains to be seen."

"As to future developments, only time will tell."

In other words, viewers are being informed that something will happen in the future but that the correspondent has no idea what it will be. Obviously the journalist has nothing useful to say, but needs to create the appearance of having an interesting final thought. Saying "what happens next remains to be seen" is about as profound as GOP nominee Thomas Dewey's statement during the 1948 presidential campaign: "You know that your future is still ahead of you."

Some of these hackneyed journalistic comments are so stupefyingly obvious that they cry out for satire. I once heard a wonderful parody of news coverage of presidential nominating conventions. It was broadcast in 1964 by WBAI, the New York affiliate of Pacifica Radio, the liberal network based in Berkeley, California. In the parody, a fictitious news organization is covering the nomination of Barry Goldwater at the Republican convention, in the Cow Palace in San Francisco. The anchor says: "We're awaiting the outcome of the vote of the delegates on the nomination. Let's go to our reporter on the floor of the convention." Next we hear the voice of the floor reporter: "Well, Steve, we're awaiting the results of the vote. Now, here's the situation: In order to *win* the nomination, Senator Goldwater needs to have a *majority* of the votes of the delegates. The big question is: *will* he get that majority? We'll only know the answer once they *count the votes.*" And on and on . . .

In the 1970s a big recurring story was shortages, and that, too, became a cliché. It seemed that every journalist was doing stories about shortages of one thing or another: Oil shortage. Power shortage. Food shortage. One day in the Bonn bureau of *Newsweek* I came across a story in the *Süddeutsche Zeitung* newspaper about a bee shortage. Apparently there were not enough of them in the world to maintain the balance of nature. The article noted that the headquarters of a world association of bee experts, called the International Institute of Beekeeping Technology and Economy, was located in Bucharest, Romania. Since Eastern Europe was part of my bailiwick, I Telexed a story proposal to *Newsweek* editors in New York, telling them that, believe it or not, now there was apparently a shortage of bees. The editors agreed that this would make an offbeat feature story. They scheduled it for the next issue. But when I phoned the head of the institute I discovered that he did not speak English. He did speak French, and I spoke some French but I soon realized that there was one crucial word missing from my vocabulary.

"I'm doing a story," I told him in French, "about the shortage of . . . the shortage of . . ."

"Of what?"

"The little thing . . ."

"What little thing?" he asked.

"Uh, what you study," I said.

"What?"

And so on, like a comedy routine. At last he figured out that this strange American journalist was interviewing him about bees, and I finally got the quote and the story.

Why do reporters write a cliché story when they know that it gets in the way of the truth? I think one reason is laziness. The cliché story is easy to do. The editor and the reader/viewer are already predisposed to accept the story, so the journalist doesn't have to work very hard to make it credible. People are more receptive to a familiar concept than one that challenges conventional thinking. As I think back on my own time as a reporter, and on the profession in general, I see that this is one of the greatest problems of journalism, the laziness that leads to simplistic, formulaic, and unoriginal stories that are easy to produce but may be harmful in their effect.

In order for journalism to fulfill its higher duty, it must provide the public with the full truth, no matter how difficult and confusing and inconclusive it might be. Just as a doctor must tell a patient the full truth about his or her health condition, including the fact that in some cases it is impossible to know for sure how dangerous an illness might be, so, too, a journalist must give the public the most complete, honest, and impartial account of what is really happening, including a full rendering of the state of messy ignorance and uncertainty that experts have rather than a reassuringly pat answer to all questions.

Such honesty is especially needed in vital issues, such as the issue of peace or war, where journalists play an important role. Whether nations go to war depends partly on how their leaders and citizens perceive the world around them. False perceptions may increase the danger of war. Journalists are partly responsible for the perceptions citizens have about the outside world, and clichés and stereotypes contribute to a distorted view.

The stereotypical and superficial view of the world, from the American perspective, includes the ooh-la-la French, the charmingly eccentric English, the humorlessly efficient Germans, the terroristic Arabs and Muslims, and so forth, but there are many French who are efficient, Germans who love life, English who are boringly conformist, and Arabs and Muslims who are peaceful and law-abiding and opposed to violence. The stereotypes are fantasies and totally misleading if we want to understand other people. Part of the problem is generalizing. When we say, "The French," we are talking about sixty-two million people, but what can we say that is true about all sixty-two million of them other than that they speak French and most of them live in France? There is no way one person can truthfully generalize about the typical behavior of millions of other people. Obviously a single individual can never meet all of those people. In fact, all that the single individual has are scraps of information—a bit of travel here, a viewed documentary there, and somewhere in between a newspaper article or two. Overwhelmed by complexity, it's tempting for us to fall back on the simplicity of a stereotype, but if we do so we are not basing our opinions about other people on objective reality.

"War on terror" is another cliché that distorts reality. So is "Arab terrorist" or "Islamic terrorist." (Timothy McVeigh, the Oklahoma City bomber, said he was raised as a Catholic, but would a journalist ever describe him as a "Catholic terrorist?") Partly because they are poorly educated and given only superficial tidbits of information about the world, and partly because they do not make enough of an effort to find out, many Americans have little idea about the reality of their current enemy, known as "terrorism" or "terrorists." What is this phenomenon? News media do not explain the causes and context, at least not deeply enough and with enough impact for the public to be well informed and able to detect governmental mendacity. In 2002 the Bush administration, building up the case for invading Iraq, conflated a real Al Qaeda threat with a false Iraqi one. The public's ignorance and its superficial view of the world made it easier for the U.S. government to get away with this duplicity. Former CBS News senior foreign correspondent Tom Fenton points out, in his book *Bad News,* that the public is dangerously uninformed about the perils it faces in the outside world, and this is due partly to journalists failing their duty and resorting to meaningless clichés.

From killer bees to bee shortages, the cliché is firmly entrenched in journalism. Getting rid of it is needed, but will that ever happen?

Only time will tell . . .

Epilogue

After thirty-four years as a journalist I decided to fulfill a longtime desire to teach and to have enough time to reflect. (There was never time when I was under deadline pressure to do anything but concentrate on the current story and plan the next one.) I accepted an offer of a teaching position at the University of Michigan in Ann Arbor in 1997 and have been here ever since, first as a visiting professor and then as a lecturer in communication studies. I miss reporting and yet I also don't miss it. I dream about it at night, but by day I enjoy having more freedom to read and think and help mentor young journalists.

One of them, a former student of mine, is a strapping young man who is eager, hard-working (at UM he worked at both WOLV-TV, the student station, and at the *Michigan Daily,* the student newspaper), fallible (in one story written after graduation he said police had found marijuana in a female singer's lipstick, and I e-mailed him that he needed to say that police *said* they found it since the reporter himself hadn't witnessed the search), and enterprising (he did some intensive digging for his story about anti-torture protesters at the U.S. Army's School of the Americas). As part of his training to be a journalist he was a summer intern at the CNN Washington bureau with my friend Jim Barnett, one of the producers there, and at UM he took my course in Supreme Court news coverage. After graduating he got a job as a reporter on a Florida television station and did live shots of hurricanes, and in one of them he fell down in a hotel parking lot because of the force of the wind. He sent me tapes of his stories from Miami, and wrote in black marker on the cassette box: *God bless you, professor.* And he sent me a wedding invitation and a photo of his baby son.

Maybe I'm reading too much into this situation, the older former journalist seeing himself in the cub reporter, but in many ways what my former student is experiencing sums up some of the main points of this book: that journalism is fun, it is flawed, it is full of surprises, it is hard work, it can bring out the best in people, and, for all its shortcomings, it is a noble profession. At its best, it is the pursuit of the truth.

Some things have changed in journalism since my day. I am happy to see that there are more women and minorities advancing in the profession. But I am unhappy to see the deaths of some print newspapers and their replacement by Web sites that may not survive very long as legitimate news organizations. I am concerned to see news organizations trying to save money by making more use of unpaid, untrained amateurs instead of careful, experienced, professional journalists.

Journalism is undergoing change, and it is difficult to predict what will emerge from this turmoil. News may or may not end up being delivered primarily to cell phones, or laptops, or desktop computers, or perhaps some new handheld devices such as Kindles. How news organizations can generate enough revenue to survive is uncertain.

But I do believe that people will continue to want real news. They will continue to seek out a reliable account of the day's events. They will still want the truth. It will still be difficult for journalists to overcome the obstacles to truth—perhaps even more difficult than before—but they will continue to find ways to do that.

Today when I read the *New York Times* or watch CNN, I can imagine the hardships that the journalists went through to get their stories, just as my former student does today, trying to dig out a few facts, straining to come up with a few bits of truth, a few glimpses behind the closed doors. I see a journalist as being not so much a witness to history as a kind of glorified Peeping Tom, getting tantalizing glimpses that may or may not mean something. I think about the glimpses I experienced: Arafat trying to hug me, Khrushchev voting, Kay Graham at her London hotel as John Mitchell entered prison, the Pope in Gemelli Hospital, Israeli planes bombing Beirut, the coffins of Marines in Beirut, Qaddafi's deranged look, the death of Clark Todd, the trial of Oliver North, "Christmas presents" in Poland, being held captive in Lebanon.

So many surprises along the way.

As a journalist I always saw telling the truth as a kind of sacred goal, something to cherish as if it were an object of almost religious devotion. There is one sentence I love in the James Joyce story, "Araby," in *Dubliners.* Although he is referring to a young man's devotion to a young woman who is the object of his infatuation, the words resonate for me in a different sense. He wrote: "I imagined that I bore my chalice safely through a throng of foes." For me, truth is the chalice, and to bear it safely the journalist must overcome the obstacles I confronted. The story of a journalist's life is what happens along the way while trying to overcome those obstacles. That was the story of my life as a reporter, and it will be the story of my former student's life and the lives of all the other journalists at work today.

Notes

Most of this book is based on my memory of events, especially the details of how I and others covered news stories. Wherever possible I have tried to make up for memory lapses or distorted recollections by looking up dates and facts, and by consulting the journalists who were with me, although sadly enough some of them are now deceased.

A special note about quotations: One thing that bothers me in reading an author's memoir or autobiography is seeing direct quotes from people in conversation, although I know that the author had made no audio recording of that conversation and that whatever notes the author jotted down were not necessarily verbatim. But when I went to write this book, I realized that if I wanted to catch the flavor of conversations, I, too, would have to put quotation marks around comments made by me and others, even if I did not have a transcript of what was said to make sure that every word in quotes was exactly what that person said. So I plead guilty to doing the very thing that bothers me in others. My only defense is that I am confessing it here, and I am cautioning readers that the conversations quoted in this book are my best recollection of what was said, rather than verbatim transcripts.

Prologue: Beirut 1981

For a description of the difficulties and dangers of reporting from Beirut in the 1980s, see Robert Fisk's article, "Please, Sam, We'll Pay You Not To Play It Again," in *The Independent,* June 2, 1993. See also "Reporter for ABC Killed in Beirut," *Washington Post,* July 15, 1981.

Chapter One No Building Collapsed

For background on covering Soviet dissidents including Andrei Amalrik, see Bernard Gwertzman's "News From Moscow," *New York Times,* May 20, 1971. See also Harlow Robinson's "Dissident's Window on Soviet Life," *Christian Science Monitor,* July 9, 1982, a review of Amalrik's *Notes of a Revolutionary.* See also John Leonard, "Books of the Times," *New York Times,* July 7, 1982, a review of the same Amalrik book. News of his death, and a tribute to him, were published in "Andrei Amalrik, Emigre, Is Dead; Predicted Soviet Breakup By '84," *New York Times,* November 13, 1980.

A report on *Pravda* attacking me and Ennio Caretto may be found in "Russia May Prosecute Foreign Protesters," Associated Press, January 21, 1970, as retrieved from the *Virgin Islands Daily News,* http://news.google.com/newspapers?nid=757&dat=19700121 &id=PO4JAAAAIBAJ&sjid=xUQDAAAAIBAJ&pg=5788,1260648.

For details of the defection of Stalin's daughter, see "1967: Stalin's daughter defects to the West," in *On This Day,* BBC Web site, retrieved from http://news.bbc.co.uk/onthis-day/hi/dates/stories/march/9/newsid_2801000/2801709.stm.

Chapter Two   Christmas Presents

One report put the total number of Solidarity activists detained in internment camps at 10,131. See "For Most Poles, the Future Looks as Gray as the Past," by John Kifner, *New York Times,* December 12, 1982.

Chapter Three   The Pope Has VD

For a colorful description of the early days at CNN, see Reese Schonfeld's *Me and Ted Against the World: The Unauthorized Story of the Founding of CNN* (New York: HarperCollins, 2001). In it he has some kind words about me, which I probably don't deserve but will gladly accept.

Chapter Four   Line of Death

The incident with the chartered jet flying near the "Line of Death" is reported by Eleanor Randolph in "The Networks' Libyan Fly-By; Plane Escorted from Combat Zone," *Washington Post,* March 26, 1986.

The bomb explosion at the Alexandre Hotel and life in Beirut during the Israeli bombing are described in "Crossing the Green Line; A Maze of War Devastation Separates Armed Forces of Two Beiruts," by William Branigin, in the *Washington Post,* August 6, 1982.

Many journalists have written about life in the Commodore Hotel in West Beirut. For example, see Thomas Friedman's *From Beirut to Jerusalem* (New York: Anchor, 1990).

Chapter Five   Welcome to Tripoli

For a summary of the PanAm 103 incident and its aftermath, see "Libya Admits Culpability in Crash of Pan Am Plane," by Felicity Barringer, *New York Times,* August 16, 2003.

The 1986 U.S. bombing of Libya is covered in "U.S. Jets Hit 'Terrorist Centers' in Libya; Reagan Warns of New Attacks If Needed; One Plane Missing in Raids on 5 Targets," by Bernard Weinraub, *New York Times,* April 15, 1986. See also "Pentagon Details 2-Pronged Attack," by Michael R. Gordon, *New York Times,* April 15, 1986.

Chapter Six   Call the Palace

For a good description of what it was like to cross the border from Jordan into Iraq, see "Road to Baghdad: A Humanitarian Worker's Uneasy Desert Car Ride from Jordan Into Iraq," by Alina Labrada of CARE, Special to ABCNEWS.com, May 10, 2003, retrieved from http://www.abcnews.go.com/sections/world/Travel/AmmantoBaghdad030510.html.

The toll in human lives of the Iran-Iraq war was enormous, but it is difficult to obtain an accurate count. Official versions on both sides are unreliable. At best we have estimates by independent analysts. One very conservative estimate, upward of 300,000, comes from Nathan J. Brown, "Iran-Iraq War," in Encarta Online Encyclopedia 2004, retrieved from http://encarta.msn.com/text_761580640___7/Iran-Iraq_War.html. A BBC report lists the death toll as ranging from 500,000 to 1.5 million. ("The Iran-Iraq war: 25 years on," by Roger Hardy, September 22, 2005, retrieved from http://news.bbc.co.uk/2/hi/middle_east/4260420.stm.) A military analysis by the Federation of American Scientists ("Iran-Iraq War (1980–1988)," retrieved from http://www.fas.org/man/dod-101/ops/war/iran-iraq.html), says that "perhaps as many as a million people died." An Associated Press report refers to "more than 1 million people killed or wounded" ("Iran Wants Saddam to be Tried for Iran-Iraq War," Ali Akbar Dareini, Associated Press Writer, December 15, 2003.) In addition to the deaths, it is highly likely that the number of wounded was in the millions.

Chapter Seven   You Said That Yesterday

The assassination of Aldo Moro and its political implications are covered in "Death in Rome," by Alexander Stille, a review of *The Aldo Moro Murder Case* by Richard Drake (Cambridge, Mass.: Harvard University Press, 1996), published in the Book Review section of the *New York Times,* December 10, 1995.

To understand the context of my being arrested with the CNN crew in Rome, there is evidence that Italian police may have been justified in suspecting that terrorists might pose as television reporters. See "Italian 'Brigades' Plotted a Massacre, Police Say," *Christian Science Monitor,* January 19, 1982.

The exact number of people killed by the atomic bomb explosion in Hiroshima, both immediately as a result of the blast and later as a result of radiation sickness, varies from one report to another. More than 140,000 is a conservative estimate. One report ("Japanese Leaders Call for Bans on Nuclear Arms and Tests," *New York Times,* August 6, 1995) estimated the toll at "probably" more than 150,000 and "perhaps" more than 200,000.

For a description of Begin's past, see "Menachem Begin, Guerrilla Leader Who Became Peacemaker," *New York Times,* March 10, 1992.

Chapter Eight   Two Endings

The death of Clark Todd was covered in many articles. Among the most detailed reports were these: "117 Bodies Found in Lebanese Village Recaptured from Christians," *New York Times,* February 17, 1984; Maria Cook, "Ultimate Price of Reporting a War: Journalist Clark Todd Was Killed During War in Lebanon in 1983. His Daughter Describes the Ordeal," *Ottowa Citizen,* February 23, 2002; Anna Todd, "In Search of the Truth about My Father," *Independent,* February 18, 2002. See also "A Little Accident," by Anna Todd, *Maclean's,* April 15, 2002.

Former CIA agent Robert Baer mentions the Jerry Levin incident in his book, *See No Evil: The True Story of a Ground Soldier in the CIA's War on Terrorism* (New York: Crown Publishers, 2002). Baer cites information that Levin was kidnapped by the same young Lebanese Shiite man who kidnapped CIA station chief William Buckley. Baer says Buckley had been held in an Iranian-run compound near Baalbek, in the Bekaa Valley, where other American hostages were held.

Since his release from captivity, Jerry Levin has campaigned for nonviolence in the Middle East and has written and lectured about the issues faced by Palestinians.

Chapter Nine   Face Down in the Mud

Oliver North's bombastic comments about his Fifth Amendment rights are quoted in "North Says He Will Not Relinquish His Rights," by Susanne M. Schafer, Associated Press, December 18, 1986.

The mysterious reference to an alleged plan to suspend the Constitution is found in "Report Says North Authored Plan to Suspend Constitution," UPI, July 6, 1987. See also "Film Review: Cover Up; On the Trail of Iran-Contra Quarry," *Globe and Mail,* June 16, 1989.

McFarlane's explanation of why he deceived the public about taking a cake to Iran may be found in "Let Them Eat Nuance," *Washington Post,* January 22, 1987.

Details of the Bush administration's attempts to explain away their apparently illegal Contra resupply talks may be found in "The Tightening Loop," an editorial in the *St. Petersburg Times,* May 10, 1990. Also see "Bush Denies Adviser Lied on Contra Issue; Gregg 'Forgot' Meeting Resupply Expert," *Washington Post,* March 16, 1987.

Chapter Ten   All the Earmarks

As to CBS's live shot early in the day of the Oklahoma City bombing playing up speculation of a Middle East connection, by that evening the network had toned it down a bit but still repeatedly raised the possibility. See "Terror in the Heartland; the Bombing of the Alfred P. Murrah Building In Oklahoma City," CBS News Transcripts, 8 p.m., April 19, 1995, retrieved from Lexis-Nexis.

The rush to find a supposed Middle Eastern connection with the Oklahoma City bombing may be seen in "McCurdy Urges Investigation of Fundamentalist Groups," transcript #920-22 of CNN live show at 12:07 p.m. ET, April 19, 1995, retrieved from Lexis-Nexis.

Details of the hype over a supposed Jordanian suspect are found in "TERROR IN OKLAHOMA: THE INVESTIGATION; A Piece of a Rented Truck Offers a Clue to 2 Suspects," by David Johnston, *New York Times,* April 21, 1995. See also "Muslim Community Pained by Harassment," by Thaddeus Herrick, *Houston Chronicle,* April 25, 1995, and "Jumping to Conclusions in Oklahoma City?" by Penny Bender Fuchs, *American Journalism Review,* June 1995.

The cryptic fax episode in the Oklahoma City bombing coverage is reported in "Stockman Office Sent Fax Quickly, FBI Says," *Houston Chronicle,* April 25, 1995, and "Oklahoma City Tragedy: Threat or a Promise? Stockman Reveals Fax Author's Taped Vow to 'Go Ballistic,'" *Houston Chronicle,* April 27, 1995. My live shot transcript is at "Feds Appear to Be Casting Wide Net in Bombing Probe," transcript #52-2 of CNN live show at 7:09 a.m. ET, April 24, 1995, retrieved from Lexis-Nexis.

Chapter Eleven   Scoop

The satire on journalism is Evelyn Waugh's *Scoop* (New York: Little, Brown, 1977).

Details of the problems with CBS's Texas Air National Guard story may be found in the report of the independent investigation by Thornburgh and Boccardi: *Report of the Independent Review Panel,* January 5, 2005, retrieved from www.cbsnews.com/htdocs/pdf/complete_report/CBS_Report.pdf.

The story reported by Lea Donosky and me about the Iranian embassy terrorist attack was "A Rescue That Worked," *Newsweek,* May 19, 1980.

The secret report about Ed Meese is covered in "Still-Secret Report May Criticize Meese's Conduct, Favors for Friend," *Washington Post,* July 6, 1988.

Chapter Twelve   Dead Baby

The earthquake story was published as "Villages of the Dead," *Newsweek,* December 6, 1976.

The North Star reference is found in David Mindich's *Just the Facts: How "Objectivity" Came to Define American Journalism* (New York: New York University Press, 1998).

(Note: Mindich himself doubts the existence of journalistic objectivity and thus puts it in quotes in his history and analysis of the evolution of the concept.)

The divided Czech family story was published as "Czechoslovakia: The Child Hostages," *Newsweek,* March 15, 1976.

The Peace People story was published as "Two Women of Ulster," *Newsweek,* October 24, 1977.

Chapter Thirteen   Down, Down

The first and second *Time* stories about Air Force pilot David Steeves were published as: "ARMED FORCES: The Bad Earth," *Time,* July 15, 1957, and "ARMED FORCES: Certain Discrepancies," *Time,* August 26, 1957.

The finding of possible wreckage of Steeves's plane was reported in "Boy Scouts Verify Pilot Survival Tale," Associated Press, published in the *Pittsburgh Post-Gazette,* October 14, 1978.

The story of Jessica Lynch was originally reported in "'She Was Fighting to the Death'; Details Emerging of W. Va. Soldier's Capture and Rescue," *Washington Post,* April 3, 2003. The *Post*'s ombudsman, Michael Getler, later criticized his newspaper for its poor handling of this story. See "A Long, and Incomplete, Correction," *Washington Post,* June 29, 2003.

For details of public journalism, see Jay Rosen's *What Are Journalists For?* (New Haven, Conn.: Yale University Press, 2001). Also, Merritt's definition of public journalism is found in "Media Matters: Can Public Radio Journalism Be Re-Invented?" by Jeffrey A. Dvorkin, Ombudsman, National Public Radio, July 5, 2001, retrieved from http://www.npr.org/yourturn/ombudsman/2001/010705.html.

The section about the coverage of Winnie Mandela is from Peter Godwin's "Lessons from South Africa," *Newsweek,* September 29, 1997.

Coverage of the NRA is discussed in Brian Patrick's *The National Rifle Association and the Media: The Motivating Force of Negative Coverage* (Frontiers in Political Communications, Vol. 1), (New York: Peter Lang Publishing, 2003).

The Hutchins Commission report is found in *A Free and Responsible Press: A General Report on Mass Communication: Newspapers, Radio, Motion Pictures, Magazines and Books,* ed. Robert D. Leigh (Chicago: University of Chicago Press, 1947).

The section on perception of bias draws partly from the report of the independent investigation by Thornburgh and Boccardi: *Report of the Independent Review Panel,* January 5, 2005, retrieved from www.cbsnews.com/htdocs/pdf/complete_report/CBS_Report.pdf.

The reference to punditry is from *Warp Speed: America in the Age of Mixed Media,* by Bill Kovach and Tom Rosenstiel (New York: The Century Foundation Press, 1999).

The example of news analysis is "Smaller Goals for U.S. in Iraq," by Steven R. Weisman, *New York Times,* August 29, 2005.

Chapter Fourteen   Firewall

Details of the Staples incident may be found in "Newspaper Promotes Editor Who Criticized Profits Deal," by Felicity Barringer, *New York Times,* January 10, 2000.

The "bazooka" quote from Mark Willes may be found in "He Built a Great Paper. Then He Quit," by Chris Welles, *Business Week,* June 11, 2001.

Krugman's defense of his taking money from Enron may be found in his blog: http://www.pkarchive.org. See the entries "My Connection With Enron, One More Time" and "Short Version of the Enron Stint."

The first Krugman *New York Times* column to mention Enron does disclose his serving on its advisory committee but does not mention being paid. It is "Reckonings: Power and Profits," January 24, 2001. Krugman also mentions his Enron connection (but again not the money) in his *Fortune* column "The Ascent of E-Man," May 1999.

The *New York Times* mentions Krugman's $50,000 Enron deal near the bottom of "ENRON'S COLLAPSE: THE REVIEW; White House Says Economics Adviser Saw Little Risk on Enron," January 17, 2002. The next day Andrew Sullivan in his "The Daily Dish" blog in the *Atlantic* attacked Krugman for taking money from Enron. See January 18, 2002, item in http://sullivanarchives.theatlantic.com/index.php.dish_inc-archives.2002_01_01_dish_archive.html.

See also Sullivan's comments in "Has Media Reported on Enron Scandal Responsibly? Was 'Talk' Magazine Victim of 9/11? Battle of the 'West Wings,'" RELIABLE SOURCES, CNN, January 26, 2002, retrieved from http://transcripts.cnn.com/TRAN-SCRIPTS/0201/26/rs.00.html.

Sullivan's own alleged conflict of interest is cited in "When Site Sponsorship Threatens Credibility," *New York Times,* July 16, 2001.

For more on the Krugman controversy, see "Ethics: Enron's Helpers," Joshua Lipton, *Columbia Journalism Review* 40 (March–April 2002).

Chapter Fifteen   Only Time Will Tell

Tom Fenton's excellent book is *Bad News: The Decline of Reporting, the Business of News, and the Danger to Us All* (New York: Harper Paperbacks, 2005).

Epilogue

The quote from the short story "Araby" is in James Joyce, *Dubliners* (London: Penguin Classics, 2000).

Index